TEACHING
JAPANESE
POPULAR
CULTURE

Asia Past & Present: New Research from AAS

Published by the Association for Asian Studies (AAS) "Asia Past & Present" features the finest scholarly work from all areas and disciplines of Asian studies. For further information, visit **www.asian-studies.org**.

- "East Meets East: Chinese Discover the Modern World in Japan, 1854–1898. A Window on the Intellectual and Social Transformation of Modern China" by Douglas R. Reynolds with Carol T. Reynolds

- "A Scholarly Review of Chinese Studies in North America" (e-book), edited by Haihui Zhang, Zhaohui Xue, Shuyong Jiang, and Gary Lance Lugar

- "Changing Lives: The "Postwar" in Japanese Women's Autobiographies and Memoirs," by Ronald P. Loftus

- "Memory, Violence, Queues: Lu Xun Interprets China," by Eva Shan Chou

- "Scattered Goddesses: Travels with the Yoginis," by Padma Kaimal

- "South Asian Texts in History: Critical Engagements with Sheldon Pollock," edited by Yigal Bronner, Whitney Cox, and Lawrence McCrea

- "Beating Devils and Burning Their Books: Views of Japan, China, and the West," edited by Anthony E. Clark

- "To Die and Not Decay: Autobiography and the Pursuit of Immortality in Early China," by Matthew V. Wells

- "Collecting Asia: East Asian Libraries in North America, 1868–2008," edited by Peter X. Zhou

- "Prescribing Colonization: The Role of Medical Practices and Policies in Japan-Ruled Taiwan, 1895–1945," by Michael Shiyung Liu

- "Tools of Culture: Japan's Cultural, Intellectual, Medical, and Technological Contacts in East Asia, 1000s to 1500s," edited by Andrew Edmund Goble, Kenneth R. Robinson, and Haruko Wakabayashi

- "Modern Short Fiction of Southeast Asia: A Literary History," edited by Teri Shaffer Yamada

Teaching Japanese Popular Culture

Edited by
Deborah Shamoon
And Chris McMorran

Asia Past & Present

Published by the Association for Asian Studies, Inc.
Asia Past & Present: New Research from AAS, Number 13

The Association for Asian Studies (AAS)

Formed in 1941, the Association for Asian Studies (AAS)—the largest society of its kind, with approximately 8,000 members worldwide—is a scholarly, non-political, non-profit professional association open to all persons interested in Asia.

For further information, please visit www.asian-studies.org.

Published by:
Association for Asian Studies, Inc.
825 Victors Way, Suite 310
Ann Arbor, MI 48108 USA
www.asian-studies.org

Printed in the United States of America on acid-free, archival quality paper.

Library of Congress Cataloging-in-Publication Data

Names: Shamoon, Deborah Michelle, editor. | McMorran, Chris, editor.

Title: Teaching Japanese popular culture / edited by Deborah Shamoon and Chris McMorran.

Description: Ann Arbor, Michigan : Association for Asian Studies, Inc., 2016. | Series: Asia past & present: new research from AAS ; no. 13 | Includes index.

Identifiers: LCCN 2016005433 | ISBN 9780924304781 (pbk. : alk. paper)

Subjects: LCSH: Popular culture—Japan—Study and teaching.

Classification: LCC DS822.5 .T3964 2016 | DDC 952.0071—dc23 LC record available at http://lccn.loc.gov/2016005433

CONTENTS

PART III. Using Popular Culture in Teaching

FIGURES AND TABLES

Acknowledgments

Inspiration for this book came in part from the Teaching Japanese Popular Culture Conference, organized by Deborah Shamoon, Chris McMorran, and Kam Thiam Huat, held in November 2012 at the National University of Singapore. We are grateful to all the participants for their contributions, thoughtful comments, and engaging discussions. The conference was generously supported by the Japan Foundation, and hosted by the National University of Singapore Faculty of Arts and Social Sciences, and the Department of Japanese Studies. Thanks to the staff and students who helped organize and run the conference. We thank our colleagues in Japanese Studies for their encouragement, particularly Hendrik Meyer-Ohle for getting us started on this project.

We are grateful to the Association for Asian Studies for seeing the utility of this volume, and especially to our editor Jon Wilson for his support and guidance. We also thank Dominic Pang and Vivian Goh Yit Min for their hard work in helping ensure the book's completion.

Deborah Shamoon acknowledges the National University of Singapore and Ministry of Education Start Up Grant. She is greatly indebted to Hanabusa Noriko at the University of Notre Dame for her generous and fruitful collaboration, and for thoughtful guidance in exploring new directions in Japanese language teaching pedagogy. She thanks her husband Jason Banta for his unwavering support, encouragement, and advice.

Chris McMorran thanks his colleagues at the National University of Singapore for their genuine concern with improving teaching and learning. He also thanks his wife Hisako for her constant love and support.

Introduction

Deborah Shamoon
and Chris McMorran

Japanese popular culture has had a tremendous global impact, particularly on the current generation of high school and university students. These students are likely to have grown up watching *Pokemon* and *Power Rangers* on television, possibly without realizing they were watching imports from Japan. Japanese animation, manga, video games, live action films, pop music, and more are available worldwide, due to unprecedented consumer demand, as well as government efforts like the Cool Japan initiative (2005–present). Casual fans can easily find the biggest current hits in anime and music in translation, while hard-core fans of even the most minor subcultural trends can access them through online communities. The popularity of Japanese popular culture outside Japan can be seen not only in North America but also in Europe, Latin America, Australia, and particularly Asia, where Japanese pop culture has dominated local markets for decades.[1] Mega-events focused on Japanese popular culture can be found throughout the world, from Singapore's Anime Festival Asia, with an attendance of 90,669 in 2015, to Japan Expo in Paris, which welcomed over 240,000 attendees in 2014, making it the largest fan event outside Japan.[2]

Robust fan communities have been driving global student interest in Japan-related courses in higher education. In turn, leading universities have been offering courses and recruiting scholars who can teach these subjects. A quick look at university job postings in contemporary Japanese studies, for instance, reveals many positions that require or prefer candidates who can offer courses on popular culture. Secondary schools are also encouraging teachers of art, literature, social studies, and more to teach manga, film, and other forms of Japanese pop culture to excited students.

Additionally, in recent years there has been a critical mass of scholars who take Japanese pop culture seriously and want to include it in their teaching as well as research. At the same time, more translations into English of manga and anime series, as well as the work of key critics such as Azuma Hiroki and Saitō Tamaki, make the study of Japanese popular culture more accessible to students without Japanese-language ability. Despite this convergence of increased student and institutional demand, growing research expertise, and improved access to primary and secondary texts, however, there has been a lack of serious discussion on teaching about, and with, Japanese popular culture. It is time for such critical reflection. This book aims to fill this gap.

Defining Japanese Popular Culture

Defining a field as varied as popular culture, or even Japanese popular culture, is a nearly impossible task. As a necessary limit, the essays in this volume only discuss popular culture of the postwar period (1945–present). We have also chosen to limit what constitutes popular culture. The majority of chapters deal with film, manga, and anime; there are also chapters on fashion, TV drama, art, design, and music. Partly due to student interest, most topics are associated with youth culture. However, ours is not meant to be a prescriptive list. There are limitless pedagogical possibilities for using other forms of popular culture in the classroom, including sports, video or online games, television game shows, news broadcasts, advertising, food, newspapers, magazines, fan cultures, festivals, karaoke, tea ceremony, and more. Indeed, deciding what constitutes popular culture, in both the present and the past, could be a course itself.

As an area of study, Japanese popular culture is a diffuse concept. In terms of pedagogical possibilities, it seems more productive to leave the parameters of what constitutes popular culture flexible, open to multiple disciplinary interpretations by individual instructors. As John Whittier Treat points out in the introduction to his seminal anthology *Contemporary Japan and Popular Culture*, there is no Department of Popular Culture, either in Japanese institutions or at most universities worldwide. Instead of popular culture belonging to any single discipline, he writes, "[T]he popular is the proprietary concern of nearly all the social sciences and the humanities. … [E]ach of the interpretive disciplines is, like it or not, implicated not only in its inquiry but in its enactment, too."[3]

Since the appearance of Treat's volume in 1996, there has been a surge in programs specializing in aspects of popular culture, particularly at larger universities, and Japanese popular culture has become a trendy topic in the secondary classroom, too. In Japan manga studies has begun to emerge as a topic of serious inquiry, led in part by Kyoto Seika University's establishment of the School of Manga and the International Manga Museum, and by Meiji University's Library of Manga and Subculture. However, manga is only one element in the broader field of popular culture. Specialists in Japanese popular culture may be housed in area studies, film, anthropology, sociology, or history departments; specialists who completed their graduate training in those fields typically take on a pedagogy associated with each field. As William M. Tsutsui points out, the majority of scholars writing in English on Japanese popular culture have a background in anthropology or Japanese literature.[4] While many use cultural studies as a disciplinary guideline, most came up through graduate programs in area studies. At the same time, secondary school teachers bringing Japanese popular culture into the classroom might have extensive pedagogical foundations in secondary education but lack Japanese-language training or graduate training in a discipline associated with popular culture.

The diversity of disciplinary approaches to the study of Japanese popular culture enriches scholarly discourse, but it has also tended to make the creation of a coherent pedagogy difficult. Our goal in this volume is not to enforce a single approach but instead to present critical reflections and concrete examples from many types of courses across disciplines. While most of the chapters in this volume address teaching in undergraduate courses, some also touch on graduate courses and high school classrooms. Selections cover a range of institutions and student populations, including schools in the United States, Canada, Australia, Germany, Singapore, and Japan, as well as study abroad programs and English-language programs at Japanese universities.

Critical Pedagogy and Public Pedagogy: Theoretical Approaches to Teaching Popular Culture

For instructors looking to create a new course in Japanese popular culture, or to add popular culture material to an existing course, there is little theoretical writing to serve as a guide. This is due in part to the fact that pedagogical scholarship has not been a priority in Japanese studies, because of the way the tenure system ranks and rewards different types of academic publishing. Publications on pedagogy simply do not count for much in most universities' systems, apart from language teaching. Therefore, scholarship on teaching Japanese popular culture specifically has been scant. When we began our respective teaching careers and started developing courses for the first time, we felt very keenly our lack of experience in creating courses using popular culture. For Shamoon, graduate training had given models for literature and film courses, and a pedagogical background in language teaching, but not for popular culture. For McMorran, graduate training in geography and Japanese studies did not include any coursework in the use of popular culture in teaching, only a general sense of its importance in interrogating students' geographic imaginations of Japan.

As Shamoon searched for a model syllabus online, she was dismayed to find some that offered students a bait and switch: the course title contained the word *manga* or *anime*, but the majority of the course materials were on something else, such as classical literature. She wanted to offer a course that takes the teaching of popular culture seriously. For McMorran the challenge was how to incorporate Japanese popular culture into courses on the geography and anthropology of Japan without it simply being a filler or distraction.

Examples of courses can be useful, and some are included here. However, there is a large body of work on the pedagogy of teaching popular culture outside area studies. This material provides a starting point for taking seriously the teaching of Japanese popular culture. For instance, in *Disturbing Pleasures: Learning Popular Culture*, Henry A. Giroux argues for what he calls a critical pedagogy based on political engagement, encouraging students to recognize patterns of authority and power particularly in mass media. Giroux also advocates decentering the instructor's authority by encouraging students to introduce popular culture texts that are meaningful to them, and to engage with their own out-of-school experiences.[5] This is particularly useful for instructors who may feel intimidated or uneasy about introducing material such as anime or manga precisely because of the issue of student expertise. Indeed, many of us who purport to be experts on Japan have been humbled by students asking after a lecture what we know about a particular trend in music, fashion, gaming, manga, and so on. The level of student knowledge in the particularities of such trends can be encyclopedic. Unsettling traditional classroom power dynamics is one way to begin thinking about how to incorporate student knowledge into instructional goals.

One example of this kind of pedagogy appears in chapter 6, "Confessions of an Anime and Manga Ignoramus," where Melanie King discusses bringing Japanese popular culture to undergraduates. She describes negotiating her training in art history with the pop culture interests of students. While King is not a fan by her own admission, she finds many popular culture texts, including appropriation of Japanese themes in US pop music videos, to be a useful way to get students thinking critically about stereotypes and orientalism. By respecting and incorporating student knowledge of popular culture, she is able to get students to engage with the material as more than passive entertainment. Similarly in chapter 2, "Talking Japanese Popular Culture at an Australian University," William S. Armour and Sumiko Iida describe a learner-centered course that builds awareness of formal versus informal knowledge. While providing a framework for approaching the material in a critical, academic way (as opposed to as fans), they report greater success when encouraging students to draw on their own knowledge of Japanese pop culture in class discussions rather than on older, unfamiliar texts.

Giroux's ideas about promoting recognition of out-of-school or informal knowledge, which he terms "public pedagogy," have inspired many instructors writing about teaching popular culture. Göran Folkestad, for instance, writing on music education, encourages changing the classroom dynamic from instructor-centered teaching to student-centered learning: "a shift of focus, from how to teach (teaching methods) and the outcome of teaching in terms of results as seen from the teacher's perspective, to what to learn, the content of learning, and how to learn, the way of learning."[6] This approach to teaching is always politically engaged, writes Patrick Roberts, for "The inclusion of popular culture in the curriculum represents an area of potential counterhegemonic practice because popular culture relates to lived experience. ... The goal is not to study popular culture as artifact or use popular culture as a vehicle for making the standard school curriculum more palatable and engaging. Rather, popular culture is engaged performatively, as a signifying practice, in the interest of critiquing structures of power and oppression."[7] This mode of teaching avoids the bait and switch to focus not on the cultural artifact or text alone but on training students to see larger ideological discourses and become aware of their own role in learning.

There are some limits to the utility of public pedagogy in the university classroom, however, particularly in area studies. The concept of public pedagogy was first developed to address issues pertaining to adult and secondary education, particularly that aimed at disadvantaged and minority students.[8] As Jennifer A. Sandlin, Brian D. Schultz, and Jake Burdick explain, "public pedagogy has come to signify a crucial concept—that schools are not the sole sites of teaching, learning, or curricula, and that they are perhaps not even the most influential."[9] While this is a powerful concept for including popular culture in the classroom, such an approach is based on an assumption that texts or other materials are operating within a single culture, that is, encouraging students to bring their own culture into the classroom. Japanese popular culture exists at an interesting nexus between out-of-school knowledge and area studies. Some students, including those outside Japan, have such an encyclopedic knowledge of manga, anime, J-pop, or TV dramas that these comprise the students' own culture. This level of familiarity may be daunting for the instructor. At the same time, other students in the same class may find the material entirely foreign. As Akiko Sugawa-Shimada shows in chapter 4, "Contested Classrooms," this can be true even of Japanese students learning about Japanese popular culture in Japan. While public pedagogy is a useful way to rethink classroom dynamics, it does not fully encompass the issues that arise in teaching across cultures, or in area studies.

While Japanese studies has neglected pedagogical research, Japanese language teaching pedagogy has offered more insight into incorporating popular culture in teaching as part of a larger movement within second-language acquisition pedagogy promoting more widespread use of authentic materials. For instance, several textbooks use manga and anime to teach Japanese to English speakers.[10] Manga, anime, film, and television are often used as authentic materials in Japanese language courses. Natsuki Fukunaga describes how anime fan activities enhance the Japanese-language-learning experience for college students in the United States, while Kelly Chandler-Olcott and Donna Mahar suggest ways in which anime-based fan fiction can help junior high school students improve their English writing skills.[11]

The present volume includes several chapters on using popular culture in language teaching. However, simply using authentic materials without a larger pedagogy can be counterproductive, and the tendency to separate language teaching from so-called "content" (i.e. informed by critical theory) teaching is problematic. For this reason, we have included chapters on both language teaching and area studies in hopes that these two related but often separate fields can come into dialogue.

As William S. Armour points out, accepting manga, film, or other pop culture texts uncritically in the language classroom has pitfalls, not least that students and teachers might have differing ideas about what is authentic.[12] Armour's larger concern, however, is with how using soft power commercial products in a language classroom positions the students as consumers. He particularly warns of the combined dangers of exposing students to culturally encoded language containing markers of gender and class, which they may not fully grasp, and using the authority of the classroom to perpetrate soft power, or branded consumerism, concluding, "Authentic texts such as MANGA do not always conflate with the notion of a correct text in terms of content and form. ... [T]his view may be a reasonable springboard from which to consider other issues such as the types of inputs both teachers and learners want to have to achieve mutually negotiable outcomes, as well as matters of trust that learners place in what teachers, texts and the like inform them about the target language."[13] In other words, we must be careful not only of unreflectively replicating stereotypes and prejudices contained in pop culture texts but also of uncritically promoting consumerism to students in a classroom setting.

Several chapters in this volume address these issues. James Dorsey in chapter 9, "Performing Gender in the Prisonhouse of a (Foreign) Language," demonstrates how drawing students' attention to gendered roles embedded in music lyrics can help them analyze and critique sexist stereotypes. Marc Yamada in chapter 8, "Using Japanese Television Media in Content-Based Language Learning," similarly shows how he gets students to discuss gender while teaching Japanese using TV dramas. It is particularly important to highlight this kind of critical stance in classes that are not focused specifically on textual or media analysis, such as in a Japanese language class. On a more theoretical level, Sally McLaren and Alwyn Spies in chapter 1, "Risk and Potential," and Melanie King in chapter 6 argue that an uncritical approach to teaching popular culture not only positions students as consumers but also can potentially falsely present Japanese culture as monolithic or reproduce orientalist or self-orientalizing discourses.

Furthermore, there are legal considerations of which instructors in all disciplines must be aware. The guidelines on fair use of copyrighted material, particularly visual material, are not well known. The Society for Cinema and Media Studies has outlined best practices for teaching on its website, although its guidelines pertain specifically to the United States.[14] Lack of access to legally distributed, subtitled, or translated material is a serious hindrance to effective teaching. The issue of copyright is far more complex in the case of online teaching, as Chris McMorran discusses in the conclusion to this volume, "The Online Future(s) of Teaching Japanese Popular Culture." Obscenity laws also have an impact on materials students and instructors may want to use, particularly manga and anime, as Mark McLelland points out.[15] Instructors must be aware of potential problems with both copyright and obscenity. All these issues make the effort to include authentic materials and engage in critical pedagogy with respect to Japanese popular culture, in either area studies or language classrooms, difficult but rewarding to achieve.

Overview of Chapters

The essays in this volume focus on teaching *about* popular culture and teaching *with* popular culture, including language teaching. More specifically, teaching *about* popular culture refers to courses that take popular culture itself as a topic of study, such as courses in film or television studies, on the history or visual analysis of manga and anime, or on music, fashion, or sports, to name a few examples. Ideally, such courses present methodological tools for analysis (such as formal analysis of film) and readings/viewings of key primary texts, as well as introduce relevant scholarly discourse on those texts. On the other hand, teaching *with* popular culture refers to courses that use primary texts to teach a related topic, for instance, using a film in a Japanese history course or a television commercial in a language course. In this case, the study of the primary text is in service to the larger goals of the course. Both teaching *about* and *with* popular culture are valid pedagogies, and the chapters in this volume address both types.

Part I covers broad issues related to using popular culture in teaching. Chapter 1, by McLaren and Spies, provides a conceptual framework for understanding several critical issues associated with teaching Japanese pop culture, drawing inspiration from Anglophone pedagogy scholarship on popular culture, critical area studies, and postcolonial theory. Their framework is not exhaustive or prescriptive. However, it provides an excellent overview of the controversies and roles played by Japanese popular culture in all classrooms, thus giving readers food for thought. In addition it provides a call to action, arguing for a more concerted and research-based effort to continually reflect on and improve teaching practices in general, and specifically when it comes to Japanese popular culture. In this way, it sets the tone for the remaining chapters, in which all contributors carefully analyze their own practices, not based on instinct or habit but on careful reflection and engagement with broader theoretical and pedagogical scholarship.

For instance, in chapter 2 Armour and Iida reflect on their use of pop culture in both content and language courses in Australia, including further discussion of the problems with what they term soft power pedagogy. In particular, they discuss the challenges associated with shifting Japanese popular culture along a continuum from entertainment to analysis, as well as the many ways in which new technologies have enabled incorporation of popular culture into their courses. While Armour and Iida discuss the ways in which pedagogical, theoretical, and technological changes have impacted their courses over the long term, Cosima Wagner, in chapter 3, "Goethe Goes Cool Japan," introduces a potential short-term remedy to a dearth of course offerings on Japanese popular culture. Specifically, she charts her experiences in creating the Cool Japan Working Group at Goethe-University in Germany, which she developed to help students conduct independent study projects in Japanese popular culture despite a lack of such courses at her institution. Such a project can avoid trying to make popular culture "fit" into existing courses and instead push students to use popular culture as the starting point for a learner-centered approach to research. Wagner also discusses a study trip she conducted with her students, an example of a short-term study abroad program focused on the study of manga and anime industries, which also gives students the flexibility to pursue their interests in popular culture.

Part II contains essays on teaching about popular culture, primarily courses dealing with media studies. In chapter 4, Sugawa-Shimada discusses teaching anime in Japan, comparing classroom dynamics of courses taught to Japanese students to courses taught in English to a mix of Japanese and foreign students. She compares not only differing cultural knowledge but also variations in media literacy and the problem of conflicting classroom behaviors among Japanese and foreign students. In chapter 5, "Teaching Fashion as Japanese Popular Culture," Jan Bardsley describes how to develop students' skills in observation, writing, and analysis by exploring a wide range of fashions, including kimono, avant-garde, Ivy prep, and Lolita cuteness. Students learn to discuss popular fashions in their historical and cultural context as a way to understand the potential of dress to shape and subvert notions of gender, race, nation, and class.

The chapters in part III describe various approaches and roadblocks to teaching *with* popular culture in a range of history, language, and area studies courses. In chapter 6, Melanie King begins by discussing ways to take advantage of student interest in pop culture. Specifically, she explains how she parlays her background in art history to help students unpack the meanings behind both the widespread success of artist Murakami Takashi and the cultural appropriations of Japan by popular singers such as Katy Perry. Moreover, based on her outreach experience with K–12 teachers, she explains how one can teach *with* Japanese popular culture while addressing the needs of the controversial Common Core Standards. Overall, she shows how Japanese popular culture can effectively bridge gaps between K–12 institutions and universities, offering hope for both providing younger students with critical tools for understanding the choices of their favorite stars and combating enduring orientalism in US popular culture.

Japanese language teaching has long utilized manga, anime, film, and television as authentic materials.[16] The chapters here suggest ways in which those materials can be used more productively beyond simple grammar lessons, to combine cultural analysis with language teaching. In chapter 7, "Co-Teaching and Foreign Language across the Curriculum Using Japanese Popular Culture," Deborah Shamoon discusses co-teaching a Foreign Languages across the Curriculum course in the United States with language instructor Hanabusa Noriko. In creating a weekly section taught in Japanese as a supplement to a pop culture course taught in English, they were able to provide new opportunities for advanced students to approach the material critically in the target language. Similarly, in chapter 8 Marc Yamada shows how he uses Japanese television drama to combine language and media studies instruction in the United States. In chapter 9, James Dorsey also combines language teaching and cultural analysis, in this case in a course for US students on a summer study abroad program in Japan. Through analysis of song lyrics in courses at the novice and intermediate levels, Dorsey introduces new grammar constructions while also encouraging students to recognize speech patterns marked by gender and class, and to contemplate how the songs rely on cultural expectations to convey meaning with few words.

In chapter 10, "Pop(ular) Culture in the Japanese History Classroom," Philip Seaton explores the potential uses of films, manga, and anime as both primary and secondary sources in history classes. He argues that instructors should not view these texts merely as entertainment or a lure for students but as primary sources when considering the era in which they were produced or as secondary sources when they reflect a certain interpretation of a past era. He also includes tourist sites and museums under the rubric of popular culture, explaining how they can be impacted by television dramas. Through virtual tours to such destinations, students can see how these locations are implicated in both popular and official histories.

One theme that runs through this volume is the importance of technology in teaching *about* and *with* Japanese popular culture. The contributors acknowledge the role of technologies in helping students find Japanese popular culture on their own and providing instructors with ways to build on and complicate student understandings. These technologies include television, film, CDs, and DVDs, but recently the Internet has proven indispensable, thanks to services like YouTube (for music videos and film and television clips), pop culture fan websites, online manga in translation (often called "scanlations"), and even virtual tours to museums and historically related tourist websites. Overall, there is a consensus that teaching Japanese popular culture is greatly enhanced by the Internet and would be virtually impossible without it. However, in the conclusion to this volume, McMorran further analyzes the Internet's impact by outlining some of the obstacles and rewards associated with courses that are completely online. MOOCs—or massive open online courses—promise to vastly expand the global population of students learning about Japanese popular culture. However, the issue of copyright may limit the number and quality of MOOCs on Japanese popular culture, since so much content is not protected by fair use when taught online. Instructors hoping to reach more students through online courses must make some difficult choices when it comes to incorporating popular culture. McMorran discusses those choices and how they might impact the future of teaching Japanese popular culture.

As these essays suggest, the possibilities for using Japanese popular culture in the classroom are limitless. Popular culture, widely defined, can provide students with a way to apply critical analysis to everyday life and other cultures, including their own. It is our hope that this volume will bring Japanese studies to the larger discourse on popular culture pedagogy, and that it will expand the conversation on teaching about, as well as teaching with, Japanese popular culture. We feel that this conversation is long past due. Together the contributors share a sense of frustration and liberation: frustration at the lack of published scholarship on teaching Japanese popular culture and liberation on realizing they are not alone. There is no single, perfect way to approach teaching Japanese popular culture. For one thing, there is no single definition of what it encompasses. Second, the fact that our contributors were trained in a variety of disciplines means that their skills and intuitions are bound to be different. As editors, we too feel a sense of liberation in not mandating a particular conceptual framework or pedagogical model for the contributors to follow. Instead, we provide them with space in which to share their thoughts and experiences on teaching Japanese popular culture, and a way to expose themselves to critical feedback on their ideas and methods.

For readers with experience teaching Japanese popular culture (or any popular culture, for that matter), we hope the chapters resonate in some way, either inducing critical reflection as you plan your next semester or inspiring you to try something new. For those planning their first course on Japanese popular culture, we hope the chapters provide insight on how and why to use Japanese popular culture content, as well as on understanding the importance of reflecting on one's decisions at every step of the way, not only when deciding learning objectives, writing the syllabus, and choosing assessments but during the course and upon its completion. More important, we hope the volume causes all readers to grasp the complexity of teaching popular culture and the importance of critical reflection on the preparation and practice of teaching as a whole.

Notes

1 Chua Beng Huat, *Structure, Audience, and Soft Power in East Asian Pop Culture* (Hong Kong: Hong Kong University Press, 2012).

2 Anime Festival Asia, http://www.animefestival.asia; Japan Expo, http://www.japan-expo-paris.com/en/menu_info/past-impacts_475.htm.

3 John Whittier Treat, "Introduction: Japanese Studies into Cultural Studies," in *Contemporary Japan and Popular Culture*, ed. John Whittier Treat (Honolulu: University of Hawai'i Press, 1996), 3.

4 William M. Tsutsui, "Teaching History and/of/or Japanese Popular Culture," *electronic journal of contemporary japanese studies* 13, no. 2 (2013), http://www.japanesestudies.org.uk/ejcjs/vol13/iss2/tsutsui.html.

5 Henry A. Giroux, *Disturbing Pleasures: Learning Popular Culture* (New York: Routledge, 1994), 121.

6 Göran Folkestad, "Formal and Informal Learning Situations or Practices vs. Formal and Informal Ways of Learning," *British Journal of Music Education* 23, no. 2 (July 2006): 136.

7 Patrick Roberts, "Cultural Studies in Relation to Curriculum Studies," in *Encyclopedia of Curriculum Studies,* ed. Craig Cridel (Thousand Oaks: Sage Publications, 2010), 178.

8 Michael P. O'Malley, Jennifer A. Sandlin, and Jake Burdick, "Public Pedagogy," in *Encyclopedia of Curriculum Studies* ed. Craig Cridel (Thousand Oaks: Sage Publications, 2010), 697.

9 Jennifer A. Sandlin, Brian D. Schultz, and Jake Burdick, "Understanding, Mapping, and Exploring the Terrain of Public Pedagogy," in *Handbook of Public Pedagogy: Education and Learning beyond Schooling,* ed. Jennifer A. Sandlin, Brian D. Schultz, and Jake Burdick (New York: Routledge, 2010), 2.

10 Marc Bernabe, *Japanese in Mangaland: Learning the Basics*, vol. 1 (Tokyo: Japan Publications Trading Company, 2004); Wayne P. Lammers, *Japanese the Manga Way: An Illustrated Guide to Grammar and Structure* (Berkeley: Stone Bridge Press, 2005).

11 Natsuki Fukunaga, "'Those Anime Students': Foreign Language Literacy Development through Japanese Popular Culture," *Journal of Adolescent and Adult Literacy* 50, no. 3 (November 2006): 206–22. Kelly Chandler-Olcott and Donna Mahar, "Adolescents' Anime-Inspired 'Fanfictions': An Exploration of Multiliteracies," *Journal of Adolescent and Adult Literacy* 46, no. 7 (2003): 556–66.

12 William Spencer Armour, "Learning Japanese by Reading 'Manga': The Rise of 'Soft Power Pedagogy,'" *RELC Journal* 42, no. 2 (2011): 130.

[13] Ibid., 137.

[14] Society for Cinema and Media Studies, "Fair Use Policies," http://www.cmstudies.org/?page=fair_use.

[15] Mark McLelland, "Ethical and Legal Issues in Teaching about Japanese Popular Culture to Undergraduate Students in Australia," *electronic journal of contemporary japanese studies* 13, no. 2 (2013), http://www.japanesestudies.org.uk/ejcjs/vol13/iss2/mclelland.html.

[16] Armour, "Learning Japanese by Reading 'Manga.'"

Works Cited

Anime Festival Asia, http://www.animefestival.asia

Armour, William Spencer. "Learning Japanese by Reading 'Manga': The Rise of 'Soft Power Pedagogy.'" *RELC Journal* 42, no. 2 (2011): 125–40.

Bernabe, Marc. *Japanese in Mangaland: Learning the Basics*. Vol. 1. Tokyo: Japan Publications Trading Company, 2004.

Chandler-Olcott, Kelly, and Donna Mahar. "Adolescents' Anime-Inspired 'Fanfictions': An Exploration of Multiliteracies." *Journal of Adolescent and Adult Literacy* 46, no. 7 (2003): 556–66.

Chua Beng Huat. *Structure, Audience, and Soft Power in East Asian Pop Culture*. Hong Kong: Hong Kong University Press, 2012.

Folkestad, Göran. "Formal and Informal Learning Situations or Practices vs. Formal and Informal Ways of Learning." *British Journal of Music Education* 23, no. 2 (July 2006): 135–45.

Fukunaga, Natsuki. "'Those Anime Students': Foreign Language Literacy Development through Japanese Popular Culture." *Journal of Adolescent and Adult Literacy* 50, no. 3 (November 2006): 206–22.

Giroux, Henry A. *Disturbing Pleasures: Learning Popular Culture*. New York: Routledge, 1994.

Japan Expo, http://www.japan-expo-paris.com/en/menu_info/past-impacts_475.htm

Lammers, Wayne P. *Japanese the Manga Way: An Illustrated Guide to Grammar and Structure*. Berkeley: Stone Bridge Press, 2005.

McLelland, Mark. "Ethical and Legal Issues in Teaching about Japanese Popular Culture to Undergraduate Students in Australia." *electronic journal of contemporary japanese studies* 13, no. 2 (2013). http://www.japanesestudies.org.uk/ejcjs/vol13/iss2/mclelland.html.

O'Malley, Michael P., Jennifer A. Sandlin, and Jake Burdick. "Public Pedagogy." In *Encyclopedia of Curriculum Studies,* edited by Craig Cridel, 697–701. Thousand Oaks: Sage Publications, 2010.

Roberts, Patrick. "Cultural Studies in Relation to Curriculum Studies." In *Encyclopedia of Curriculum Studies,* edited by Craig Cridel, 171–78. Thousand Oaks: Sage Publications, 2010.

Sandlin, Jennifer A., Brian D. Schultz, and Jake Burdick. "Understanding, Mapping, and Exploring the Terrain of Public Pedagogy." In *Handbook of Public Pedagogy: Education and Learning beyond Schooling,* edited by Jennifer A. Sandlin, Brian D. Schultz, and Jake Burdick, 1–5. New York: Routledge, 2010.

Society for Cinema and Media Studies, "Fair Use Policies."
http://www.cmstudies.org/?page=fair_use.

Treat, John Whittier. "Introduction: Japanese Studies into Cultural Studies." In *Contemporary Japan and Popular Culture,* edited by John Whittier Treat, 1–16. Honolulu: University of Hawai'i Press, 1996.

Tsutsui, William M. "Teaching History and/of/or Japanese Popular Culture." *electronic journal of contemporary japanese studies* 13, no. 2 (2013). http://www.japanesestudies.org.uk/ejcjs/vol13/iss2/tsutsui.html.

PART I

THE BIG PICTURE

ON CURRICULUM DESIGN

1

Risk and Potential: Establishing Critical Pedagogy in Japanese Popular Culture Courses

Sally McLaren and Alwyn Spies

Introduction

This chapter problematizes the teaching of Japanese popular culture through a survey of recent research and by drawing on observations and reflections from personal experiences of teaching in a variety of programs and universities. Essentially, we are aiming to explore how research on the teaching of Japanese popular culture can be developed and strengthened. We identify tensions surrounding Japanese studies and Japanese popular culture courses in the academy caused by lingering issues with area studies, as well as the current trend toward teaching and research on "Cool Japan," which has a propensity to ignore historical, gender, and labor issues and precludes discussions of diversity and dissent inside Japan. Persistent problems with orientalism, self-orientalization (*Nihonjinron*), and the othering of "exotic" Japan continue to haunt Japanese popular culture programs. We examine and identify risks and potentials, with possible pitfalls, in various ideological and methodological approaches to teaching Japanese popular culture. We also point out that if future discussions of pedagogical methods are to move beyond descriptions of content, we (as a fledgling association of scholars of teaching and learning in Japanese popular culture) need to consider the other key aspects of curriculum design—statements of student learning outcomes, alignment of assignments and assessments, and instruments for assessing the achievement of these outcomes. Reading widely across academic disciplines, we have found five common paradigmatic approaches to the teaching of popular culture in general and, more specifically, to discussions of Japanese popular culture.

1. "Pop to prop," which uses Japanese popular culture courses to prop up ailing or aging programs and attract students or tuition revenue

2. "Proper pop," which aims to establish, legitimize, and institutionalize new disciplines such as manga studies and video game studies in a more traditional academic manner

3. "Pop as propaganda," which promotes Cool Japan and tends to celebrate rather than critique

4. "Poco pop," which takes a postcolonial view of the study of Japanese popular culture by including cultural studies theory

5. "Pop to prep," in which the study of Japanese popular culture is seen as equivalent to teaching intercultural skills or as a way to learn twenty-first-century literacies and skills, which will purportedly prepare students for future employment

These approaches intersect in many ways and raise additional questions. There are also very different issues and concerns when Japanese pop culture courses, or topics within a course, are housed in an Asian studies or Japanese studies department rather than a cultural studies, film studies, or other interdisciplinary, interregional department. We acknowledge that there is no unproblematic way to study and teach Japanese popular culture, either inside or outside Japan, in Japanese or in another language context. Each and every approach outlined below has both risks and potentials involved. We think that "better teaching" requires critiquing and combining parts of the five approaches—and needs to include a metacritique of the university itself and the program curriculum—in order to produce positive and measurable outcomes across postsecondary pedagogical contexts.

We also believe, at this juncture in time, that it is particularly crucial to the future of Japanese popular culture studies that pedagogical issues are addressed. As Graeme Turner has noted in his post-assessment of the institutionalization of cultural studies programs in Australia, teaching has gradually become marginalized within the academy.[1] It "amplifies problems within the practice of the field because it can't help but consolidate tendencies into templates or prescriptive structures."[2]

As the title of this chapter indicates, we are arguing for the establishment of critical pedagogy in Japanese popular culture courses. While pedagogical issues are central to this concern, it is important to distinguish between thinking critically about pedagogy and incorporating critical pedagogical practices into the teaching of Japanese popular culture. We find Peter McLaren's definition of critical pedagogy to be most relevant to our argument.

> Critical pedagogy is both a way of thinking about and negotiating through praxis the relationship among classroom teaching, the production of knowledge, the larger institutional structures of the school, and the social and material relations of the wider community, society and nation state.[3]

Therefore, discussions about institutional politics and the production of knowledge are just as important as discussions about content. Over twenty years ago, Henry A. Giroux stated that there is a "need to develop a critical pedagogy in order to navigate the terrains of popular culture texts."[4] John Weaver and Toby A. Daspit have supplemented Giroux's assertion by emphasizing that it should be a critical pedagogy that promotes "the creation of interdisciplinary, border crossing students, teachers and administrators."[5] To this end, we believe that critical reflection on our teaching of Japanese popular culture needs more attention.

It is also important to consider the Japanese pop culture classroom as a potential "site of struggle." Tamara Swenson's observations and interviews with American students studying Japanese language indicate that Japanese media and cultural products are most certainly "triggers" for interest in studying Japan at the tertiary level.[6] Unfortunately, this interest has not changed the perception of Japan as the "exotic other."[7] Her interviewees also reported that for them the Internet is a major source of information about Japan, a further indication of the mediated nature of students' engagement with and knowledge of Japan. Swenson discovered that it is primarily manga and anime, with their "cybernetic, futuristic culture," that appeals to her interviewees and creates an "imaginary" for them.[8] It is the existence of this imaginary that gives Japan exotic appeal.[9] She locates the source of this interest in the concept of the "Techno Orient," the idea that "if the Orient was constructed and invented by the west to build up its cultural identity, then the techno Orient has been invented to define images of information capitalism and the information society."[10]

Swenson argues that it is important to know how students "read and understand the tension between technology and humanity" in the Techno Orient, as a direction for future research.[11] These findings certainly resonate with our own classroom experiences and our concern that, with students obviously obtaining such pleasure from the text, issues of orientalism and the study of Japanese popular culture need to be carefully addressed. Henry Jenkins has also noted that:

> these patterns of consumption generate a hunger for knowledge, a point of entry into a larger consideration of cultural geography and political economy. ... What kinds of pedagogical interventions might displace orientalist stereotypes with a more nuanced account of cultural difference and national specificity?[12]

One way to deal with this is to establish critical pedagogy in Japanese popular culture courses and to problematize "the role of popular culture in relation to knowledge construction, social desire, and student agency."[13] While recognizing that the shared experiences of popular culture are important and meaningful to students, Kevin M. Tavin has argued that educators also need to problematize their own relationship with popular culture.[14] Certainly, the goal of these "struggles" in the classroom should be to develop a more sophisticated and complex understanding of Japanese popular culture.[15] Therefore, with these concerns in mind, we hope that the approaches we outline below will contribute to a debate and discussion on establishing critical pedagogy in Japanese popular culture courses.

Pop to Prop

Using Japanese popular culture to attract students has become commonplace in universities in North America, Europe, and the Asia-Pacific, including universities in Japan wishing to increase numbers of foreign students. Often this results in random one-off Japanese popular culture courses or thematically related popular content tacked onto already established courses or into preexisting programs—sometimes in quite separate fields, such as when Japanese fictional narrative films are used to introduce historical figures in a history course or anthropological films are used to study Japanese culture.

Academically, if done effectively, the addition of popular culture texts to traditional course materials can draw students farther into the "main" field and lead them to more rigorous or specialized popular culture content,[16] bridge the gap between intermediate and advanced levels in language learning, or motivate language learners to continue with formal language courses.[17] This does require a larger context for the learning goals or a well-designed program curriculum and conscious framing of the materials. Done poorly, it could "cheapen" the academic value of the text, the course, and the program. If there is nowhere to go after the sexy "hook," from the perspective of students it could be seen as a "bait-and-switch" scam. It can also lead to inaccurate interpretations of the text (because it has been taken out of discursive or historical context of its conception and reception) or methodologically problematic uses (such as fictional characters used as case studies in social science courses or papers, or documentary films used to illustrate "reality").

An interesting variant of the "pop to prop" approach is to make less attractive or underpopulated courses prerequisites for the more popular courses on popular culture. Turner describes how cultural studies introductory courses have become canonized theory courses that are slowly choking program numbers and represent a return to an academic elitism that contradicts the original "grassroots, for the people" concept of cultural studies. He states that while everyone in his department agreed on the necessity of a common core of theoretical knowledge for their majors, there were "genuine and legitimate differences of opinion" on how to get there.[18]

Turner warns that our decisions now, in regard to teaching, could spell the end of our jobs in the near future. In October 2010, immediately after the State University of New York at Albany permanently closed its French, Italian, classics, Russian and theater programs, there was a series of editorials in the *New York Times* by prominent humanities professors discussing the demise of the humanities. Stanley Fish, in his editorial, identified much about required courses that is elitist and coercive—similar to Turner's examples—but was far more blunt about what is at stake for those in the teaching profession.

> I have always had trouble believing in the high-minded case for a core curriculum—that it preserves and transmits the best that has been thought and said—but I believe fully in the core curriculum as a device of employment for me and my fellow humanists. But the point seems to be moot. It's too late to turn back the clock.[19]

It would be smart to learn from Fish and Turner that, when planning curriculum changes via popular culture studies, it is necessary to consider carefully a symbiotic balance between student popularity (in terms of both numbers and tuition fees), disciplinary rigor, and academic labor conditions. It is not just what gets taught but also when, how, and with what else. While our personal experience shows that Japanese manga classes have consistently higher enrollment rates than Japanese literature classes, we need to point out that we were not able to find any publications with quantitative or qualitative data to support the concept that popular culture courses, Japanese or otherwise, attract students, grow programs, or increase revenues.[20] The only large-scale longitudinal research being done is by the Japan Foundation in its Survey on Japanese-Language Education Abroad, which has been conducted approximately every three to five years since 1974. The 2012 international survey results show a significant increase in the number of Japanese-language students who claim to be studying Japanese because of an interest in Japanese popular culture. However, the foundation only began asking specifically about popular culture in 2009 and is therefore only comparing two sets of data.[21] Until more pedagogical research is done, discussions about Japanese popular culture pedagogies and administration will remain unsubstantiated "opinions."

Proper Pop

We are using the term *proper pop* to describe the establishment, legitimization, or institutionalization of new disciplines in traditional academic systems. The various manga programs at Kyoto Seika University and the video game programs at the IT University of Copenhagen, and its Centre for Video Game Studies are concrete examples. Both were founded around 2000 and began with production (design or tech) courses, added social science/humanities analysis streams, and finally bridged the two with international graduate studies programs. This follows a path set fifty years ago by film studies and somewhat more recently by cultural studies.[22] The new programs and faculty also immediately founded new professional associations, annual conferences, and specialized journals to house research findings. Antithetical to the shallow, often isolated nature of "pop to prop," the presence of a solid set of steps through which to progress, intellectual depths into which to delve, and colleagues with whom to collaborate is very attractive. The flip side of methodological rigor, standards, and transferable credits, though, is, as Turner has so concisely observed, canonization, ossification, and elitism.[23]

Also, more specifically with regard to manga studies, establishing this new discipline as its own department may not be a sustainable model, particularly outside Japan. At the graduate level, it would be very hard to motivate students to specialize entirely in Japanese manga. Many graduate students enter PhD programs hoping to get academic jobs after graduating, and the better students carefully consider entry-level academic job conditions and trends before they choose their advanced degree program and the school that houses it. In a country with a small and widely dispersed population such as Canada, for example, there are only a few universities, in major cities such as Toronto, Montreal, and Vancouver, where undergraduate students can major in Japanese studies. As a result, there are few tenure-track jobs for PhDs in Japanese in Canada at all, let alone recently graduated Japanese manga experts without a primary field of expertise such as history, art history, or business management. Unless manga or pop culture departments suddenly spring up all over the world (or universities in Japan start hiring more non-Japanese), those wanting to do a PhD dissertation on Japanese popular culture may be more likely to do it in older departments with larger research profiles, higher rankings, and more status (particularly with the large government funding agencies) and will combine their manga studies with some other field that offers more job opportunities. A quick survey of job postings for 2015 on the H-Japan listserv shows quite clearly that popular culture as a secondary area of expertise would be an advantage.

Furthermore, one of the biggest practical issues in running a full set of undergraduate Japanese pop culture courses of any kind lies in the challenge of acquiring texts for classroom use. The fast-paced developments in Japanese pop culture mean that it is an extremely expensive field in which to keep abreast, particularly from outside Japan. Not only are the costs of shipping exorbitant, but e-books from online retailers in Japan are often regionally protected and legally unavailable in other regions. Legal copies of TV anime or TV shows, especially with reliable English subtitles, are almost impossible to obtain and require special equipment in classrooms (e.g., different zones, PAL vs. NTSC video formats). Public performance rights are difficult for non-Japanese-speaking librarians to even begin to negotiate and can be expensive (depending on the company that owns the license). Video games are very difficult to utilize in a regular classroom during a single semester, with the average role-playing game (RPG) taking about seventy hours to complete. Even if the materials are available for purchase, libraries are not very willing to buy, store, or lend games, and console equipment is expensive and regionally restricted. As it can take years of study for students to reach a language proficiency level sufficient to play games, read manga, or watch anime in the original Japanese, English translations of most materials are necessary—thereby potentially doubling the cost. Furthermore, the choices game companies and publishers make in terms of what to translate and market outside Japan are not the same ones that academics would make. This also makes it difficult to match popular content with sound theoretical or methodological approaches—often resulting in either a misrepresentation of Japanese popular genres or an academically thin syllabus. In summary it is often too complicated, time consuming, and expensive to accumulate enough Japanese pop culture materials, particularly recent ones, to build a "proper" program outside Japan or in a language other than Japanese.

Pop as Propaganda

The celebratory nature of the Cool Japan phenomenon has had wide implications, from its validation both within Japan and internationally by "academic fans," to its appropriation by the Japanese government for foreign policy and tourism promotion. To some extent this has made it difficult to critique in a classroom of manga and anime fans, and therefore a risk. As Laura Miller has pointed out, "Cool Japan is saturated with so much visual delight and so many creative aspects that it is difficult to convey the sense that there is . . . something troubling about it."[24] From our review of the literature, many of the issues we have identified as being problematic in current research and teaching of Japanese popular culture, were actually identified many years before Cool Japan began to receive attention in the academy, and will be examined in the following section, "Poco Pop." Somehow these critiques and debates have been sidelined as the global success of Japanese popular culture products has tended to occupy scholars.

We have identified three major issues concerning the Cool Japan phenomenon in the research literature that we think are pertinent to the risks and potentials inherent in the teaching of Japanese pop culture: the marketing of a national brand, the eradication of history, and cultural hegemony.[25] Essentially, and as some scholars point out, these are all just recycled forms of colonialism, capitalism, and industrialization. However, it is not our intention to chart the development of Cool Japan and Japanese "soft power" here. Instead, we found that the research literature has tended to overlook gender and labor issues, which are central to co-optation by the Japanese government of the global success of Japanese popular culture. These kinds of political issues must be included in Japanese popular culture courses that deal with Cool Japan. Otherwise, as Tavin argues, if the politics of culture are erased, then insider practices and privileged myths are reified and reproduce the status quo.[26]

Here we think it is beneficial to highlight Miller's research, since her analysis of the "Ambassadors of Cute" (Kawaii Taishi), a 2009 initiative of the Ministry of Foreign Affairs (MOFA), has argued that Cool Japan is a gendered ideology, a male enterprise that has objectified and commodified women. In particular, she notes, "Women and girls as subjects rather than objects are often missing in enthusiastic celebrations of Cool Japan, particularly in formulations that are sponsored or promoted by mainstream and government institutions."[27] The Ambassadors of Cute were three young women who were chosen to promote Japanese fashion overseas by wearing the uniforms or costumes of carefully chosen subcultures. They were categorized as the schoolgirl, the Lolita, and the Harajuku teen.[28] All wore teen-oriented fashions, although they were no longer teenagers. All were professionals—a singer, an actress, and a model. Miller's concern is that "the selection, media production, and strategic deployment of the Ambassadors of Cute were primarily in the hands of middle-aged men."[29] Her analysis reveals two main patterns: reinforcement of gender norms and paternalistic control of women and girls.

According to Miller, the Ambassadors of Cute reinforce gender norms in two ways. First, the fashions and models "conform to conventional gender norms and reinforce a non-threatening girlhood."[30] They are "kooky or edgy enough to a foreign audience to suggest putative coolness, but ... not disrupt gender norms and gender politics."[31] The second way in which the Ambassadors of Cute reinforce gender norms is through control by exclusion. Miller writes that the Cool Japan project has promoted male geek culture "by displacing female innovations and creativity in cultural production to the margins," which she sees as a deliberate tactic that maintains and promotes gender stratification.[32] Additionally, this exclusion is practiced because there are "forms of innovative girl culture that are not easily packaged and exported as part of these soft power initiatives."[33] Overall, MOFA has simplified girl culture into a kind of mindless consumption of lace and sweetness, which completely excludes "female agency and resistance through aesthetic forms" in Japanese girl culture.[34]

In terms of labor, the Cool Japan project is built on contradictions and inequities that have been largely overlooked in the research literature. For teaching purposes, these issues are highly relevant. For example, one of the key tenets of the media literacy research model advocates including an analysis of the sociocultural context in which media texts are created, in conjunction with media content and audiences.[35] Certainly, the labor conditions in which Japanese cultural products are produced have not received as much academic attention as the actual products themselves. Moreover, it has been pointed out that, although international fans of Japanese pop culture are usually extremely knowledgeable about the content of the anime or manga they consume, they are much less familiar with the artists, animators, producers, or publishers who create them.[36]

Even the current limited research on the *shōjo* manga (girls' comics) industry and the background to its gendered division of labor provides an important indicator of gendered labor inequities. As with most manga genres, *shōjo* manga is gender segregated and specifically aimed at a young female audience. However, Jennifer S. Prough reports that, although 99 percent of *shōjo* manga artists are women, 75 to 80 percent of editors in *shōjo* manga publishing companies are men.[37] This gendered division of labor is also in line with Japanese media industries that employ much higher numbers of young women.[38] In the case of the *shōjo* manga industry, Prough writes that 80 percent of the artists published in most *shōjo* manga magazines are new, and therefore younger than the other 20 percent, who are "veteran artists."[39] The income of young artists, whether they are female or male, is also very low. According to a 2012 media report, young animators earn on average just over a million yen (about 12,185 US dollars) per year.[40]

Anne Allison's research highlights another aspect of the contradictions in the labor conditions of the Cool Japan project (which she refers to as "J-cool"). She argues that Japanese youth is now in a precarious position, as under neoliberal policies an increasingly flexible economy is shifting from manufacturing with materials to the immateriality of information and communications industries.[41] Due to unstable and insecure employment conditions, young Japanese are marrying later, if at all, or delaying starting families. They have been blamed for the low birth rate and criticised for "choosing" *freeter* lifestyles.[42] However, Allison argues that the central issue is the failure of immaterial labor, which is at the core of the Cool Japan industries, to reproduce effectively. The lack of stable and secure employment with salaries commensurate to the cost of supporting a family and the inability to contribute to the pension system have destabilized the socioeconomic order. At the same time, Allison identifies a gap.

> J-cool falls short in providing a sociological roadmap sufficient to the times. With a recursive worldview and a timeless, endless play that is addictively, narcissistically fun, J-cool tends to collapse in on itself, encouraging youth to do the same. Neither it nor calls to revive the nuclear family are adequate to deal with the crisis in reproduction facing Japan today.[43]

Thus, the cool, cute, and fun consumer lifestyles that Cool Japan promotes ignore the realities of gendered hierarchies and socioeconomic realities in contemporary Japanese society. Bringing these issues into the classroom is by no means without friction. As Miller notes, "to criticize Cool Japan opens one up to charges of being a disapproving prude, after all it's just fantasy, entertainment and cute fun!"[44] However, because the Japanese government has appropriated Cool Japan, stripping it of its "potential to question and challenge culture," and "taking away its cutting-edge, counter-culture appeal" in order to promote an apolitical, ahistorical and homogenous Japan, dissent and diversity have been quashed.[45] This situation provides a good opportunity to critique the status quo that the government and media industries are attempting to reinforce through Cool Japan.

Poco Pop

Prior to Cool Japan becoming a significant preoccupation of the academy, scholars versed in postcolonial theory were arguing that area studies needed to transcend the confines and limitations of its colonial origins and think beyond western hegemonies of knowledge production to include cross- or pan-area gender, race, and class issues.

The traditional approach of area studies has been for the western scholar to objectively observe "the other" and then explain and interpret the cultural, social, and historical peculiarities of specific geographic regions through established disciplines.[46] In the Zadankai (roundtable) discussion paper with historians Tessa Morris-Suzuki and Narita Ryūichi, anthropologist Yao Souchou has stated that the problem of area studies is "an inability to get beyond area, and the failure to examine universal human concerns within the specificities of local anxieties and aspirations."[47] Tessa Morris-Suzuki has written on the possibility of "anti-area studies," which examines "a specific social, political or historical problem from widely differing geographical vantage points" and "aims to promote cross-border exchanges of ideas about common problems ... in our complex and globalized world" and pointedly seeks dialogue between disparate geographic spaces such as those of minority communities.[48]

Harry Harootunian, a long-standing critic of the apolitical and ahistorical tendencies in Asian area studies in the United States, describes the origins of the crises for area studies as the point at which area studies academics ignored Edward Said's warning regarding the inherent causal connections between orientalism (as a discursive system) and area studies at universities (as a state apparatus). Instead of seizing the opportunity to critique the Cold War policies that resulted in the creation of area studies programming, Japanese area studies retreated into cultural relativism and nativism, rendering itself theoretically archaic and allowing English literature to colonize the postcolonial. According to Harootunian, the major consequence of this missed opportunity:

> is that the migration of colonial discourse to English studies meant that its emphasis would be textual, semiotic, and generic, whereas if area studies had confronted the challenge posed by the Saidian critique, there would have been greater concern for the social sciences and the role played by political economy, that is to say, materiality.[49]

Correspondingly, Rey Chow has written about the risks and potentials of postcolonial cultural studies approaches for Asian area studies. Similar to Harootunian, for Chow the potential lies in a critique of orientalist methodologies and approaches. The risk, though, lies in the possibility that area studies scholars will turn postcolonial critiques around to support an antitheory position.

> Even those whose work has only to do with the most culturally chauvinistic, canonical issues and nothing to do with gender, class, or race, are suddenly able to claim not only for their objects of study but also for themselves the subject position of an oppressed, marginalized minority simply because they are the so-called "specialists" of a non-Western culture; because they are, as they always have been, straightforward Orientalists![50]

With more specific regard to popular culture in Japanese studies, the approach we are calling, "poco pop" is a methodology for researching and teaching about popular culture that is directly informed by and descended from postcolonial theory. It is more likely to be associated with cultural studies than traditional Japanese studies. Because it tends to warn of the negative effects, particularly in Asia, of the globalization and universalization of Japanese popular cultural products, it could also be called "political pop." Despite Harootunian's critique of the textual turn, postcolonial literary theory provides theoretical tools, within Anglo-Japanese studies, with which to create a speaking position between old-fashioned orientalism and the negative side of Cool Japan or the "narcissistic discourse of soft nationalism" that Koichi Iwabuchi, in 2002, warned was coming. Iwabuchi explains that because of its failing economy, the "hitherto unthinkable diffusion of Japanese popular culture throughout the world seems to inspire a social and personal lift in Japan," but that uncritical discussions of this cultural power easily become "chauvinistic."[51]

This narcissism is clearly visible in Kyoto Seika University's English-language public relations webpage, advertising its Faculty of Manga.

Now Japanese manga is spreading all around the world and is widely accepted, regardless of national or cultural differences. In the same way that speaking multiple languages lets people communicate internationally, we will soon arrive at an era in which drawing manga becomes a global communication tool. SEIKA graduates are spreading around the world, enrapturing people through manga and animation. With the immense creative power of manga and animation, the Faculty aspires to contribute to world peace.[52]

Interestingly, many popular culture academics are claiming the exact opposite—that the global interest in Japanese popular culture will prevent future generations from thinking about or acting on political issues. For example, Yoshiko Shimada, writing in 2002 about a Japan-Singapore collaborative theater project in Singapore, notes that the young people involved did not want to talk to each other about the World War II issues that the project was supposed to be about, but preferred Japanese popular culture topics. She concludes, "Behind the rosy, futuristic picture of Japan-Asia, where history is eradicated and consumerism rules, there may be a darker side where Japan's strategy to obtain cultural hegemony in Asia makes any kind of questioning and resistance invalid."[53]

In addition, Nissim Kadosh Otmazgin, in his 2008 research on the effectiveness of Japanese soft power in Korea, conducted many interviews with young Koreans about their interest in Japanese pop culture. He found that they felt anger toward Japan about things they had learned in their history classes, but that they believed these things were dissociated from their interest in popular culture products from Japan. He concludes: "As the case in East Asia shows, consumer reception points strongly to apolitical consumers who remain politicized only by the politics of memory (war, textbooks, etc.) but who refuse to see any politics in their affection to popular culture."[54]

Despite the risks of postcolonial theory privileging literary approaches to Japanese popular culture, if encouraging students to politicize their consumption of Japanese popular culture products is an important learning goal, then much more time in the curriculum will need to be allocated to teaching and learning critical theory than is currently common in many Japanese popular culture courses and publications.

Consequently, we believe that establishing critical pedagogy as part of the teaching and research of Japanese popular culture could help improve this situation because it provides a "pedagogy of possibility." As Weaver and Daspit have argued, "[W]e need to study the ways in which popular culture offers alternative possibilities just as much as it articulates or resists the agenda of power blocs."[55] Similarly, David W. Livingstone made a case at an earlier time that critical pedagogy must persist so as "to expose the dynamics of cultural power and to enable popular engagement in creating alternative futures."[56] These are approaches that could be used to engage students, as well as inspiring more critical, and ethical, teaching and research.

Pop to Prep

With the "pop to prep" approach, the study of Japanese popular culture is seen as equivalent to, or a way toward, teaching intercultural communication skills—a method for learning twenty-first-century literacies and digital media skills that will purportedly prepare students for future employment. In the case of Australia, it has long been recognized that "whatever the political future of the Asia-Pacific region, Australian society will increasingly need citizens who possess a good knowledge of neighboring regions."[57] Successive governments have funded language-education programs to increase "Asia literacy." The most recent was the National Asian Languages and Studies in Schools Program (NALSSP), which aims to produce fluent speakers of Japanese, Mandarin, Bahasa Indonesia, and Hindi at the high school level by 2020.[58] In Canada the current marketability of intercultural skills or global citizenship training provides an important argument for preserving Japanese language or culture classes, particularly at smaller universities that do not offer full Japanese or area studies majors. Universities that are trying to brand themselves as international and supportive of diversity need non-western course offerings, and Japanese language and culture electives appeal to international students from Asia—a student population that universities in North America and Australia are seeking to attract, as they generate significantly higher international tuition fees.

While research shows that study abroad combined with specific learning interventions can significantly increase intercultural development, unfortunately, the kinds of teaching and learning activities that are reported to be effective require the exploration and adjustment of deep-seated personal beliefs and long-held behavioral patterns.[59] This is a time-consuming, labor-intensive, and emotionally challenging process.[60] In other words, even if students could be convinced to do the extra work and self-reflection required for intercultural skills development, on top of reading the literature, writing papers, and conjugating verbs correctly, we could not properly mentor, supervise, or evaluate it if our classes stay the same size or shape they are now. Regrettably, many intercultural communication studies and much education research shows that the typical kinds of "university learning," such as learning about culture through literature, history, or art, learning a language, or even study abroad, do not on their own directly lead to the development of measureable intercultural skills.[61]

Furthermore, our own pedagogical practices and classroom experiences have shown that our students tend to see Japanese-language studies as a means of access to Japanese friends and Cool Japan and do not see Japanese as a tool for communicating with those who are not ethnically Japanese. They actively resist intercultural skills assignments in the classroom as a result and respond on surveys that it is a waste of time and detracts from learning *more* language (rather than *better* communication, which was the learning objective).

Twenty-first-century skills are mostly related to the digital media realm: "new" media, social media, mobile media, video production, or anything to do with video games. Real digital media literacy would require years of intensive production training, as well as mastery of the usual academic materials and practices needed for critique. Furthermore, the technical skills necessary for digital media production require up-to-date equipment and relatively small student-to-instructor ratios. One "blogging" assignment in a film theory class is not going to help students land jobs in the film industry.

The effective and successful incorporation of either intercultural or digital literacies and skills into Japanese pop culture courses would also require retraining for most instructors and curriculum redesign for all programs—a major investment of time, energy, and money that would require commitment by all faculty members involved. In addition, over-emphasis on these skills and literacies could distract from basic literacy or be seen as false advertising, since there are no data showing that more skill-based courses actually lead to better hiring rates for university graduates or better salary gains.

Discussion and Conclusion

No matter what the discipline, political underpinnings, or main learning goals are, university students in academic classes will need to do academic work—they cannot just sit around talking about their favorite manga characters or anime and get university credit for it. If students are keen to explore the imaginary in Japanese popular culture texts, as Swenson has identified it,[62] then it is also imperative that they have knowledge of the social, cultural, and economic contexts in which these texts were created. To this end, learning outcomes must be defined and clearly communicated by educators. This is not just an issue of "rigor" or "methods"; it is also one of directionality. The best way to solve this, we think, is to advocate an approach whereby students studying popular culture use Japan to explain the text, rather than using the text to explain Japan. In this way, the issues of orientalism, essentializing, and othering can be addressed as part of classroom discussions and analysis.[63] Jenkins gives examples of supplementary materials that can engender meaningful classroom discussions on cultural traditions, cultural identity, and imported cultural products, for example.[64] However, he is quick to point out that the goal of these classroom discussions should not be to push aside popular culture in favor of more authentic or refined culture but to help students develop more sophisticated understandings.[65]

As an intellectual research community, the pedagogical challenges faced in the Japanese popular culture classroom have produced an opportunity to discuss creative curricular design possibilities and argue for establishing a core of critical analysis and historical contextualization in Japanese popular culture studies. We think that this has to happen in three ways: first, by focusing on minority cultures in Japan and looking at diversity and dissent within the society in order to avoid stereotypical generalizations and assumptions; second, by recognizing labor issues and socioeconomic context, in particular cultural labor and affective labor in Japanese popular culture industries; and, last, by developing effective teaching practices with clear learning outcomes.[66]

From what we have discovered in the five paradigmatic approaches discussed above, we have identified a need to improve pedagogy, measure it and evaluate it—and not just value it. If we are to convince university administrators, as well as parents, taxpayers, and students, that the study of Japanese popular culture really is beneficial, then we need to be able to define the benefits and explain what would constitute the measure of their assessment. To this end, we are calling for cooperation in research about teaching Japanese popular culture and the development of tools and protocols for measuring the effectiveness of such teaching. We suspect that it is going to become increasingly important to be able to demonstrate, with data, the relevance of our teaching. One way to establish this is by forming action research communities.[67] Without metrics we could spend all our time on genuine and legitimate differences of opinion and make our own jobs redundant.

By establishing critical pedagogy in Japanese popular culture courses, practices of teaching and learning can be strengthened by challenging both educators and students "to investigate, understand, and intervene in the matrix of connections between schooling, ideology, power, and culture."[68] The risks we have identified are also what gives the study of Japanese popular culture the potential to be a powerful and efficient tool, making visible and comprehensible the "constructedness" of the discourse of global culture and the subjectivities available through the Japanese popular narratives consumed daily around the world.

Notes

[1] Graeme Turner, *What's Become of Cultural Studies?* (London: Sage, 2012), 71.

[2] Ibid., 89.

[3] Peter McLaren, "Revolutionary Pedagogy in Post-revolutionary Times: Rethinking the Political Economy of Critical Education," *Educational Theory* 48, no. 4 (1998): 441.

[4] Henry A. Giroux, *Disturbing Pleasures: Learning Popular Culture*. (New York: Routledge, 1994), 133.

[5] John Weaver and Toby A. Daspit, "Critical Pedagogy, Popular Culture, and the Creation of Meaning," in *Popular Culture and Critical Pedagogy: Reading, Constructing, Connecting*, ed. John Weaver and Toby A. Daspit (New York: Garland, 1999), xv.

[6] Tamara Swenson, "What Kind of Culture Could Produce These? Appeal of the Exotic as Entry into Japanese Culture," *Ōsaka Jogakuin Daigaku Kiyō* [Osaka Jogakuin College Bulletin] 4 (2007): 109.

[7] Ibid. 116.

[8] Ibid., 117.

[9] Ibid., 119.

[10] Swenson (ibid.) credits Toshiya Ueno with having originated this term in 2002, but it was actually coined (and critiqued first) by David Morley and Kevin Robins in 1995 and later paraphrased by Ueno. See Toshiya Ueno, "Japanimation: Techno-Orientalism, Media Tribes, and Rave Culture," in *Aliens R Us: The Other in Science Fiction Cinema*, ed. Ziauddin Sardar and Sean Cubitt (London: Pluto Press, 2002); and David Morley and Kevin Robins, *Spaces of Identity: Global Media, Electronic Landscapes, and Cultural Boundaries* (London: Routledge, 1995), 97.

[11] Swenson, "What Kind of Culture Could Produce These?," 118.

[12] Henry Jenkins, *Fans, Bloggers, and Gamers: Exploring Participatory Culture* (New York: New York University Press, 2006), 170.

[13] Kevin M. Tavin, "Wrestling with Angels, Searching for Ghosts: Toward a Critical Pedagogy of Visual Culture Studies," *Art Education* 44, no. 3 (2003): 198.

[14] Ibid., 200.

[15] Jenkins, *Fans, Bloggers, and Gamers,* 172.

[16] See chapter 10, by Philip Seaton, in this volume for a discussion of how Japanese popular culture can be effectively used in Japanese history courses.

[17] See chapter 7 by Deborah Shamoon and chapter 2 by William S. Armour and Sumiko Iida in this volume.

[18] Turner, *What's Become of Cultural Studies?*, 86.

[19] Stanley Fish, "The Crisis of the Humanities Officially Arrives," *New York Times*, October 11, 2010, http://opinionator.blogs.nytimes.com/2010/10/11/the-crisis-of-the-humanities-officially-arrives/?_r=0.

[20] However, there are media reports claiming that Japan's soft power is so unique that it will continue to attract students to Japanese studies. See "Aussie Students Switching to Chinese but Japan's Soft Power Still Inspires," *Japan Times*, December 21, 2012, http://www.japantimes.co.jp/text/nn20121221f2.html.

[21] Japan Foundation, "Preliminary Results of the Survey on Japanese-Language Education Abroad, 2012," Japan Foundation, http://www.jpf.go.jp/e/japanese/survey/result/survey12.html.

[22] Film studies and cultural studies has never really had a production side, especially the North American and Australian variations, which morphed out of English literature.

[23] Turner, *What's Become of Cultural Studies?*, 77.

[24] Laura Miller, "Cute Masquerade and the Pimping of Japan," *International Journal of Japanese Sociology* 20 (2011): 27.

[25] See Koichi Iwabuchi, "Soft Nationalism and Narcissism: Japanese Popular Culture Goes Global," *Asian Studies Review* 26, no. 4 (2002): 447–69; Michal Daliot-Bul, "Japan Brand Strategy: The Taming of 'Cool Japan' and the Challenges of Cultural Planning in a Postmodern Age," *Japan Social Science Journal* 12, no. 2 (2009): 247-66; Yoshiko Shimada, "Afterword: Japanese Pop Culture and the Eradication of History," in *Consuming Bodies: Sex and Contemporary Japanese Art*, ed. Fran Lloyd (London: Reaktion Books, 2002); Peng Er Lam, "Japan's Quest for 'Soft Power': Attraction and Limitation," *East Asia* 24, no. 4 (2007): 349-63; Coralie Castel, "'Nihonjinron' in the Museums of Paris: Design and Japanese Identity," *Cipango: French Journal of Japanese Studies* 1 (2012): 227; Koichi Iwabuchi, "De-westernization and the Governance of Global Cultural Connectivity: A Dialogic Approach to East Asian Media Cultures," *Postcolonial Studies* 13, no. 4 (2010): 403-19; and Nissim Kadosh Otmazgin, "Contesting Soft Power: Japanese Popular Culture in East and Southeast Asia," *International Relations of the Asia-Pacific* 8 (2008): 73-101.

[26] Tavin, "Wrestling with Angels," 197.

[27] Miller, "Cute Masquerade," 19.

[28] Unfortunately it is not within the scope of this chapter to unpack and discuss just how problematic these three categories are. Please refer to Miller's article (ibid.) for her excellent analysis of MOFA's fetishization of the Ambassadors of Cute.

[29] Ibid., 20.

[30] Ibid.

[31] Ibid., 2.

[32] Ibid., 19.

[33] Ibid.

[34] Ibid., 24.

[35] Although it has been pointed out to us that the relationship between text and context should be obvious to university instructors, we have observed that this is not always the case in the research and teaching of Japanese popular culture. Suzuki Midori, ed., *Study Guide Media Literashii: Nyūmon Hen* [Media literacy study guide: Introductory approach], rev. ed. (Tokyo: Liberta Publishing, 2013).

[36] Roland Kelts, "Japanamerica: Why Cool Japan Is Over," *3:AM*, May 17, 2010, http://www.3ammagazine.com/3am/japanamerica-why-cool-japan-is-over/.

[37] Jennifer S. Prough, *Straight from the Heart: Gender, Intimacy, and the Cultural Production of Shojo Manga* (Honolulu: University of Hawai'i Press, 2011), 96.

[38] According to annual surveys conducted by the Newspaper Publishers and Editors Association, and the state broadcaster NHK, the total number of women working at all levels in print and broadcast media organizations is approximately 13 percent, with the majority in their twenties or thirties.

[39] Prough, *Straight from the Heart,* 98.

[40] Dan Grunebaum, "Is Japan Losing Its Cool?," *Christian Science Monitor,* December 8, 2012, http://www.csmonitor.com/World/Asia-Pacific/2012/1208/Is-Japan-losing-its-cool.

[41] Anne Allison, "The Cool Brand, Affective Activism, and Japanese Youth," *Theory, Culture & Society* 26, no. 2 (2009): 90.

[42] Defined by Allison as "workers, mainly young people, who are employed in non-permanent jobs such as convenience stores" See Allison, "The Cool Brand," 98.

[43] Ibid., 106.

[44] Miller, "Cute Masquerade," 27.

[45] Daliot-Bul, "Japan Brand Strategy," 262.

[46] Tessa Morris-Suzuki, "Australia, Japan, and the Asia-Pacific Region: From the Perspective of Frontier Studies," *Otemon Journal of Australian Studies* 30 (2004): 101.

[47] Ryūichi Narita, Tessa Morris-Suzuki, and Yao Souchou, "Zadankai: On Cultural Studies, Japanese Studies, Area Studies," *Japanese Studies* 18, no. 1 (1998): 86.

[48] Morris-Suzuki, "Australia, Japan, and the Asia-Pacific Region," 101.

[49] Harry Harootunian, "Postcoloniality's Unconscious/Area Studies' Desire," in *Learning Places: The Afterlives of Area Studies*, ed. Masao Miyoshi and Harry Harootunian (Durham, NC: Duke University Press, 2002), 167.

[50] Rey Chow, "Theory, Area Studies, Cultural Studies: Issues of Pedagogy in Multiculturalism," in *Learning Places: The Afterlives of Area Studies*, ed. Masao Miyoshi and Harry Harootunian (Durham, NC: Duke University Press, 2002), 111.

[51] Koichi Iwabuchi, "Soft Nationalism," 448.

[52] Kyoto Seika University, Faculty of Manga page, n.d., www.kyoto-seika.ac.jp/eng/edu/manga/

[53] Shimada, "Afterword," 191.

[54] Otmazgin, "Contesting Soft Power," 26.

[55] Weaver and Daspit, "Critical Pedagogy," vii.

[56] David W. Livingstone, "Introduction," in *Critical Pedagogy and Cultural Power*, ed. David W. Livingstone (New York: Bergin & Harvey, 1987), 12.

[57] Morris-Suzuki, "Australia, Japan, and the Asia-Pacific Region," 100.

[58] "Aussie Students Switching to Chinese but Japan's Soft Power Still Inspires." *Japan Times*, December 21, 2012, www.japantimes.co.jp/text/nn20121221f2.html.

[59] For examples of research with specific intercultural interventions tested in university courses, see Lili Engle and John Engle. "Assessing Language Acquisition and Intercultural Sensitivity Development in Relation to Study Abroad Program Design." *Frontiers: The Interdisciplinary Journal of Study Abroad* 10, (2004): 219-36 (for French): and Paula Pedersen. "Teaching towards an Ethnorelative Worldview Through Psychology Study Abroad." *Intercultural Education* 20, sup1, (2009): S73-86 (for psychology).

[60] See Janice Abarbanel. "Moving with Emotional Resilience Between and Within Cultures." *Intercultural Education*, 20, sup1, (2009): S133-141 on the necessity of "emotional resilience." Michael R. Paige "On the Nature of Intercultural Experiences and Intercultural Education." In *Education of the Intercultural Experience*, edited by Michael.R. Paige, 1-20. Yarmouth, ME: Intercultural Press, 2003 on intercultural psychological stress factors, and Anita Mak and Monica Kennedy. "Internationalising the Student experience: Preparing Instructors to Embed Intercultural Skills in the Curriculum." *Innovative Higher Education* 37, 2012: 323-34 for their work on training instructors to embed intercultural skills in the curriculum.

[61] See Milton Bennet. "Defining, Measuring, and Facilitating Intercultural Learning: A Conceptual Introduction to the Intercultural Education Double Supplement." *Intercultural Education* 20, sup1, (2009): S1-13 for research on the Intercultural Development Inventory. See Jonathan Crichton and Angela Scarino. "How are we to Understand the 'Intercultural Dimension'? An Examination of the Intercultural dimension of Internationalisation in the Context of Higher Education in Australia." *Australian Review of Applied Linguistics* 30, no.1, (2007): 04.1-21 for their work on intercultural training in higher education in Australia. In this volume, Sugawa-Shimada's observation that Japanese students will not talk (unless in small groups) provides an example of where intercultural awareness could be built in to an academic setting and become an explicit learning goal. Because it is predictable and consistent, this kind of conflict (or, more precisely, conflict avoidance) could actually become the content of a course with learning goals focused on increasing awareness of intercultural conflict styles. Assignments that challenge students to figure out, on their own, ways to ameliorate the imbalance in discussion participation or level of engagement in classroom discussions of a political nature would be useful.

[62] Swenson, "What Kind of Culture Could Produce These?," 119.

[63] This is a point made by many of the authors in this volume. But to reach this end, Japanese popular culture courses and programs need to be planned purposefully. Those of us who teach the subject need to apply the critical thinking skills we are so keen to pass on to students to our own teaching practices and methodologies.

[64] Jenkins, *Fans, Bloggers and Gamers,* 170–71.

[65] Ibid., 172.

[66] That clearly defined and explicitly stated learning outcomes are necessary is something that is basic to good course design and is known to most. However, our point here is that, as Japanese popular culture is taught across a multitude of disciplines, critical discussions of Japanese popular culture pedagogy are imperative.

[67] Turner has also called for a discipline-wide dialogue about the teaching of cultural studies. See Turner, *What's Become of Cultural Studies?*, 91.

[68] Tavin, "Wrestling with Angels," 198.

Works Cited

Abarbanel, Janice. "Moving with Emotional Resilience between and within Cultures." *Intercultural Education* 20, sup1 (2009): S133–41.

Allison, Anne. "The Cool Brand, Affective Activism, and Japanese Youth." *Theory, Culture & Society* 26, no. 2 (2009): 89–111.

"Aussie Students Switching to Chinese but Japan's Soft Power Still Inspires." *Japan Times*, December 21, 2012, www.japantimes.co.jp/text/ nn20121221f2.html.

Bennet, Milton. "Defining, Measuring, and Facilitating Intercultural Learning: A Conceptual Introduction to the Intercultural Education Double Supplement." *Intercultural Education* 20, sup1 (2009): S1–13.

Castel, Coralie. "'Nihonjinron' in the Museums of Paris: Design and Japanese Identity." *Cipango: French Journal of Japanese Studies* 1 (2012): 227.

Chow, Rey. "Theory, Area Studies, Cultural Studies: Issues of Pedagogy in Multiculturalism." In *Learning Places: The Afterlives of Area Studies*, edited by Masao Miyoshi and Harry Harootunian, 103–18. Durham, NC: Duke University Press, 2002.

Crichton, Jonathan, and Angela Scarino. "How Are We to Understand the 'Intercultural Dimension'? An Examination of the Intercultural Dimension of Internationalisation in the Context of Higher Education in Australia." *Australian Review of Applied Linguistics* 30, no. 1 (2007): 04.1–21.

Daliot-Bul, Michal. "Japan Brand Strategy: The Taming of 'Cool Japan' and the Challenges of Cultural Planning in a Postmodern Age." *Japan Social Science Journal* 12, no. 2 (2009): 247–66.

Engle, Lili, and Engle, John. "Assessing Language Acquisition and Intercultural Sensitivity Development in Relation to Study Abroad Program Design." *Frontiers: The Interdisciplinary Journal of Study Abroad* 10 (Fall 2004): 219–36.

Fish, Stanley. "The Crisis of the Humanities Officially Arrives." *New York Times,* October 11, 2010, http://opinionator.blogs.nytimes.com/2010/10/11/ the-crisis-of-the-humanities-officially-arrives/?_r=0

Giroux, Henry A. *Disturbing Pleasures: Learning Popular Culture.* New York: Routledge, 1994.

Grunebaum, Dan. "Is Japan Losing Its Cool?" *Christian Science Monitor,* December 8, 2012. http://www.csmonitor.com/World/Asia-Pacific/2012/1208/Is-Japan-losing-its-cool.

Harootunian, Harry. "Postcoloniality's Unconscious/Area Studies' Desire." In *Learning Places: The Afterlives of Area Studies*, ed. Masao Miyoshi and Harry Harootunian, 150–74. Durham, NC: Duke University Press, 2002.

Iwabuchi, Koichi. "De-westernization and the Governance of Global Cultural Connectivity: A Dialogic Approach to East Asian Media Cultures." *Postcolonial Studies* 13, no. 4 (2010): 403–19.

———. "Soft Nationalism and Narcissism: Japanese Popular Culture Goes Global." *Asian Studies Review* 26, no. 4 (2002): 447–69.

Japan Foundation. "Preliminary Results of the Survey on Japanese-Language Education Abroad, 2012," http://www.jpf.go.jp/e/japanese/survey/result/survey12.html.

Jenkins, Henry. *Fans, Bloggers, and Gamers: Exploring Participatory Culture.* New York: New York University Press, 2006.

Kelts, Roland. "Japanamerica: Why Cool Japan Is Over." *3:AM,* May 17, 2010, http://www.3ammagazine.com/3am/japanamerica-why-cool-japan-is-over/.

Kyoto Seika University. Faculty of Manga page, n.d., http://www.kyoto-seika.ac.jp/eng/edu/manga/.

Lam, Peng Er. "Japan's Quest for 'Soft Power': Attraction and Limitation." *East Asia* 24, no. 4 (2007): 349–63.

Livingstone, David W. "Introduction." In *Critical Pedagogy and Cultural Power*, edited by David W. Livingstone, 1–12. New York: Bergin & Harvey, 1987.

Mak, Anita, and Monica Kennedy. "Internationalising the Student Experience: Preparing Instructors to Embed Intercultural Skills in the Curriculum." *Innovative Higher Education* 37 no. 4 (2012): 323–34.

McLaren, Peter. "Revolutionary Pedagogy in Post-revolutionary Times: Rethinking the Political Economy of Critical Education." *Educational Theory* 48, no. 4 (1998): 431–62.

Miller, Laura. "Cute Masquerade and the Pimping of Japan." *International Journal of Japanese Sociology* 20, no. 1 (2011): 18–29.

Morley, David, and Kevin Robins. *Spaces of Identity: Global Media, Electronic Landscapes, and Cultural Boundaries,* London: Routledge, 1995.

Morris-Suzuki, Tessa. "Australia, Japan, and the Asia-Pacific Region: From the Perspective of Frontier Studies." *Otemon Journal of Australian Studies* 30 (2004): 99–117.

Narita Ryūichi, Tessa Morris-Suzuki, and Yao Souchou. "Zadankai: On Cultural Studies, Japanese Studies, Area Studies." *Japanese Studies* 18, no. 1 (1998): 73–87.

Otmazgin, Nissim Kadosh. "Contesting Soft Power: Japanese Popular Culture in East and Southeast Asia." *International Relations of the Asia-Pacific* 8 (2008): 73–101.

Paige, Michael R. "On the Nature of Intercultural Experiences and Intercultural Education." In *Education of the Intercultural Experience,* edited by Michael R. Paige, 1–20. Yarmouth, ME: Intercultural Press, 2003.

Pedersen, Paula. "Teaching towards an Ethnorelative Worldview through Psychology Study Abroad." *Intercultural Education* 20, sup1 (2009): S73–86.

Prough, Jennifer S. *Straight from the Heart: Gender, Intimacy, and the Cultural Production of Shojo Manga.* Honolulu: University of Hawai'i Press, 2011.

Shimada, Yoshiko. "Afterword: Japanese Pop Culture and the Eradication of History." In *Consuming Bodies: Sex and Contemporary Japanese Art,* edited by Fran Lloyd, 186–91. London: Reaktion Books, 2002.

Suzuki Midori, ed. *Study Guide Media Literashii: Nyūmon Hen* [Media literacy study guide: Introductory approach]. Rev. ed. Tokyo: Liberta Publishing, 2013.

Swenson, Tamara. "What Kind of Culture Could Produce These? Appeal of the Exotic as Entry into Japanese Culture." *Ōsaka Jogakuin Daigaku Kiyo* [Osaka Jogakuin College Bulletin] 4 (2007): 103–22.

Tavin, Kevin M. "Wrestling with Angels, Searching for Ghosts: Toward a Critical Pedagogy of Visual Culture Studies." *Art Education* 44, no. 3 (2003): 197–213.

Turner, Graeme. *What's Become of Cultural Studies?* London: Sage, 2012.

Ueno, Toshiya. "Japanimation: Techno-Orientalism, Media Tribes, and Rave Culture." In *Aliens R Us: The Other in Science Fiction Cinema*, edited by Ziauddin Sardar and Sean Cubitt, 94–110. London: Pluto Press, 2002.

Weaver, John, and Toby A. Daspit. "Critical Pedagogy, Popular Culture, and the Creation of Meaning." In *Popular Culture and Critical Pedagogy: Reading, Constructing, Connecting*, edited by John Weaver and Toby A. Daspit, xiii–xxxiii. New York: Garland, 1999.

2

TALKING JAPANESE POPULAR CULTURE AT AN AUSTRALIAN UNIVERSITY

INSIGHTS FROM A LITERACIES PEDAGOGY PERSPECTIVE

WILLIAM S. ARMOUR AND SUMIKO IIDA

Introduction

Hindsight is a luxury that cannot and should not be taken for granted. Reflecting on past course designs, curriculum development endeavors, and how they were rendered into actual classroom pedagogies has provided us with the impetus for this chapter. To date we have been exploring the "Japanese popular culture effects argument" or the view that the private consumption of Japanese popular culture (hereafter JPC) in some way motivates individuals to study the Japanese language and Japan.[1] While a small literature supports this argument, there is another side to it. Drawing on data from an online survey of 451 participants, we found that, while many had been motivated to study some Japanese language and learn about Japan, most did not advance since the JPC being consumed (anime and manga) were available in Japanese and translations into other languages.[2] We considered the role that informal learning played in how these informants used JPC to learn Japanese and/or about Japan, claiming that in the case of informal learning, JPC products stand *in loco praeceptoris* (in the place of the teacher). Informal learning can be positioned along the continuum, informal to formal learning, and can be construed as rhizomatic, that is, "a learning that takes off in a variety of directions."[3]

In this chapter, however, we consider formal learning using two JPC courses, Talking JPC and Representations of Japan, which were taught consecutively from 2002 to 2013 in a university department that, at the time these courses were offered, was charged primarily with the delivery (teaching) of a range of foreign languages, including Japanese (hence echoing observations made in several chapters in this volume regarding the location where JPC courses are actually taught). As discussed in chapter 1 by Sally McLaren and Alwyn Spies and in chapter 9 by James Dorsey, what follows is a reflection in which we explore how JPC can be used in the higher education classroom. Issues that come to mind include how the consumption of JPC for entertainment has moved along the continuum to end as becoming JPC for analysis;[4] how certain types of knowledge are charged positively and negatively in relation to their legitimacy; and how the pedagogy that was created during the life of these courses developed with the advent of greater access to certain sophisticated types of technology and Internet resources such as YouTube, the increase in published information about JPC (as canon), and a more sophisticated understanding of the transcultural flows out of Japan.

Data for this chapter are based on a summary of the course outlines used in the Talking JPC and Representations of Japan courses. We analyzed these outlines using the categories (a) Information about the course, (b) Objectives, (c) Assessment, and (d) Topics on which to focus our reflection. These data represent the major aspects of each course and are set along a chronological timeline to show course evolution. We also considered the changes in technology and other kinds of milestones as part of this chronology. The literature that discusses the pedagogical practices of using JPC in the classroom is a small one, a point made in the introductory chapter to the volume by Deborah Shamoon and Chris McMorran. We have already engaged with the work of Deborah Shamoon, especially the way she deals with otaku-identifying students.[5] A recent contribution to the discussion regarding pedagogy and JPC is one by William M. Tsutsui.[6] There are many points of intersection in his discussion paper and this chapter, for example, the shift in hierarchy of instructor and students based on their apparent extensive knowledge of a range of JPC examples and the vastness of the material that comes under the umbrella of JPC.

However, what resonates is Tsutsui's reference to a culturalist approach, which may have been taken, that encourages readers "to see manga and anime as transparent windows into Japanese cultural traditions" and "to find uniquely 'Japanese' traces" in the examples presented to and by students.[7] This approach, while understandable to some extent, has also been problematized as a concern that may "keep the nation hermetically sealed, and impede contributions to, and engagement with broader academic debates outside the study of Japan."[8] In our reflections, while we are aware that our pedagogy has favored a more culturalist approach, especially in the early 2000s, it has also evolved using recent scholarship. One challenge has been to convince our students to transcend a "this is so uniquely Japanese" discourse and replace it with one that provides tools (e.g., frameworks, literature, and examples) that can be used to reveal a more comprehensive picture of what JPC might represent, as well as how and why such tools are chosen.

Theoretical Underpinning

Given the paucity of teaching pedagogy scholarship on the delivery of courses about or with JPC, the heuristic used as the basis for our reflections comes from the work of Mary Kalantzis and Bill Cope.[9] While their work is directed toward K–12, it has offered us insights that can be used as a reflection tool but also to design and construct any future courses concerning JPC since they also consider newer modalities, including video, rap, and visuals, in their discussion of meaning making.

At the outset, our courses were not designed using this heuristic. In fact they were examples of curriculum design experimentation using advice from the university's Learning and Teaching Unit (e.g., about assessment, the shift in practices from "teaching" to "learning," blended or hybrid learning) and our own intuitions from years of personal appreciation of JPC. The course Talking JPC was developed based on demands articulated by students at the time. William M. Tsutsui uses the word *pandering*,[10] and in a sense we also pandered by hitching a ride on the JPC bandwagon not only to provide a venue where students could formally engage with JPC but also to ensure revenue generation. There is a definite resonance with the view expressed by McLaren and Spies, in chapter 1 of this volume, regarding the "pop to prop" approach, which was initially the motivation to offer Talking JPC. In contrast, Representations of Japan was a much more designed course based on a revision of Talking JPC using scholarship on learning and teaching, input from students, and our reflections, and perhaps falls into a "poco pop"approach discussed by McLaren and Spies in chapter 1 of this volume.

Kalantzis and Cope capture to a great extent the pedagogical transitions that were experienced through the delivery of the two courses. For example, the advent of technological innovations during the period 2002–10, when Talking JPC was taught, radically changed the way we could approach it. Our VHS tapes were replaced with DVDs, which then changed to media files (e.g., mov, wmv, avi) along with their distribution on the Internet. These media are now even portable by means of a smart phone or tablet. These technologies changed the way in which knowledge was collected, disseminated, and consumed by instructors and students, thus providing new content, as well as new contexts for JPC literacy teaching and learning.

The Kalantzis and Cope model also addresses the formal-to-informal learning continuum by approaching students, called Generation P (for "participatory"), as learners with "different kinds of sensibilities … [who] have at hand ubiquitous smart devices … [and are communicating] with people at a distance from them at any time of day and anywhere."[11] This transition has also been a challenge for us in terms of the associated shift in our professional identities.[12] Their model advocates a range of changes under the banner of "new-learning," including the design of learning environments rather than delivering content, using new media, letting go (of the instructor identity) and allowing students to take more responsibility for their learning, and offering a variety of learning paths in the name of differentiation.[13] We present the main thrust of the literacies heuristic as figure 2.1.

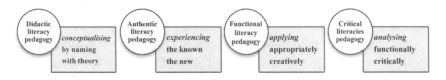

Figure 2.1. The literacy heuristic (based on
Kalantzis and Cope, *Literacies*, 355–73)

Kalantzis and Cope analyze classroom learning ecologies and literacy pedagogy on four dimensions.[14]

1. Represents the content of literacy knowledge or its subject matter, or what learners are meant to learn

2. Denotes the organization of the literacy curriculum or how the subject matter is arranged

3. Embodies learners doing literacy or the ways in which learners are intended to learn to make meanings

4. Characterizes the social relationships of literacy learning, that is, the relationships between learners and literacies knowledge, learners and other learners, and learners and instructors

Each dimension is used to judge the pros and cons of four literacy pedagogies: didactic, authentic, functional, and critical. Kalantzis and Cope describe didactic literacy pedagogy as the founding approach to reading and writing from the introduction of mass, compulsory, institutionalized education in the nineteenth century and still advocated and applied in schools (we would add universities) today.[15] The main features of didactic literacy pedagogy are learning rules, learning a "correct" way to comprehend and write, learning to respect the high cultural texts of the literary canon, and having a syllabus that tells the student what is to be learned. In contrast, authentic literacy pedagogy promotes natural growth through a learner-centered approach that provides immersion in personally meaningful reading and writing experiences, focusing on processes rather than rules and adherence to conventions.[16] The aim of functional literacy pedagogy is to help learners understand the reasons why texts exist and how this affects their shape by asking, "What is the purpose of this whole text?" and "How is the whole text structured to meet these purposes?" This pedagogy is aligned with a "genre" approach through which learners explore the ways different kinds of texts work to make different meanings in the world.[17] Last, Kalantzis and Cope explain that critical literacies pedagogy expands "literacy" into the plural by recognizing the many voices learners bring to the classroom, the many sites of popular culture and new media, and the differing perspectives that exist in real-world texts.[18] Learners are meaning makers, agents, participants, and active citizens who use the learning of literacies as a tool to enable them to take more control over the ways in which meaning is made in their lives. The pedagogy discourages the use of unfamiliar texts that make learners grudgingly compliant.

In our course designs we tended to privilege the didactic literacy pedagogy and critical literacies pedagogies over the other two. While the

Kalantzis and Cope model underpins the way we have reflected on our courses, figure 2.1 sets out the way certain "knowledge processes" (set in the rectangular boxes) cluster around each type of literacy pedagogy. Before discussing these processes in more detail, Kalantzis and Cope raise the issue of how they can be used with learners and also how they "capture some profound differences in kinds of knowing or 'epistemic moves.'"[19] These epistemic moves are also described as "things students can do to know."[20] Furthermore, while these literacy pedagogies appear to be historically sequential, moving from left to right in figure 2.1, they are in fact not so, since instructors select certain aspects of each of the four pedagogical traditions that represent goodness-of-fit in a specific context. There is also no sense of balancing the pedagogies.

> Some subject matters or learning situations might call for a lot more conceptual work, others for more experiential work. The knowledge processes require instead that teachers reflect purposefully on the mix and ordering of the epistemic moves they make in their classrooms and are able to justify their pedagogical choices on the basis of learning goals and outcomes for individuals and groups.[21]

To conclude this section, we will now consider each of the knowledge processes outlined in figure 2.1. To do this we have created figure 2.2, in which terms are further defined. For example, if we focus on "experiencing" as a knowledge process, then we can make certain claims about what each student has brought to the JPC classroom, the known. This makes sense when attempting to understand a student who identifies as otaku and brings ideas, information, and the like about anime, manga, or video games to class yet has trouble when exposed to "the new" in terms of information about these instances of JPC and more so perhaps when he or she is required to take part in some unfamiliar context such as presenting an analysis of a film or television program that might not be in his or her knowledge repertoire. The known and the new symbolize the "pedagogical weaving" between informal learning situations and the formal learning situation.[22] In some cases, however, there is actually very little weaving and more fraying as the student's known can overwhelm the instructor while the instructor's new can cause tension for the student. Kalantzis and Cope argue that "pedagogy is a careful process of choosing a suitable mix of ways of knowing and purposeful weaving between these different kinds of knowing" and "pedagogy is the design of knowledge action sequences in ways that suit different academic and social domains: choosing activity types, sequencing activities, transitioning from one activity type to another and determining the outcomes of these activities."[23] One purpose of this chapter is to provide us as instructors with an opportunity to say, in the words of Kalantzis and Cope, "Now I am using this particular way to know, and now I am using that other way, and here is the reason why I did this, then that."[24]

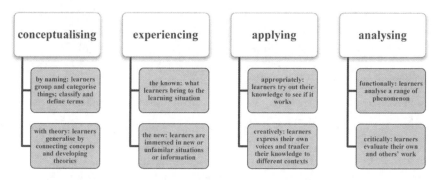

Figure 2.2. Knowledge processes in detail
(based on Kalantzis and Cope, *Literacies*, 357)

Course 1: Talking JPC (2002-10)

Talking JPC was designed for upper-level students of Japanese studies. It was originally categorized as a Japanese-language course that required students to use Japanese as part of their learning of Japanese culture, hence it assumed a certain level of Japanese proficiency so students could comprehend, in particular, popular songs and films (including anime). For manga, while there was also a language focus,[25] more emphasis was placed on their historical development, an explanation of the internal workings of the medium, and how narrative as a genre is constructed. In relation to Talking JPC, while the necessity of having some Japanese proficiency did not completely disappear toward the end of the life of this course, around 2008, the course changed its general focus from language to area studies using something more akin to the functional literacy pedagogical approach described above. It is interesting reading chapter 7 by Deborah Shamoon in this volume since Talking JPC was initially designed to co-teach across the curriculum using Japanese language. However, the course transitioned into English-only partly due to the range of the students' Japanese language proficiency and also to internal restructuring of faculty, and hence department, course offerings.

Until 2006 the course was fundamentally theme oriented: anime/ manga, film, and popular music. These themes were revised from time to time (e.g., in 2004 the thematic strands for anime included transformation of the body and human interest), while the selection of music and films also captured a range of specific themes that exposed students to a number of views about Japan. Themes for anime were expanded and film was dropped due to the departure of the film instructor/expert, leaving manga, anime, and popular music as the three basic themes. In 2005 television was introduced as a new theme. In 2007 TV dramas and comedies were studied, in 2008 shows for children and variety shows were added, in 2009 the theme was changed to TV and other visual cultures, and in 2010 the themes were broadened to reflect differences in epistemic moves generated in part by expanded access to written material and theory related to popular culture, soft power, and media studies.

The themes in Talking JPC are of particular importance since they link the evolution of each course to a pedagogy that was influenced to a great extent by materials available to both instructors and students. For example, in 2002 media were accessed through VHS tapes and students were required to engage with "essential reading material." Given the constraints of space, there are too many materials to mention in any great detail, but they represent a canon of essential works that needed to be read to satisfy the course objectives.

In the first and subsequent years of teaching this course, we drew extensively on students' own knowledge and experiences of their consumption of manga, anime, and popular music; however, there was also a didactic element to the pedagogy so as to legitimize the course by making it clear to students that JPC was an object of "study" rather than an entertainment. We drew on other experts to provide the necessary rigor considered important to guide students down the informed path. For example, Sharon Kinsella's 2000 monograph *Adult Manga: Culture and Power in Contemporary Japanese Society* provided a brief overview of the history of manga, while Scott McCloud's 1994 *Understanding Comics: The Invisible Art* offered a theory of how comics (including manga) work. Other influential resources, such as Susan Napier's 2001 *Anime from Akira to Princess Mononoke: Experiencing Contemporary Japanese Animation* and Frederik Schodt's work on manga, Carolyn Stevens's 2007 *Japanese Popular Music: Culture, Authenticity, and Power*, among others, were used in conjunction with what the students brought to class so as to, in the words of Kalantzis and Cope, transform everyday knowledge into disciplined knowledge.[26]

As the course progressed over the next few years, this canon also expanded through the publication of a series of influential monographs and academic journal articles, as well as articles in magazines and newspapers, reporting on the increasing interest in JPC in Asia, North America, Europe, and Australasia. In 2006, for example, the extent to which the canon was used to usurp any kind of authentic literacy pedagogy by formalizing and promoting a didactic literacy pedagogy is clear. Objectives that promoted informed discussion and reflection remained, and by the end of the course in 2010, the reflective portfolio (20 percent of the final grade) required students to engage with eight set readings. The year 2010 was also a turning point in thematic development. J-pop was retained almost without change from previous years, but there was much more emphasis placed on the development of JPC using "case studies"—manga, anime, media, and other, more timely examples such as the use of cell phones in Japan. Students were required to read what some might construe as a staggering twenty-three readings over the semester.

There was also an evolution in how the course was assessed. Tutorial Participation was a feature from 2002 to 2004 but was abandoned when the university directed that all courses must replace it with more "objective" measures. Individual topic assessments set in 2002 and 2003 offered a range of options for each theme, but they were teacher-centered since each instructor provided the procedures for carrying out the assignment. This task was replaced in 2004 with a Research Project and accompanying Research Proposal. This configuration lasted until 2007. The Research Proposal was created to motivate students to conduct a modest piece of original research about a JPC of interest. It utilized a critical literacies pedagogy, and, while the details of all these projects are now vague, we still recall the effort that many students put into this assessment task. The task had to be approved by the university's ethics committee given that in some cases students wished to interview people. While this was problematic at times, the effort of drafting an application to the committee each year seemed worth it.

In 2007 a major change in teaching and learning strategies in the course instigated a new approach: Cycle 1—Introduction to Japanese Popular Culture, Cycle 2—Introduction to Print and Broadcast Media and Cycle 3—Introduction to J-Pop songs. The Research Project was replaced with a Group Tutorial Presentation worth 60 percent of the total grade. Students presented three times during the semester, and the impetus for their presentations came from either readings or experience. There was an emphasis on critique, analysis, and conceptualizing, and this clouded the alignment of pedagogy with assessment. We were clear that we wanted students to read instructor-set readings to gain an informed view; however, some students tended to avoid engaging with the readings and therefore could not construct a metalanguage with which to discuss their own relationship with and consumption of JPC. The Group Tutorial Presentation assessment was repeated with some modifications in 2008, 2009, and 2010.

One consistent task was keeping a reflective journal (also called a J-pop diary or diary) in which students were required to link the course content to their thinking about JPC. The journal also gained legitimacy in terms of what it was worth in comparison to other assessment tasks. In 2002 the informal-sounding "J-pop diary" was worth 15 percent of the grade and was designed to be more of a series of impressions, reactions, and responses to students' consumption of JPC. This was prompted by a more authentic literacy pedagogy in which personally meaningful writing was rewarded. However, the diary (2003–5) was replaced in 2006 with a more formal Reflective Journal worth 40 percent of the total grade, which prompted students to be reflective rather than descriptive.

To complete this section, there is also a need to report on how the changes in technologies influenced this course. When Talking JPC began, mobile telephones, e-mail, and Internet resources existed, but we were using VHS tapes to show anime and films and cassettes to play Japanese popular music. These were either imported or brought by us from Japan, as there were few resources available in Australia at that time. A mini revolution occurred when the university introduced a Learning Management System (LMS) in 2004. It was used as a repository where learning resources were digitally stored for students to view and download and it also acted as a communications liaison between instructors and students. In 2005 it was the launch of YouTube that quickly shifted our learning and teaching materials from a limited number of VHS tapes and DVDs to the countless worlds of JPC brought directly into the classroom.

As we have pointed out, the preferred teaching approach was in a real sense the more traditional didactic literacy pedagogy. However, with increasingly sophisticated technologies being introduced, such as presenter software, hardware (including lighter laptops and tablets), and online resources, the shift toward a blended or hybrid teaching approach seemed more realistic, hence the blending of didactic literacy pedagogy with its more contemporary sibling, critical literacies pedagogy. This latter pedagogy reflected the times, in which students preferred the multimodal over the monomodal (print readings) and also allowed them to bring into the classroom other kinds of texts, which, while still conforming to the themes of the course, better represented the interests of the student body.

Course 2: Representations of Japan (2011-2013)

Following the launch of a new Bachelor of Arts degree, a revision of Talking JPC was required to fit it into the Japanese Studies major stream as a non-language course. A new course, Representations of Japan, was therefore designed to encompass Talking JPC and another course that focused on Japanese society, politics, and economics from a cultural studies perspective. Since popular culture reflects current affairs, we envisioned a course that would address a Japanese social-political-economic chronology, basic fare in courses about Japan, through an unfolding of the domestic Japanese consumption of JPC. While we cannot address all aspects of this course, we will highlight some of its more significant aspects.

Briefly, Representations of Japan explored a number of broad social themes post-1945 through the popular cultures of the time. Using didactic literacy pedagogy (again), students were required to read set materials that highlighted particular aspects of the historical time being discussed. The course was divided into an introduction as an orientation to asking, answering, and discussing questions about representation, popular culture, and cultural history. This allowed us to provide a metalanguage we could use to talk about the rest of the material presented during the semester. The rest of the course was divided by decades: 1945–59, 1960–69, 1970–79, 1980–89, 1990–2000, and post–2000. In a sense, the focus on representation was also linked to a functional literacy pedagogy more than Talking JPC had been in that we wanted to explore the purposes of texts located in a specific time. On reflection, there was certainly a degree of resistance among students to engaging with these materials due to difficulty, lack of personal interest, and a general misunderstanding that a course about popular culture required effort to gain a pass let alone high distinction.

Readings and other audiovisual materials (including links to YouTube) were uploaded into the LMS. From 2011 to 2013, we followed the movements of JPC chronologically from 1945 through watching films, anime, and television; looking at *kamishibai* (a picture story show), manga, fashions, and the popular arts of the time; and listening to songs. We wanted students to consider how the various social-political-economic events of each decade (e.g., the 1964 Olympic Games and the 1970 Osaka Expo to name just two) were being represented in the popular culture of the time.

While the instructors were excited about this, unfortunately many students were not. While assessment tasks were designed to give students opportunities to demonstrate mastery of what they had read and experienced during the semester (orally and in writing), we reflected at the end of the 2013 course that beginning in 1945 was not the best approach for most students since the period between 1945 and even the late 1970s was largely unknown, especially for those who had not studied any Japanese history. As a result of this experience, we believe it is more appropriate to begin this course with what the students already know (following a critical literacy pedagogy) and then work backward. We say this since most students during the three years in which the course has been taught appeared more animated, motivated, and prepared to discuss representations (i.e. use metalanguage derived from the set readings) when they could talk about their own experiences with contemporary JPC rather than watching some largely unknown and therefore contextless black-and-white Ozu Yasujirō movie from the 1940s.

Concluding Remarks: Looking Forward

This reflection has provided us an opportunity to consider how future courses might be designed in terms of subject matter, how this subject matter could be arranged, and the ways in which students could be helped to make meanings, as well as the changing social relationships between students and knowledge, students and students, students and instructors. We admit that we have embraced a blended type of pedagogy that attempts to join aspects of the didactic and the critical while neglecting other kinds of pedagogies. We did this in part due to our conceptions of what is expected from a formal university course (subject matter and its arrangement, i.e. the didactic) and our own experiences dealing with students (social relationships and the ways in which we wanted students to make meanings, i.e. the critical).

More recently, in 2014, Representations of Japan was taught again. However, having considered the relationships between the two pedagogies, we changed its name to Japan in Popular Culture to broaden the subject matter, how it was arranged, and how students could deal with it. The course structure was reorganized by foregrounding discussions regarding JPC post-2000 to the beginning of the semester as described above. Students became "tutorial leaders," selecting one example of Japanese popular culture from the relevant period, finding an article about it, preparing a question to pose to the tutorial, and leading the class in discussion. Significantly, student enrolments nearly tripled to sixty, compared to 2013, perhaps due to the change of name and a restructuring of courses about Japan. On reflection, while having tutorial leaders was an initially innovative approach, ironically the actual number of students per tutorial hampered time for discussion of a range of interesting topics. Despite the innovation and its impact on the pedagogy, the reality of how many students are allocated to a tutorial (largely beyond the control of the instructor) also needs to be taken into consideration.

We agree with the sentiments expressed by McLaren and Spies in this volume with regard to students who take a course about JPC needing to do academic work rather than merely chatting about their favorite manga or anime and expecting to pass the course. Furthermore, the link between teaching practices and learning outcomes cannot be stressed more strongly. Our university imposes such a link through internal checks via the faculty's Education Committee. It has become extremely difficult for any course not to link teaching practices to student learning outcomes.

This reflection reminds us of how Neil Postman characterized the media as epistemology, arguing that part of its subject matter "is the interest it takes in definitions of truth and the sources from which such definitions come."[27] Postman draws on the work of Northrop Frye, in particular his principle called "resonance" or metaphor, which generates a particular force that invests it with meaning.[28] How JPC is taught and studied now involves a media-based epistemology that draws from the resonances of the many elements that make up the objects we are calling JPC. The consequences for the higher education classroom in relation to this shift between pedagogies will be largely mediated through a media-based epistemology, and this requires further and deeper consideration since "ideas of truth move with it."[29]

Notes

[1] Armour, William S., and Sumiko Iida. "Are Australian Fans of Anime and Manga Motivated to Learn Japanese Language?" *Asia Pacific Journal of Education* (2014): 1–17.

[2] We acknowledge the somewhat haphazard conflation of manga and anime with JPC; however, in terms of expediency, in our study we concentrated on these two media since we consider them the most important in an Australian context.

[3] Robin Usher, "Consuming Learning," *Convergence* 41, no. 1 (2008): 38.

[4] See chapter 1 in this volume by Sally McLaren and Alwyn Spies for an in-depth discussion of this.

[5] Deborah Shamoon, "Teaching Japanese Popular Culture," *ASIANetwork Exchange* 17, no. 2 (2010): 9–22.

[6] William. M. Tsutsui, "Teaching History and/of/or Japanese Popular Culture," *electronic journal of contemporary japanese studies* 13, no. 2 (2013): http://www.japanesestudies.org.uk/ejcjs/vol13/iss2/tsutsui.html.

[7] Ibid.

[8] Patrick W. Galbraith and Jason G. Karlin, "The Mirror of Idols and Celebrity," in *Idols and Celebrity in Japanese Media Culture*, ed. Patrick W. Galbraith and Jason G. Karlin (Houndmills: Palgrave Macmillan, 2012), 3.

[9] Mary Kalantzis and Bill Cope, *Literacies* (Cambridge: Cambridge University Press, 2012).

[10] Tsutsui, "Teaching History."

[11] Kalantzis and Cope, *Literacies*, 9.

[12] See Tsutsui, "Teaching History" for a similar reflection.

[13] Kalantzis and Cope, *Literacies*, 9. See their table 0.2 for the full list.

[14] Ibid., 66.

[15] Ibid., 63.

[16] Ibid., 95.

[17] Ibid., 118.

[18] Ibid., 145.

[19] Ibid., 358.

[20] Ibid., 359.

[21] Ibid.

[22] Ibid.

[23] Ibid., 360.

[24] Ibid.

[25] In another course, Learning Japanese by Reading Manga, offered from 2005 to 2010, manga were used as "authentic" materials for studying the Japanese language.

[26] Sharon Kinsella, *Adult Manga: Culture and Power in Contemporary Japanese Society* (Abingdon: RoutledgeCurzon, 2000); Scott McCloud, *Understanding Comics: The Invisible Art* (New York: HarperCollins, 1993); Susan J. Napier, *Anime from Akira to Princess Mononoke: Experiencing Contemporary Japanese Animation* (New York: Palgrave, 2001). Stevens, Carolyn S., *Japanese Popular Music: Culture, Authenticity and Power* (Routledge, 2008); Frederik L. Schodt, *Inside the Robot Kingdom: Japan, Mechatronics, and the Coming Robotopia* (Tokyo: Kodansha International, 1988); Carolyn S. Stevens, *Japanese Popular Music: Culture, Authenticity and Power* (New York: Routledge, 2007); Kalantzis and Cope, *Literacies*, 348.

[27] Neil Postman, *Amusing Ourselves to Death: Public Discourse in the Age of Show Business* (New York: Penguin Books, 1985), 17.

[28] Ibid., 18.

[29] Ibid., 24.

Works Cited

Armour, William S., and Sumiko Iida. "Are Australian Fans of Anime and Manga Motivated to Learn Japanese Language?" *Asia Pacific Journal of Education* (2014): 1–17.

Galbraith, Patrick W., and Jason G. Karlin. "The Mirror of Idols and Celebrity." In *Idols and Celebrity in Japanese Media Culture*, edited by Patrick W. Galbraith and Jason. G. Karlin, 1–32. Houndmills: Palgrave Macmillan, 2012.

Kalantzis, Mary, and Bill Cope. *Literacies*. Cambridge: Cambridge University Press, 2012.

Kinsella, Sharon. *Adult Manga: Culture and Power in Contemporary Japanese Society*. Abingdon: RoutledgeCurzon, 2000.

McCloud, Scott. *Understanding Comics: The Invisible Art*. New York: HarperCollins, 1993.

Napier, Susan J. *Anime from Akira to Princess Mononoke: Experiencing Contemporary Japanese Animation*. New York: Palgrave, 2001.

Postman, Neil. *Amusing Ourselves to Death: Public Discourse in the Age of Show Business*. New York: Penguin Books, 1985.

Schodt, Frederik L. *Inside the Robot Kingdom: Japan, Mechatronics, and the Coming Robotopia*. Tokyo: Kodansha International, 1988.

Shamoon, Deborah. "Teaching Japanese Popular Culture." *ASIANetwork Exchange* 17, no. 2 (2010): 9–22.

Stevens, Carolyn S. *Japanese Popular Music: Culture, Authenticity and Power*. New York: Routledge, 2008.

Tsutsui, William M. "Teaching History and/of/or Japanese Popular Culture." *electronic journal of contemporary japanese studies* 13, no. 2 (2013). http://www.japanesestudies.org.uk/ejcjs/vol13/iss2/index.html

Usher, Robin. "Consuming Learning." *Convergence* 41, no. 1 (2008): 29–45.

3

Goethe Goes Cool Japan

Teaching Popular Culture through Research-Oriented Learning at a German University

Cosima Wagner

Introduction

Since the 1990s, Japanese popular culture products—especially manga, anime, computer games, cosplay, and J-pop—have become a prominent part of the youth culture in Germany, inspiring more students to academically engage with Japanese culture, society, and language at university. For instance, at Goethe-University in Frankfurt, Germany, the number of students enrolled in undergraduate and graduate degree programs in the Japanese Studies Department has increased steadily since the end of the 1990s, with a dramatic doubling of student numbers from 2009 to 2010 alone (a jump from 90 to 190 freshmen).[1] As of November 2012, a total of 549 students were enrolled in Japanese studies bachelors and masters degree courses at Goethe-University. A poll taken by the Japanese Studies Department in the summer of 2011 confirmed that 70 percent of the freshmen in the bachelors courses were motivated to study Japan because of their interest in Japanese popular culture.[2]

At the same time, the German university system underwent fundamental structural changes in line with the reform of the education systems of all countries in the European Union (the so-called Bologna

Process).[3] This has meant that since 1999 all German universities have had to discard the former degree programs of Magister (masters) or Diplom (diploma) and develop bachelors and masters programs. As opposed to the previous system, which provided flexibility for students, as well as staff, on the choice and scheduling of courses, the new "structured curricula" have proven to be a challenge for small departments like Japanese Studies. It has had to establish a set sequence of courses and restrict the number of courses and the introduction of new courses in order to accommodate the needs of each cohort of students year by year.

Given this situation, the department introduced a new teaching and learning format, the "working group," to challenge what the department saw as an overregulated new curriculum. This innovation helped create a space of creative learning according to the interests of students, regardless of their year, and supervised by senior researchers in line with their academic expertise. The idea was to provide an environment for research-oriented teaching and learning in small, non-homogeneous groups on an ever-shifting variety of Japan-related subjects (Japanese literature, popular culture, theater, Kanbun reading, and, more recently, translation of texts about the triple disaster of March 2011, which indicates the earthquake, tsunami and meltdown of the Fukushima Daiichi nuclear power plant (the "Fukushima Text Initiative"). In order to integrate these activities into the bachelors and masters curricula, project-oriented learning/applied Japanese studies modules were created as part of the study course, wherein students can choose which working group to join or which other activity to pursue (i.e. department workshops, working as tutors or student representatives, etc.) and earn one credit point for each thirty hours of activity.

This chapter introduces the activities of one such group, the Cool Japan working group, which emerged in mid-2007 after a course, Cultural Globalization of Japanese Popular Culture, was taught by the author. Student interest in further discussion and readings on the topic was very high, but given the strict new curriculum requirements, there was no possibility of teaching another class the following term on a similar topic. Therefore, it was decided to continue our activities within the framework of a study group. The Cool Japan working group is an example of a "creative" course design within structured curriculum guidelines that makes it possible to integrate research-oriented learning activities on Japanese popular culture into curricula for undergraduate students. Furthermore the working group format provides a means of coping with a situation in which students are often more knowledgeable in the field of Japanese popular culture than their instructors—what William M. Tsutsui has described as the uncanny feeling of educators about the "'inverted' classroom studying popular culture" and a "forbidding loss of control in the classroom."[4]

This chapter demonstrates how a working group can facilitate student-centered learning about Japanese popular culture despite decreased staff time and limits on the development of new courses. The author hopes that the experiences of this working group will inspire others to develop such learning-rich practices and encourage institutions to formalize such groups (e.g., via course credit) as nonstructured parts of university curricula, providing a collaborative study environment for (Japanese) popular culture studies. After a description of the didactic concept and outcome examples of the Cool Japan working group, a study trip to Japan in 2010 will be documented.

Didactic Concept and Outcomes of the Cool Japan Working Group

How to integrate popular culture into university curricula and how to use popular culture as a starting point for developing critical scholarly thinking have become academic topics in their own right.[5] The grounding idea of the Cool Japan working group connects to this discussion and recognizes that "one of the most common and meaningful shared experiences for students is through popular culture."[6] Therefore the recent global boom in Japanese popular culture provides a way to use it as a valuable source for transforming students' fan knowledge into critical scholarly thinking on popular culture in general and Japan in particular. With regard to the images students gain through the contact and consumption of popular culture, the scholar of art education Kevin M. Tavin has described the classroom situation in the following way.

> By beginning with these images, teachers can help students articulate their particular investments—naming their pleasures, desires, and passions that derive from popular cultural texts. ... By embracing differentiated interpretations (of popular culture) and linking them to critical social theories students can understand that popular culture is not simply a terrain of unproblematic entertainment or static manipulative propaganda. Instead, students' relationship to popular culture is seen as "a layering process in which meanings are altered and always already contested by the very fact that popular culture is being interpreted or

read...identities are not only shifting but the meaning of [the] texts constantly shift also as [students] need them" (Weaver & Daspit, 1999, p. xv).[7]

Providing a forum for this "layering process" and assisting students in developing a scientific perspective on Japanese popular culture and their own research projects within this area became the basic idea for establishing the Cool Japan working group—connecting to what is described in chapter 1, by Sally McLaren and Alwyn Spies, in this volume as the paradigmatic approach of "poco pop," "which takes a postcolonial view of the study of Japanese popular culture by including cultural studies theory." Here the worldwide boom in Japanese popular culture and Japan's role as an exporter of culture and a lifestyle nation in the twenty-first century is a special field of investigation. In the working group the following questions are addressed:

- How can the worldwide interest in Japan's popular culture be explained? Which groups are attracted to this "neo-Japonism"?

- How does the Japan boom manifest itself in different countries and cultures (especially in Germany)?

- What view of Japan as a country is disseminated? Is there danger of another "orientalized" view of Japan ("coolest nation on earth," etc.) and can popular culture be analyzed through a nation-framework perspective?

- How is the Japanese government supporting the globalization of popular culture? Is it able to steer Japan fandom through campaigns like the Cool Japan strategy of the Ministry of Foreign Affairs (MOFA)? What is the role of the Ministry of Economy, Trade and Industry (METI)?[8]

- What is the position of Japanese intellectuals and content creators on the appropriation of popular culture through politics?

- Which political promotion activities have been continued or discontinued since the triple disaster of March 2011?

- What methodological approaches are appropriate for research on Japanese popular culture in a global-local perspective (especially that of fan culture)?

To answer these questions, various manifestations of Japanese popular culture in both Japan and Germany, as well as academic papers in Japanese and western languages, were analyzed and discussed.

The didactic concept of the working group aims to create an informal learning situation that "is not sequenced beforehand, the activity steers the way of working, … and the process proceeds by [means of] the interaction of the participants in the activity."[9] Developing soft skills such as proactiveness, intercultural competence, the ability to work in teams, creativity, and a sense of responsibility is a further important point of didactic interest.

Therefore, the Cool Japan working group relies on the initiative of its student members. The role of the teacher lies only in coordinating the joint syllabus planning, moderating discussions, posing critical questions, proposing reading material, and supervising project teams. Furthermore, additional information (texts, Internet links, conference advertisements, etc.) on the working groups' topics is provided through an e-learning platform.

While part of each working group's activities is based on analysis, another part is based on activities such as editing the Cool Japan web journal (http://cooljapan.de), which provides a central storage platform for reports and academic essays written by group members, as well as term papers by other interested Japanese studies students. Currently the website contains reviews of manga and anime, a (partly) annotated, work-in-progress bibliography of scholarly literature on the subject of Japanese popular culture, results of student projects (e.g., a report titled "Definition and Use of the Term Otaku within a German Internet Community," based on guided interviews with German fans of Japanese popular culture who call themselves otaku with reference to the Japanese understanding of the term as "obsessive fans" of popular culture products like manga and anime), and information on upcoming conferences and workshops on Japanese popular culture (see figure 3.1).

In addition, group members prepared talks and contributed to conferences on Japanese popular culture, such as the symposium "Robots in Manga and Anime" held in 2008 at the Museum of Applied Arts in Frankfurt; "Japantag 2009" (Japan Day) in Frankfurt; a student panel titled "Reading Manga, Studying Japanese Studies" at the annual conference of the Association for Social Science Research on Japan (VSJF) at Goethe-University in Frankfurt on the subject of "Cultural Power Japan—Impact

Figure 3.1. Screenshot of the Cool Japan web journal
(http://cooljapan.de/pages/projekte/otaku.php)

and Intellectual Dimensions," in 2010; and a presentation on the study trip
to Japan in 2010 at the film festival Nippon Connection in 2011.

The "Goethe Explores Cool Japan" Study Trip

The largest project carried out by the Cool Japan working group has been
a fifteen-day study trip to Japan in 2010. Under the title "Goethe Explores
Cool Japan: Angewandte Studien zur Japanischen Populärkultur" (Goethe
Explores Cool Japan: Applied Studies of Japanese Pop Culture), fifteen
students visited institutions and locations connected to the Japanese
culture industry and took part in discussions with academics and experts in
the field of Japanese popular culture research. The excursion was carried
out under the direction of the author and was the first trip to Japan in
the history of the institution. It was made possible with financial support
from various institutional and external sources, thus giving a "hands-on"
experience to students, for whom a trip to Japan and to institutions related
to Japanese popular culture had long been a dream.

In order to understand the production, distribution, and promotion
processes of Japanese popular culture and the attitude of Japanese citizens,
notably students of the same age as the working group members, the
didactic concept of the study trip consisted of three elements.

1. Achieving greater proficiency in discussing one's research interest in Japanese, along with acquiring a deeper understanding of the role of popular culture in everyday life in Japan in general and as a university subject in particular. Here, we organized an exchange of ideas between Japanese and German students on the topic "Pop Culture between Fandom and Research: The Significance of Manga, Anime, and Video Games in the Lives of German and Japanese Students." By taking part in shared seminars at a Tokyo and a Kyoto university, the didactic emphasis was on practicing language skills through group presentations in Japanese and providing insight into the Japanese university system, as well as Japanese students' worldviews with regard to popular culture. Furthermore, by visiting newly established partner universities during the trip, possibilities for long-term exchange study trips could be introduced through face-to-face contact.

2. Furthering the understanding of Japanese creative industries, particularly the production and promotion of Japanese popular culture products by visiting institutions related to the Japanese culture industry and culture promotion.

3. Acquisition of knowledge of different areas of Japanese culture and society in order to obtain insight into present-day and historical Japan from the students' own perspective for the first time.

While the study trip was conceived with these goals in mind, the final itinerary and selection of institutions to visit was made part of the students' discussion in the classroom in order to allow a bottom-up commitment by all participants. Therefore, the program for the study trip was developed beginning in October 2009 over a year-long period, which included the preparation of short presentations in Japanese for a joint seminar at Kyoto Seika University. Furthermore, taking turns leading each day's proceedings during the visits to individual institutions was another part of the participants' involvement in arranging the tour. Last, it was agreed that the participants would write detailed reports about each day of the trip in the form of a blog (see fig. 3.2). The texts and photos can be viewed at http://cooljapan.de/pages/projekte/japan-exkursion-blog.php. The blog

Tag 9 - 20.09.2010

Gegen 9 Uhr haben wir heute unser Zimmer im Hômeikan geräumt. Da die Angestellten des Ryokan freundlicherweise unsere Koffer zum Bahnhof brachten, machten wir uns nur noch mit der Hälfte unseres Gepäcks auf den Weg zum Technikmuseum „Miraikan" (日本科学未来館, *Nippon kagaku miraikan*) in der Nähe von Odaiba (お台場), in dem eine Sondervorführung des Roboter-Maskottchens Doraemon auf uns wartete.

Aufgrund unserer Buchung als Gruppe mussten wir uns nicht in der relativ langen Schlange vor dem Museum anstellen, sondern wurden vom Personal direkt hinein geführt. Bereits im Erdgeschoss war eine separate Ausstellungsfläche für Doraemon reserviert – die hauptsächlich an Kinder gerichtete Sonderausstellung sollte den Besuchern nahebringen, wie die Beziehung zwischen Mensch und Roboter in Zukunft gestaltet werden kann. Der Fokus lag dabei hauptsächlich darauf, den Kindern die Angst vor dem Umgang mit Robotern und Technik im Allgemeinen zu nehmen. Einige Ausstellungsstücke luden zu diesem Zweck zum direkten Kontakt und zum spielerischen Umgang mit unbekannten Dingen ein. Obwohl sich dieser Teil der Ausstellung in erster Linie auf Kinder bezog, war auch der restliche Teil des Museums in derartiger Form gestaltet. Auf mehreren Ebenen wurden den Besuchern sowohl vergangene als auch zeitgenössische Forschungsergebnisse aus den Gebieten der Computer- oder Gentechnik sowie etwa der Raumfahrt näher gebracht.

Figure 3.2. Screenshot of the blog for day nine, a visit to
the National Museum of Emerging Science and
Innovation (Nihon Kagaku Miraikan) at Odaiba
http://cooljapan.de/pages/projekte/japan-exkursion-blog.php

strengthened teamwork among the students and helped them reflect and gain insights on each day of the tour. It attracted a great deal of attention, even beyond the Japanese studies academic community, and had been visited 41,184 times by January 30, 2016.

The trip began with an eight-day stay in Tokyo with two to three appointments each day. The group met with two companies in the creative industries, the Shūeisha publishing house, which publishes manga and magazines, and the video game producer Bandai Namco Games. The companies offered presentations on the production process between 90 and 120 minutes long. Shūeisha illustrated the manga production process through the example of the magazine *Shōnen Jump,* while Bandai explained video games production with the help of presentations and visual aids. Both presentations made it clear that the products are heavily shaped by the tastes of Japanese customers of all ages, who are constantly asked for their opinions through consumer research.

A particular highlight were the visits to MOFA and METI, where the working group received a detailed explanation of the significance of Japanese pop culture to the state. METI representatives explained that in July 2010 Japanese popular culture had been elevated to one of seven pillars of the future of the Japanese economy.[10] At MOFA young fashion models (Gothic and Lolita style) had been appointed official ambassadors for Japan, and were sent to trade shows and events around the world.[11]

During the trip, the group experienced the popularity of video games in Japan at a visit to the Tokyo Game Show, the largest video game trade show in the world, during which over two hundred thousand people packed themselves into the exhibition center, sometimes queuing for over six hours just to try new games for up to ten minutes.

Alongside Japanese pop culture, the program sought to expand students' sociocultural knowledge through visits to museums dealing with Japanese national history, Buddhist temples and Shintō shrines, famous Tokyo neighborhoods (Akihabara, Asakusa, etc.), and cities such as Nara. The visit to the National Museum of Emerging Science and Innovation (Nihon Kagaku Miraikan) in Odaiba proved particularly impressive as it portrayed robots as future household helpers and partners of humans by connecting famous popular culture stories of robot manga and anime to existing robot prototypes.[12]

Exchange with Japanese university students was a further highlight of the trip. For instance, the Japanese Studies Department has been in contact with Senshū University in Tokyo for several years through a shared virtual classroom project, and thankfully, Senshū students were able to accompany the group to both the Ghibli Museum of Animated Film, founded by anime artist and director Miyazaki Hayao, and a showroom of Sony Corporation. While in Kyoto, the group had an exchange at Dōshisha University and a seminar with Kyoto Seika University's master students at the Manga Museum in Kyōto.[13] Seminar preparation took many months, from deciding the seminar topic on "'Cool Japan' in Germany: Societal Phenomena and Japanese Studies' Research Topics," to organizing presentation groups, and collaborating on presentations in Japanese. The result was an intensive discussion with Japanese students, which not only gave the members of the working group many new ideas for research on Japanese popular culture, but also boosted their confidence in their Japanese language skills. In addition, the seminar added to the questioning of stereotypes regarding the construction of a monolithic "Japaneseness" of manga (and anime), similar to the "contested classroom situation" described in chapter 4, by Akiko Sugawa-Shimada, in this volume. Interestingly, the Japanese students did not perceive their drawings as "Japanese manga" but as artworks bearing no relation to the government's Cool Japan initiative. A further stimulating debate developed through the comparison of the multiple interpretations of the term otaku in German and Japanese.

This project shows that visiting Japan is an ideal way—albeit an expensive one—to promote consolidation of the topics studied both in class and in the working group sessions.[14] It thus helped to further facilitate problem-orientated learning and research, thereby expanding the scope of students' knowledge beyond the curriculum. Additionally, creative work in small groups and group planning of the study trip to Japan contributed to the learning atmosphere and can be executed even in cases where a real tour to Japan is not affordable.

Conclusion

As described above, the goal of the Cool Japan working group is to promote independent engagement with current academic topics in the field of Japanese popular culture within a free working environment beyond the fixed modules of the structured curriculum.

Participants in the group have the opportunity to research a topic of their choice and thereby to explore academic sources in depth, not least in the Japanese language, in order to develop a nuanced scientific perspective on Japanese popular culture. Through these activities students acquire more experience in developing research questions, improve their language skills, and have a positive study experience in times of crowded university courses. The proactiveness of the students, who bring with them their specific Japanese popular culture expertise, and the informal teaching-learning atmosphere, allow for the pursuit of fruitful and critical discussions of popular culture as a Japanese studies topic. The project work carried out by students in the bachelors and masters degree programs can be credited as part of a practical module, "Applied Japanese Studies," and, additionally can be published in the group's web journal. As of December 2013, five dissertations had been developed based on project work carried out within the working group, resulting in the motivation to continue to take courses in masters and PhD programs. In 2010, the project was nominated for the Hessischen Hochschulpreis Exzellenz in der Lehre (Hesse University Prize for Excellence in Education).

After the triple disaster of March 2011, Japan's focus turned to the role of popular culture in "reconstructing Cool Japan" and the question of a caesura of the incident became a politically and intellectually debated topic. Members of the working group took part in a symposium organized by the author in February 2013 titled "Reconstructing Cool Japan: Japanese Identities after Fukushima," where the literature scholar and cotranslator of Azuma Hiroki's well-known book *Otaku: Japan's Database Animals* (2009), Kōno Shion, and Japanese studies scholar Steffi Richter took part.[15] Finally, in June 2013, a member of the working group arranged a lecture by a former METI bureaucrat and researcher, Mihara Ryōtarō, deputy director of the Creative Industries Division and Design Policy Office of METI and the individual in charge of the Cool Japan policy from 2011 to 2012.[16] All of these efforts have continued to reinforce the importance of tapping into student interest in Japanese popular culture outside the classroom setting and approaching the subject in a more rigorous way.

Although the working group has proved to be a successful teaching and learning tool since 2007, a few limitations of the study group format also have to be mentioned. Despite the general introduction of critical perspectives on Japanese popular culture production and consumption, it often proves difficult for students to adopt a scholarly attitude toward the subject because it might mean abandoning one's fan idealization of the object. Also individual research projects are often designed as empirical studies, without methodological background knowledge on how to facilitate qualitative and quantitative surveys in Japan. Students have many questions about Japanese popular culture that have not been researched and published, and they struggle with the limitations of the existing research.

I agree with Tsutsui that there has to be "more substantive research on pop culture. … Only when pop's place in the scholarly literature has been secured, only when pop culture is not a supplement to our standard narratives of history but fully integrated as a constitutive component of Japanese past and present, will the teaching of manga and anime, Godzilla and Hello Kitty, SMAP and Harajuku street style reach its full potential."[17] I believe that one way to inspire such substantive research is by providing a nonstructured place within the university where it is possible to begin to develop research questions and critical thinking through a collaboration between scholars and students, all willing to share their expertise and fascination with Japanese popular culture.

Notes

The author wishes to cordially thank all institutions and individuals supporting the project, especially: Executive Committee Goethe-University, Vice President Prof. Dr. Manfred Schubert-Zsilavecz, International Office Goethe University, Almuth Rhode, Dr. Guido Woldering (Goethe-University), Prof. Dr. Noriko Itasaka and Dr. Yasuoka Mitsuhara (Senshū University), Prof. Dr. Jaqueline Berndt (Kyoto Seika University), Consulate General of Japan in Frankfurt, Hirakawa Shingo (Bandai Namco Games), *Shōnen Jump* editorial office, Isseidō Booksellers, and International Center Dōshisha University.

[1] This growth in numbers was largely due to the abolition of admissions restrictions. It should be mentioned that public universities in the federal state of Hesse, like Goethe-University, receive part of their funding based on student head count. Therefore a high number of freshman students results in larger budget allocations to the university from the state. However, the budget increase does not trickle down to departments in the form of increases in permanent teaching staff. Growing student numbers have resulted in high loads of grading and consultation hours and an increase in the temporary employment of young scholars.

[2] Japanese Studies Department, Goethe-University Frankfurt, ed., *Auswertung Japanologramm: Sommersemester 2011* [Japanologram questionnaire results: Summer term, 2011], (Frankfurt: Japanese Studies Department, Goethe-University Frankfurt, 2011), 6.

[3] More information about the Bologna Process is available on the European Higher Education Area (EHEA) website, http://www.ehea.info

[4] William M. Tsutsui, "Teaching History and /of/or Japanese Popular Culture," *electronic journal of contemporary japanese studies* 13, no. 2 (2013), http://www.japanesestudies.org.uk/ejcjs/vol13/iss2/tsutsui.html.

[5] See, for example, Göran Folkestad, "Formal and Informal Learning Situations or Practices vs. Formal and Informal Ways of Learning," *British Journal of Music Education* 23, no. 2 (July 2006): : 135–45. Henry A. Giroux, "Public Pedagogy and the Politics of Resistance," *Educational Philosophy and Theory* 35, no. 1, (2003): 5–16. Hilaria Gössmann, "Medien und Populärkultur" [Media and popular culture], in *Grundriß der Japanologie* [Outline of Japanology], ed. Klaus Kracht and Markus Rüttermann (Wiesbaden: Harrassowitz, 2001), 555–86; Henry Jenkins, *Confronting the Challenges of Participatory Culture: Media Education for the 21st Century* (Cambridge, MA: MIT Press, 2009); Kevin M. Tavin, "Wrestling with Angels, Searching for Ghosts: Toward a Critical Pedagogy of Visual Culture" *Studies in Art Education* 44, no. 3 (Spring 2003): 197–213; and chapters 1, 2, 4, 9, and 10 in this volume.

[6] Tavin, "Wrestling with Angels," 198.

[7] Ibid., 199–200.

[8] For further information on the "Pop Culture Diplomacy" initiative of MOFA, see the ministry's website, www.mofa.go.jp/mofaj/gaiko/culture/koryu/pop/index.html. For the Cool Japan/Creative Industries initiative of METI, see the ministry's website, www.meti.go.jp/policy/mono_info_service/mono/creative/index.html.

[9] Folkestad, "Formal and Informal Learning Situations," 141.

[10] See "New Growth Strategy: Blueprint for Revitalizing Japan," p. 55, Ministry of Economy, Trade, and Industry, http://www.meti.go.jp/english/policy/economy/growth/report20100618.pdf.

[11] See "Commission of Trend Communicator of Japanese Pop Culture in the Field of Fashion," Ministry of Foreign Affairs, http://www.mofa.go.jp/mofaj/gaiko/culture/koryu/pop/kawaii/. For a critical analysis of the "Kawaii ambassadors" from a gender studies point of view, see Laura Miller, "Cute Masquerade and the Pimping of 'Cool Japan,'" *International Journal of Japanese Sociology*, no. 20 (2011): 18–29.

[12] The group visited the exhibition *Doraemon Kagaku Miraiten* (Doraemon's Scientific Future, see http://www.miraikan.jst.go.jp/spexhibition/doraemon), which toured museums all over Japan. For further information on the influence of popular culture on the development of "social" robots in Japan, see Frederik L. Schodt, *Inside the Robot Kingdom: Japan, Mechatronics, and the Coming Robotopia* (Tokyo: Kodansha International, 1988); and Cosima Wagner, *Robotopia Nipponica: Recherchen zur Akzeptanz von Robotern in Japan* [Robotopia Nipponica: Research into the acceptance of robots in Japan] (Marburg: Tectum, 2013).

[13] The museum is a research center belonging to the University. For further information on the Manga Museum see the homepage of the institution, http://www.kyotomm.jp/english/about/mm. The joint seminar was organized in cooperation with Jaqueline Berndt, Professor in Manga/Comics Theory at the Graduate School for Manga Studies.

[14] For an analysis of didactical concepts as well as outcomes of fieldtrips to Japan "between fan pilgrimage and dark tourism" see Chris McMorran, "Between fan pilgrimage and dark tourism: competing agendas in overseas field learning," *Journal of Geography in Higher Education* 39, no. 4 (2015): 568-83.

[15] See the announcement for the symposium (in German): http://www.japanologie.uni-frankfurt.de/58656065/Reconstructing.pdf. The papers from the symposium and further contributions are expected to be published in the near future.

[16] See the announcement of the lecture on the Japanese Studies Department website: http://www.japanologie.uni-frankfurt.de/58720175/Vortrag_R_Mihara--Goethe-Universitaet.pdf.

[17] Tsutsui, "Teaching History," 2013.

Works Cited

"Commission of Trend Communicator of Japanese Pop Culture in the Field of Fashion." Ministry of Foreign Affairs, http://www.mofa.go.jp/mofaj/gaiko/culture/koryu/pop/kawaii/.

Folkestad, Göran. "Formal and Informal Learning Situations or Practices vs. Formal and Informal Ways of Learning." *British Journal of Music Education* 23 (July 2006): 135–45.

Giroux, Henry A. "Public Pedagogy and the Politics of Resistance." *Educational Philosophy and Theory* 35, no. 1 (2003): 5–16.

Gössmann, Hilaria. "Medien und Populärkultur" [Media and popular culture]. In *Grundriß der Japanologie* [Outline of Japanology], edited by Klaus Kracht and Markus Rüttermann, 555–86. Wiesbaden: Harrassowitz, 2001.

Japanese Studies Department, Goethe-University Frankfurt, ed. *Auswertung Japanologramm: Sommersemester 2011* [Japanologram questionnaire results: Summer term, 2011]. Frankfurt: Japanese Studies Department, Goethe-University Frankfurt, 2011.

Jenkins, Henry. *Confronting the Challenges of Participatory Culture: Media Education for the 21st Century*. Cambridge, MA: MIT Press, 2009.

Miller, Laura. "Cute Masquerade and the Pimping of 'Cool Japan.'" *International Journal of Japanese Sociology*, no. 20 (2011): 18–29.

"New Growth Strategy: Blueprint for Revitalizing Japan." Ministry of Economy, Trade, and Industry, http://www.meti.go.jp/english/policy/economy/growth/report20100618.pdf.

Schodt, Frederik L. *Inside the Robot Kingdom: Japan, Mechatronics, and the Coming Robotopia*. Tokyo: Kodansha International, 1988.

Tavin, Kevin M. "Wrestling with Angels, Searching for Ghosts: Toward a Critical Pedagogy of Visual Culture." *Studies in Art Education* 44, no. 3 (Spring 2003): 197–213.

Tsutsui, William M. "Teaching History and/of/or Japanese Popular Culture." *electronic journal of contemporary japanese studies* 13, no. 2 (2013), http://www.japanesestudies.org.uk/ejcjs/vol13/iss2/tsutsui.html.

Wagner, Cosima. *Robotopia Nipponica: Recherchen zur Akzeptanz von Robotern in Japan* [Robotopia Nipponica: Research into the acceptance of robots in Japan]. Marburg: Tectum, 2013.

Weaver, John, and Toby A. Daspit. "Critical Pedagogy, Popular Culture, and the Creation of Meaning." In *Popular Culture and Critical Pedagogy: Reading, Constructing, Connecting*, edited by John Weaver and Toby A. Daspit, xiii–xxxiii. New York: Garland, 1999.

PART II

IN THE MEDIA STUDIES CLASSROOM

TEACHING ABOUT POPULAR CULTURE

4

CONTESTED CLASSROOMS

RECONSTRUCTIONS OF "JAPANESENESS" THROUGH ANIME

AKIKO SUGAWA-SHIMADA

Introduction

The global reach of Japanese popular culture is reflected not only in its widespread consumption among fans but also in its growing adoption as a subject in university classrooms. In fact, courses that teach about Japanese culture through anime (Japanese animated works), manga (Japanese-style comics), and other forms of popular culture regularly attract eager students around the world.[1] Several Japanese universities have responded to young people's growing interest by offering pop culture courses in English (see chapter 10, by Philip Seaton, in this volume).[2] Such courses are designed for international students who are not fluent in Japanese, but they are also popular among local students. However, as this chapter demonstrates, students are often drawn to these courses for vastly different reasons, leading to classrooms in which the relevance of popular culture and the meaning of Japaneseness itself are contested.

In this chapter I analyze the divergent motivations of both Japanese and international students in Japan who learn about Japan through popular culture. Specifically, I show that Japanese students who are not regular anime viewers or manga readers are less interested in the anime and manga themselves than in the Cool Japan phenomenon, that is, the presumed international acclaim for Japanese pop cultural products.[3] Japanese students tend to focus on the reasons why Japan's popular culture has gained popularity overseas in order to learn aspects of their culture about which they are ignorant and to "discover" Japanese cultural values through an appreciation and evaluation of these values by non-Japanese. In other words, the growing interest in Japanese popular culture overseas has forced Japanese students to reevaluate their own culture and construct a sense of national identity through the perspective of non-Japanese. On the other hand, a growing number of international students are motivated to study in Japan by products such as anime, manga, and video games, through which they project a particular fantasy onto Japanese culture and society (see the discussion of orientalism in chapter 1, by Alwyn Spies and Sally McLaren, in this volume). While in Japan they expect to learn about the Japaneseness of anime and/or manga, as these products are linked to Japanese traditional culture and subsequently aid in constructing students' conception of a "true Japan." The result is often a contested classroom in which the Japaneseness of popular culture and its representations of sexuality, violence, religion, morality, and more is constantly debated.

I begin this chapter by outlining the reasons why Japanese universities have recently begun offering courses on Japanese pop culture as a subject in the liberal arts curriculum. Then I introduce my teaching experiences at two private universities in Osaka and Tokyo and analyze my students' constructions of Japaneseness through a survey conducted in three classes, all taught in English: one solely for Japanese students, one with a majority of international students, and one with a majority of Japanese students. I then explore how Japaneseness is constructed and deconstructed through anime in each of these classes. I suggest that discussing these constructions and deconstructions in class enables students to gain intercultural competence and fill the perceptual gap that exists between Japanese and international students. Overall, I show how teaching about Japanese culture through popular culture both reveals divergent student learning motives and enables frank discussion about stereotypes and fantasies associated with Japanese culture.

Anime in Japan's Liberal Arts Agenda

A number of universities in Japan today offer courses on anime, manga, and other popular culture/popular art forms. However, it is only in the past decade or so that universities have taught about more than the practical and artistic elements of such popular culture products. For instance, the College of Art of Nihon University offered the earliest university course on animation. Animēshon kōza (Lecture on Animation) was offered in 1971 by Hiroshi Ikeda of the Toei Animation Company, director of *Soratobu yūreisen* (The Flying Phantom Ship, 1969).[4] It taught art students how to produce animation (or theatrical/TV anime, not "art animation"). Other art universities nationwide soon followed. Yet those lectures were generally designed for students who planned to become creators and artists, making the courses less suitable for general education in the liberal arts offerings of non-art universities. Since 2000, however, a growing number of Japanese universities have been offering courses on Japanese pop culture, such as anime, manga, and J-pop, with an academic agenda in the general program of study, targeting even non-art students.[5]

Japanese universities that offer pop culture courses in the fields of literature, sociology, media studies, cultural studies, and communications intend to appeal to students born after 1990, who are perceived as having grown up amid the proliferation of Japanese popular culture. This trend of attracting students with popular topics has become more obvious since 2007, when the number of openings for university students outnumbered applicants for the first time, caused in part by Japan's low fertility rate and shrinking student population. Universities such as Kansai Gaidai and Meiji intentionally began to offer courses on anime, manga, and other popular culture products in Japanese and English in order to appeal to both local and international students, and thereby hopefully increase enrollments. Japanese universities have seen recent growth in numbers of international students from countries such as China and South Korea[6], many of whom go to Japan specifically to learn about Japanese popular culture. Courses on anime and manga have caught their attention.[7] Their interests range from acquiring language skills and learning about the "contents business" (business related to anime, manga, video games, etc.), to the simple enjoyment of Japanese pop culture.

Universities' financial situations after 2007, coupled with student demand for classes on Japanese popular culture, has prompted the creation of such courses. However, sufficiently academic examination of popular culture products has become a significant issue. Although using popular movies and TV programs in higher education is still controversial due to its dissemination of stereotypes and the impoverishment of teachers' and students' perception of higher education,[8] popular culture can afford a rich text for examination in general education because anime, manga, and video games can "reflect the political, ideological, and socio/cultural characteristics of contemporary Japanese society."[9] By utilizing popular culture products as visual texts, teachers can "attempt to position particular forms of popular culture in a hermeneutical field of contradictory meanings."[10] Moreover, students can acknowledge "how certain forms of popular culture may have helped maintain hegemonic beliefs in ways that seem natural or unproblematic."[11] Thus, popular culture products such as anime and manga provide students with a significant site to investigate ideologies and hegemonic norms that affect their lives, thus requiring serious academic research.

The government has intervened recently to raise the academic profile of popular culture studies. Specifically, in 2012 the Japanese Agency for Cultural Affairs commissioned a study of academic scholarship on manga and anime. The report of the initial study, "Report of Manga and Animation Research Mapping Project" aims to build an academic database on manga and anime studies accessible to students and scholars at all institutional levels.[12] Through these efforts and an increase in the number of courses on Japanese popular culture targeting nonart students, given both in Japanese and English, Japanese popular culture now has a greater presence in the liberal arts curriculum of Japanese universities. In the next section, I introduce several case studies based on my experiences in teaching Japanese culture through anime and manga. As I demonstrate, the choice of language of instruction and the demographics of each class affect student understandings of Japanese culture.

Case Studies: Teaching Japanese Popular Culture to Diverse Populations

As more universities have begun to offer Japanese pop culture courses in English in Japan, several problems have emerged. One issue concerns the construction and authentication of Japaneseness through an examination of ideology and sociocultural issues represented in anime (see chapter 2, by William S. Armour and Sumiko Iida, in this volume). I have found this to be particularly common in Japanese pop culture courses when the class consists of both Japanese and international students. This setting creates a contested classroom in which these students of different backgrounds debate the meaning of Japanese culture through careful analysis of Japanese popular culture. Here I share three case studies of such contested classrooms which have emerged through two types of cultural study courses in English that use anime as texts: the courses Japanese Studies at Kansai Gaidai University in Osaka since 2010 and Animation Culture at Meiji University in Tokyo since 2011.

Kansai Gaidai University receives the majority of its international students through its Asian Studies Program (ASP). As a non-degree program, international students enrolled in ASP take Japanese-language courses in the morning and courses in Asian studies, taught in English, in the afternoon. They can transfer their credits to their home universities. I was in charge of Japanese Studies as an elective course taught in English to Japanese students in the Department of Foreign Languages and to international students in the ASP. My first case study, case A (table 4.1) concerns Japanese Studies, which consisted solely of upper-level Japanese students. Case B (table 4.2) was the same course, but it was primarily designed for international students. Local students with a high TOEFL (Test of English as a Foreign Language) score could also take it, but the majority were international students.

Meiji University offers pop culture courses, especially about manga and otaku (obsessive fan) culture, through its department of Global Japanese Studies. It started an English-based program in 2011 in which international students can take all courses in English and earn a bachelors degree in four years. Although the course Animation Culture is aimed at international students, it is open to all departments. In fact the majority of students are Japanese, including returnees (Japanese students who have returned from abroad after a certain period of stay), those who wish to study abroad, and/or those who are interested in studying with international students (case C, table 4.3).

In order to examine student impressions of learning Japanese pop culture via English in Japan, I conducted a survey about the lectures in the spring (June 2012) and fall (October 2012) semesters at both universities.[13] I used a paper questionnaire, and all responses were anonymous. The questionnaire incorporates Máire M. Davis and Nick Mosdell's model of qualitative research and contains two types of questions: multiple choice questions about the reading manga/viewing anime experience and motives for studying Japanese pop culture in English, and open-ended questions about the advantages and disadvantages of studying pop culture via English in Japan.[14]

Case A: Classes with Only Japanese Students (Nonmixed)

	Spring semester, 2012	Fall semester, 2012
Number of students	Female 8; Male 4	Female 4; Male 6
Experience living abroad	F: 4 persons (12 years in Germany; 1 year in Australia etc.) M: 3 persons (1 year in New Zealand)	F: 1 person (1 year in the U.S.A.)
Time watching anime	1.68 hours/week on average	0.4 hours/week on average
Time reading manga	0.14 hours/week on average	0.5 hours/week on average

Table 4.1. Nonmixed Classes at Kansai Gaidai University, 2012

Table 4.1 shows student backgrounds in the Japanese Studies course, held in the spring and fall semesters of 2012. Both were small, discussion-based classes conducted in English. It is of note that most students in my courses rarely watch anime or read manga regularly. Some said that they were particularly interested not in anime or manga but in their overseas popularity. They have experienced non-Japanese young people's enthusiasm toward Japanese popular culture while staying outside Japan, and they realized how ignorant they were about their own culture, especially anime and manga. This experience primarily motivated them to study anime and manga, and they hoped to better explain them when traveling abroad in the future.[15]

These students' primary purpose in taking my course in English was to improve their English skills and learn about Japanese culture in general, not pop culture specifically. There is indeed another course, Japanese Culture, offered in another Kansai Gaidai department in Japanese. However, according to their answers, the students who took my course were convinced that learning Japanese culture through anime and manga would not only be easy and fun but would enable them to brush up their

English. As mentioned above, they were highly motivated to take English-based classes, hoping to gain enough English skills to explain Japanese culture represented in anime and manga in English when next asked about it by non-Japanese.

The survey asked students about the advantages and disadvantages of learning Japanese culture through popular culture in the English language. Since they were highly motivated to study abroad, they regarded English-based courses as advantageous regardless of the subject. However, in terms of culture, most students assumed that Japanese culture is opposed to "western" culture, especially American and British, and they believed that they would be able to "discover" a Japanese culture distinct from western culture by using English and reading English materials written by western authors. According to one respondent (a Japanese, female, third-year student), "I can discover Japanese culture from non-Japanese perspectives."[16] Students tended to locate Japanese culture in a binary opposition to western culture, thus constructing "Japaneseness" (something very Japanese or imagined to be originally of Japanese culture). As O Young Lee points out, Japanese ideology and cultural behavior tended to be compared to those of the West until the 1980s, which thus served to construct Japanese culture as unique and exclusive in relation to western culture. However, he suggests that such "illuminated clothes," which veil the essence of Japanese culture, should be criticized and carefully investigated from nonwestern perspectives.[17] Although Lee's account is important, the use of English in class serves to make students privilege western views of Japanese culture.

Responding to the question "What do you think are the disadvantages of studying Japanese pop culture in English in Japan?," students mostly pointed out their poor command of English and their passivity—a typical Japanese cultural attitude. For instance, one student in the fall semester remarked clearly on the first day, "I hate Japanese, because they are shy and quiet" (JF4). Despite her remark, she was very quiet in class during the rest of the semester, likely due to her poor English-speaking ability or a fear of being critical. As Ian Hosak argues about Japanese students' attitudes in his writing class at a Japanese university, they tend to be afraid of offending others by being critical of them in public.[18] This can apply to class discussion, too. Japanese students who rarely speak in class often speak more freely in private settings, for instance, in a small group or pairing.

Inability to express themselves clearly in English often causes Japanese students to feel inhibited in classes with native English speakers. One Japanese student suggested that learning Japanese culture in English through anime was awkward, making him feel that "Japanese language seems to be disrespected" (JM3). Some students assumed that Japanese concepts or ideologies might be distorted when expressed in English. In this regard, another student wrote, "Good aspects of Japanese language are lost in translation" (JF3). This is probably true when they view animated works with English subtitles in the classroom. Japanese youth jargon, slang, and special terms that convey subtle nuances in anime are often mistranslated or not translated. The students' construction of "Japaneseness" included the assumption that only native Japanese speakers could understand the "true" Japan. This is exemplified by the remark of another student, who claimed, "Japanese unique cultural aspects cannot be translated" (JF4). This clearly shows how notions of the uniqueness of Japanese culture are emphasized by learning Japanese culture through anime in English.

Case B—Mixed Class with a Majority of International Students

The Japanese Studies course at Kansai Gaidai University in 2012 included thirteen international students (twelve from the United States) and three Japanese students who planned to study abroad the following year (table 4.2).

Table 4.2 shows that both international and Japanese students did not usually watch anime or read manga for long periods of time; however, international students were slightly more exposed to anime and manga than local students. The primary reason why the international students were studying in Japan was to learn about Japanese culture and language in general. Although only one student clearly indicated that he was motivated to come to Japan because of anime, all were fond of anime and more familiar with anime titles than local students. The advantages of taking a Japanese culture through anime course in English in Japan mentioned by the international students were:

> "It's easy to understand the complex ideas in my native language" (IF3).

> "This course probably would not be offered in most US universities" (IM3).

	International students	Japanese students
Number of students	Female 9; Male 4	Female 2; Male 1
Nationality	U.S. 12; Estonia 1	Japanese 3
Main objective of coming to Japan	To learn Japanese culture: 5 To learn Japanese language: 2 To learn Japanese pop culture: 1 Others: 5	N/A
Time watching anime	2 hours/week on average	1 hour/week on average
Time reading manga	1 hour/week on average	0.8 hours/week on average

Table 4.2. Mixed Class in the ASP at Kansai Gaidai University, Fall 2012

"We are able to discuss [topics] with Japanese students" (IF2).

"We are able to apply what I learned to what I observe in my daily life in Japan, giving me the insight to see the deeper meaning of pop culture" (IM2).

The final comment specifically articulates the meaning of learning Japanese pop culture in Japan. However, most international students rarely cared whether or not anime was appropriate as an academic subject. They readily accepted representations in Japanese anime as academic issues to be discussed simply because they grew up with them.

On the other hand, Japanese students tended to construct "Japaneseness" or something purely "Japanese" in class. One Japanese student wrote, "I can study Japanese culture from different [non-Japanese] perspectives" (JF2). Another student said, "I can reevaluate Japanese culture from comments of the non-Japanese" (JM3). Reevaluation itself is not a problem. However, Japanese students distinguished themselves from international students and tended to agree with international students' analysis of Japanese culture as different, unique, and sometimes strange.

Disadvantages that international students mentioned were similar to those of Japanese students in the nonmixed class: "the problem of inaccurate English translation" (IF3, IF2, and others). They assumed that translations (English subtitles) were inaccurate and some elements could not be translated. Since no international students in this course had a perfect command of Japanese, they imagined that English translations did not convey "genuine" Japanese narratives. This assumption kept them convinced that they would be able to fully understand the ideologies and philosophy that anime represented if they acquired complete Japanese language skills. Although such a language-oriented approach to texts can motivate them to improve their language skills, an excessive association between intercultural understandings and language abilities might blur the purpose of the course. Although it is not a language course, students might avoid tackling their confusion caused by interpreting visual texts and eventually end up concluding that they will never understand Japanese culture without a good command of Japanese.

Another comment—"Non-Japanese perspectives, as opposed to the perspectives of Japanese people, are disadvantageous" (IM3)—reveals that the international students were conscious of the western inclination to place Japanese (or eastern) culture in opposition to their own. Another international student remarked self-critically that a "western lens and technique are often applied to eastern materials" (IF3). Ironically, however, this idea also served to construct the binary opposition between the West and the East. They assumed that western scholarship is often inappropriate, while Japanese scholarship would be more appropriate to understanding Japanese culture. It should be noted that the Japanese students in this course considered clear differences between Japanese and western cultures to be advantageous, while the international students disagreed.

Case C—Mixed Classes with a Majority of Japanese Students

In 2012 I taught Animation Culture over two semesters at Meiji University. The spring course attracted three international students (one American, one Hungarian, and one French) and twenty-four Japanese. Among the Japanese students, five had experienced living in English-speaking countries for over three months. The fall semester attracted seven international students (two Koreans, one Thai, one Malaysian, one Hungarian, one Australian, and one French) and twenty-five Japanese. Interestingly, in the fall semester no Japanese students had studied or lived abroad.

Although international students were exposed to anime and manga more than Japanese students, I observed no significant differences in viewing or reading experiences between them. The specific purpose of this course, to teach about animation culture, likely explains why student interest in anime at Meiji University was slightly higher than in Kansai Gaidai University.

	Spring 2012		Fall 2012	
	International students	Japanese students	International students	Japanese students
Number	Female 2; Male 1	Female 15; Male 9	Female 3; Male 5	Female 10; Male 15
The purpose of coming to Japan	To study anime and manga To study Japanese culture	N/A	To study Japanese culture To study Japanese pop culture	N/A
Time viewing anime	1.3 hours/ week on average	1 hour/week on average	1.4 hours/ week on average	1.4 hours/ week on average
Time reading manga	1.3 hours/ week on average	1.3 hours/ week on average	4 hours/week on average	0.9 hours/ week on average

Table 4.3. Mixed Classes at Meiji University, 2012

When asked about the advantages of learning about Japanese popular culture in Japan in English, the international students in the spring semester pointed out things similar to those noted by the international students at Kansai Gaidai University, for example, "There is no similar class in the United States" (IM2) and "We are able to discuss [popular culture] with Japanese students" (IF2). Students also commented, "It is good to learn from a Japanese teacher" (IF3). Other international students made similar remarks. These revealed that they authenticated and valued my national identity, which legitimized their new knowledge about Japanese culture. In the English-track program at Meiji University, most faculty members are non-Japanese, due in part to the exclusive use of English in the classroom. The high expectations of international students concerning lectures on Japanese subjects conducted by a Japanese teacher can influence instructors' practices as well. In fact, these comments made me feel that I could offer something non-Japanese instructors could not. This presented a problematic moment in which I was driven to attempt to construct Japaneseness in the classroom.

In the fall semester, table 4.3 shows that international students more seriously considered anime as reflecting Japanese sociocultural issues than the Japanese students did. An American student explained that an advantage of hearing a lecture on anime in English was that it could provide a "better understanding of Japanese culture because pop culture is consumed tremendously in Japanese society" (IM2). He attempted to seek connections between anime and Japanese society, which could offer him an opportunity to expand his perspective beyond discourses of anime per se. On the other hand, most Japanese students were reluctant to distance themselves from their own culture, which was usually naturalized and invisible to them. They neglected to problematize their own ideologies and behavior, except when international students intervened and defamiliarized their dominant ideologies and behavior. In this regard, the diverse backgrounds of the international students helped produce alternative points of view. As a Thai student suggested, "Leaning Japanese culture from different perspectives is advantageous" (IF3).

The comments of Japanese students in the spring semester are intriguingly similar to those found at Kansai Gaidai University. Many students confessed that they were asked about Japanese anime and manga when they visited foreign countries, but they were too ignorant about them to answer. This embarrassing experience had motivated them to learn Japanese culture through anime in my course. As indicated in the survey at Kansai Gaidai University, Japanese students at Meiji University tended to view learning Japanese culture in English as advantageous, as it would allow them to answer such questions in English in future travels. However, one student's comment struck me as particularly troubling: "I can learn Japanese culture 'objectively'" (JM4). This student assumed that learning about Japanese culture through English would enable him to grasp Japanese culture (or the "essence" of Japanese culture) objectively. It is important for Japanese students to distance themselves from the hegemonic norms that control their behavior and attitudes. However, the simple association of using English with the objectification or distancing might enhance a false dichotomy—the idea that western perspectives always differ from Japanese ones and are more objective.

The disadvantages that Japanese students at Meiji University mentioned focused on the inconvenience of communication in English due to their "poor English-speaking ability" (JM2) and their passive behavior in the classroom, saying, for instance, "Japanese are very quiet" (JF3). Because of their feelings of inferiority vis-à-vis international students, a female Japanese student commented, "We [Japanese] have to think 'subjectively'" (JF3). This evokes a serious question: if the student thinks that learning Japanese culture through anime in English is "objective," what can make it "subjective"?

Japanese students brought up this objective/subjective issue in the fall semester as well. When asked about the disadvantages of English lectures on anime, one student answered, "Japanese students do not completely understand in English" (JF3). Some students claimed, "There are many things that can be expressed only in Japanese" (JF4) and "Nuance [of Japanese culture and language] is lost in English" (JM3). It is true that translations do not completely convey the original meanings; however, these comments reveal that the "uniqueness" of Japanese culture is constructed among Japanese students by distinguishing their perspectives from others, especially western ones.

Effects of Small-Group Discussions

The empirical data in the mixed and nonmixed classes with different demographic compositions disclosed the gap between Japanese and international students in their understandings of Japanese culture attained through the study of anime in English. On one hand, Japanese students positively accepted "western" views of Japanese culture represented in anime, which is often negatively acknowledged by international students. However, both Japanese and international students expressed concerns about the limits of English translations and critical pedagogy written in English for understanding Japanese culture. In both cases, Japaneseness is constructed as an absolute status that is distinct from others, and hence it is assumed that only Japanese native speakers can fully understand Japan. The gap between international students' enthusiasm about Japanese popular culture and young Japanese students' relative indifference to it also produced theoretical and technical problems in the classroom.

Takashi Ikuta and Yasushi Gotoh suggest that media literacy has three aspects: the instrumental, the interactive, and the critical. In the interactive dimension, "[M]eanings do not objectively exist outside, but are acquired through mutual interactions between the learners and objects, [and] interpretation becomes deep or shallow according to the 'receiver's' knowledge and education."[19] Interactions between people with different cultural values are also important for students to nurture their literacy. Thus, although various confusions occur in my mixed and nonmixed classes, the interactions, or exchange of opinions, can offer a critical space for students to deconstruct their hegemonic ideologies.

Regarding the critical dimension of media literacy, Ikuta and Gotoh emphasize the significance of critical thinking, suggesting, "[W]hen knowledge is viewed to be objectively existing outside its receiver and when a teacher tries to inject this knowledge into a student, such education results in changing the student into 'a content to be filled by the teacher.'"[20] Because Japanese education in primary schools generally places less emphasis on fostering critical thinking, Japanese students are relatively passive in university classrooms, as some of my students indicated in the surveys. In this regard, the interactions between students through student-led discussions can be an effective way to nurture their critical-thinking skills.

Therefore, one may solve the problems of students' belief that language skill leads to full comprehension of culture, different cultural behavior, and simplified constructions of Japaneseness by introducing small-group discussions in mixed and nonmixed classes. In a group of four or five people, less peer pressure is created, allowing passive Japanese students to more easily participate. In the nonmixed class at Kansai Gaidai University, Japanese students do not usually take initiative to speak in class. To solve this problem, I have students select a discussion leader in their group and ask him or her to start the discussion. All students are assigned the role of leader at least once in a semester, and the leader is obliged to make a short oral report about what his or her group discussed. This forced responsibility can break the cultural barrier of passivity that Japanese students usually have. Also, in a small group, students pay more attention to group members and carefully listen to and respond to each other. This style has also been effective in the mixed classes at both universities. Intentional groupings of three or more Japanese students and fewer international students can successfully alleviate Japanese students' feelings of inferiority about their English speaking skills in front of international students.

Several discussions about sexuality in popular culture demonstrate how conceptual issues can be treated in small-group discussions and turned into significant teaching moments that allow deconstruction and reconstruction of Japaneseness. In a mixed class at Kansai Gaidai University, we watched *Magical Angel Creamy Mami* (1983–84), in which a ten-year-old girl named Yū is magically transformed into her adult self, an idol singer named Creamy Mami. In analyzing representations of girls and magical power in a small-group discussion, an American student asked his group members, "Why do Japanese anime often feature such kids as Yū and have them involved in romance with boys?" For him, having grown up with cartoons that rarely feature romance between children, a ten-year-old girl's interest in heterosexual love prompted him to generalize about representations of little girls as sexualized objects in anime and thus to construct a particular notion of Japaneseness.

The student's question was soon shared with other groups, and gradually all the students participated in a single discussion, with the reserved Japanese students even becoming excited to speak. The student's question offered a great opportunity to discuss cultural differences and the way little girls are represented in Japanese anime and consumed in Japanese society. At first the Japanese students passively accepted the American student's view of a distinctively pedophilic quality in anime. However, eventually a Japanese student disputed the matter by suggesting that, although young Japanese viewers consumed ideally represented girls and their sexuality, they hardly connected those fantasies to the real world. Meanwhile, an Estonian student introduced the example of European (especially French) cultural preferences for innocence represented by little girls and boys, especially in films. This student's suggestion made both American and Japanese students reconsider their assumptions and allowed the discussion to expand to the issue of how one should consider the relationship between representations of child exploitation and sex in anime and child abuse in Japanese society and beyond.

In a similar case, in the mixed class at Meiji University, after watching *Sailor Moon* (1992), an American student pointed out how Japanese anime sexualizes girls. Regarding the almost naked body of the protagonist Usagi Tsukino in the transformation scene, in particular, he suggested that excessive sexual depictions were characteristic of Japanese anime, meaning that representations of sexualized girls in anime play a part in his construction of Japaneseness. In the small-group discussions of the way sexuality is represented in anime, many female students, both Japanese and international, countered that Usagi's transformation had a positive quality, arguing that the body of Sailor Moon (Usagi) in this scene is flexible and beautiful in silhouette surrounded by shining particles, which drew their attention. Male Japanese students, who at first agreed with the American student's remark about deviant depictions of the female body in anime, deconstructed their own perceptions of sexuality and started to consider differences between what American men and others consider sexual. This matter prompted passive Japanese students to talk within the groups, and the discussion ultimately expanded beyond the groups.

Conclusion

Besides sexuality, discussions in my courses involved such controversial issues as morality, religion, justice, death, and violence, all of which are represented in anime. Regardless of the topic, Japanese students rarely expressed their opinions in front of others in class, whereas international students usually spoke out aggressively. However, even Japanese students who are usually silent listeners in class discussions often talk in a small group. Thus, small-group discussion successfully changed the passive attitude of Japanese students. The small-group discussion among students with different cultural backgrounds also effectively offered alternative views to cultural values of their own. The imagined binary opposition between the West (America) and the East (Japan) was deconstructed in discussions, especially when European and other Asian students showed alternative perspectives. In my 2014 survey at Meiji University, some similar cases were observed: more European and Asian students were in class, and more diverse perspectives were expressed. In addition, among native English speakers (American and British), different ethnic backgrounds also allowed students, particularly Japanese students, to realize that some Japanese anime include ethnically diverse depictions and often challenge ethnic, religious, and/or gender taboos.[21]

This study does not conclude that small-group discussion is the only way to solve the cultural and pedagogical problems that often arise in learning Japanese culture through anime. However, the results suggest that a small-group-discussion style positively stimulates students' (especially Japanese students') motivation to challenge issues brought up in class when analyzing representations in anime. For Japanese students without a strong command of English and no particular interest in Japanese pop culture, my course is considerably challenging. Without offering their own opinions, they are easily persuaded by the analysis and interpretations about Japanese culture and society constructed by international students. However, through interactions with international students, who have more knowledge about anime but less knowledge about Japanese culture, all students can find a way to examine and negotiate their own and other cultural values from multiple perspectives, avoiding the construction of a simplified image of Japan.

Notes

1 Ministry of Education, Culture, Sports, Science, and Technology—Japan, "Sugureta Ryūgakusei Senryakuteki Kakutoku," http://www.mext.go.jp/b_menu/ shingi/chukyo/chukyo4/houkoku/attach/1249705.htm; Deborah Shamoon, "Teaching Japanese Popular Culture." *ASIANetwork Exchange* 17, no. 2 (2010): 9; "Nihon manga e no kanshin takamaru" ("Growing Interest in Japanese Manga"). *Asahi Newspaper*, April 6, 2009, morning ed.

2 For instance, Kansai Gaidai University, Meiji University, Ōita University, Ritsumeikan Asia Pacific University, Ryūkoku University, and others offer popular culture courses in English.

3 The Cool Japan/Creative Industry Policy was launched by the Ministry of Economy, Trade, and Industry in 2010. In 2013 fifty billion yen was allotted to promote Cool Japan. "New Entity in Works to Promote Cool Japan Themes for Export," *Japan Times*, March 5, 2013.

4 Ikeda Hiroshi, "Daigaku niokeru animēshon kyoiku no taidō" ("The Movements of Animation Studies at Universities"). *Animeshon Kenkyū* (*Japanese Journal of Animation Studies*) 13 (2013): 27.

5 A number of vocational schools have focused on teaching animation production. Currently in Japan approximately fifty universities describe their programs or syllabi for animation-related courses on their websites. See Koyama Masahiro and Sugawa Akiko, "Anime de ronbun wo kakitai hitono tameni," in *Anime kenkyū nyūmon: Anime wo kiwameru 9tsu no tsubo* ("For Those who Want to Write a Thesis on Anime" in *Introduction to Anime Studies: The Nine Tips for Mastering Anime*) ed. Koyama Masahiro and Sugawa Akiko (Tokyo: Gendai Shokan, 2013), 5.

6 Japan Student Services Organization [JASSO], "Heisei 24nendo gaikokujin ryūgakusei zaiseki jōkyō chōsa kekka," 6, http://www.jasso.go.jp/statistics/ intl_student/data12.html.

7 Wakō Masakazu, Hasegawa Yuri, and Nakayama Aoi, "Nihon ryūgaku no dōki, taiken, kōka: Kōkan ryūgakusei wo chūshinni" ("Motivations, Experiences, and Consequences of Staying in Japan: Cases of Exchange Students") in *Osaka Kyōiku Daigaku Kiyō* (*Journal of Osaka Kyōiku University*) 61 (2012): 172–73.

8 Marshall Gregory, "Real Teaching and Real Learning vs. Narrative Myths about Education," *Arts and Humanities in Higher Education* 6, no. 1 (2007): 7–27.

9 Kazumi Nagaike, "Elegant Caucasians, Amorous Arabs, and Invisible Others: Signs and Images of Foreigners in Japanese BL Manga," *Intersections: Gender and Sexuality in Asia and the Pacific* 20 (April 2009): 1–11, http://intersections. anu.edu.au/issue20/nagaike.htm.

[10] Kevin M. Tavin, "Wrestling with Angels, Searching for Ghosts: Toward a Critical Pedagogy of Visual Culture," *Studies in Art Education* 44, no. 3 (2003): 199.

[11] Ibid.

[12] Japanese Agency for Cultural Affairs, "Manga, Animēshon Kenkyū Mappingu Purojekuto" [Report of Manga and Animation Research Mapping Project] 2013. http://mediag.jp/project/project/images/Report%20of%20Mapping%20 Project2012.pdf.

[13] Because my course in the ASP at Kansai Gaidai University was offered only in the fall, the survey was not conducted in the spring of 2012.

[14] Máire M. Davis and Nick Mosdell, *Practical Research Methods for Media and Cultural Studies: Making People Count* (Athens: University of Georgia Press, 2007).

[15] Most of the students in my classes know little about *NARUTO* and *Bleach*, which, along with *One Piece*, are arguably the current the "Big Three" anime or manga most popular overseas. *One Piece* is more familiar to my students than the other two, although they rarely view the anime or read the manga. This tendency is often observed in my Japanese Studies course.

[16] Hereafter I shorten student descriptors as follows: JF3 to mean Japanese female third-year student and IM2 to mean international male second-year student, for instance.

[17] Lee O Young, *"Chijimi" shikou no nihonjin* (*The Japanese Preference for "Shrinking"*). (Tokyo: Kōdansha, [1982] 2007), 9–21.

[18] Ian Hosak, "The Effects of Anonymous Feedback on Japanese University Students' Attitudes towards Peer Review," in "Memorial Issue for the Retirement of Professor Yamamoto Iwao," special issue, *Kotoba to sono hirogari* (*Language and Its Expansion*). (Ritsumeikan University) 3 (2005): 309–11.

[19] Takashi Ikuta, and Yasushi Gotoh, *Towards the Construction of Media Literacy in Japan* (Niigata: Niigata University, 2009), 298.

[20] Ibid., 308.

[21] For instance, an African American student (IM3) commented that *Super Dimension Fortress Macross* (1982) depicts an interracial marriage and *Neon Genesis Evangelion* (1995) has an antichrist theme. A LGBT student (IF3) mentioned that *Revolutionary Girl Utena* (1997) subverts heteronormativity and observed that her country would never allow such a TV anime to be aired.

Works Cited

Davis, Máire M., and Nick Mosdell. *Practical Research Methods for Media and Cultural Studies: Making People Count.* Athens: University of Georgia Press, 2007.

Gregory, Marshall. "Real Teaching and Real Learning vs. Narrative Myths about Education." *Arts and Humanities in Higher Education* 6, no. 1 (2007): 7–27.

Hosak, Ian. "The Effects of Anonymous Feedback on Japanese University Students' Attitudes towards Peer Review." In "Memorial Issue for the Retirement of Professor Iwao Yamamoto." *Kotoba to sono hirogari* (Ritsumeikan University) 3 (2005): 297–319.

Ikeda Hiroshi. "Daigaku niokeru animēshon kyoiku no taidō." *Japanese Journal of Animation Studies* 13 (2013): 27–32.

Ikuta, Takashi, and Yasushi Gotoh. *Towards the Construction of Media Literacy in Japan.* Niigata University's Scholarly Series, vol. 10,: Niigata University, 2009.

Japanese Agency for Cultural Affairs, "Manga, Animēshon Kenkyū Mappingu Purojekuto" (Report of Manga and Animation Research Mapping Project) 2013. http://mediag.jp/project/project/images/Report%20of%20 Mapping%20Project2012.pdf.

Japan Student Services Organization [JASSO]. "Heisei 24nendo gaikokujin ryūgakusei zaiseki jōkyō chōsa kekka." http://www.jasso.go.jp/statistics/ intl_student/data12.html.

Koyama, Masahiro, and Sugawa Akiko. "Anime de ronbun wo kakitai hitono tameni." In *Anime kenkyū nyūmon: Anime wo kiwameru 9tsu no tsubo,* edited by Koyama Masahiro and Sugawa Akiko, 3–15. Tokyo: Gendai Shokan, 2013.

Lee O Young. *"Chijimi" shikou no nihonjin.* Tokyo: Kōdansha, [1982] 2007.

Ministry of Education, Culture, Sports, Science, and Technology—Japan. "Sugureta Ryūgakusei Senryakuteki Kakutoku." http://www.mext.go.jp/b_ menu/shingi/chukyo/chukyo4/houkoku/attach/1249705.htm.

Nagaike, Kazumi. "Elegant Caucasians, Amorous Arabs, and Invisible Others: Signs and Images of Foreigners in Japanese BL Manga." *Intersections: Gender and Sexuality in Asia and the Pacific* 20 (April 2009): 1–11. http:// intersections.anu.edu.au/issue20/nagaike.htm.

"New Entity in Works to Promote Cool Japan Themes for Export." *Japan Times,* March 5, 2013.

Shamoon, Deborah. "Teaching Japanese Popular Culture." *ASIANetwork Exchange* 17, no. 2 (2010): 9–22.

Tavin, Kevin M. "Wrestling with Angels, Searching for Ghosts: Toward a Critical Pedagogy of Visual Culture." *Studies in Art Education* 44, no. 3 (2003): 197–213.

Wakō Masakazu, Hasegawa Yuri, and Nakayama Aoi. "Nihon ryūgaku no dōki, taiken, kōka: Kōkan ryūgakusei wo chūshinni." *Journal of Osaka Kyōiku University* 61 (2012): 169–84.

5

TEACHING FASHION AS JAPANESE POPULAR CULTURE

JAN BARDSLEY

L acey white Lolita looks and their murky Goth counterparts, schoolgirls sporting long, loose socks kept in place with glue, and the new Tokyo street style of young men donning skirts over their jeans have all captured attention as signs of "cool Japanese fashion." Fascination with these styles parallels global intrigue with the kimono in the early twentieth century and avant-garde Japanese designs of the late 1980s. Students in Japanese language and popular culture classes enjoy exploring these topics, especially contemporary ones, by scouting images and facts over the Internet and discovering material from around the world and in multiple languages. This curiosity has taken shape at a time when trends of the moment, celebrity styles, and fashion reviews spiral constantly across all media platforms and the overproduction of cheap clothing threatens the globe.[1] Taking fashion seriously has never been more critical.

Investigating fashion—past and present—enhances the study of Japanese popular culture by provoking questions about its production, dissemination, and reception domestically and transnationally. Exploring Japanese fashion interrogates the relationship between the popular and the established, the taboo and the proscribed, and the commercial systems that appropriate street style and folk traditions to construct haute couture and mass production. Fashion makes statements about national culture, often in ways that index social position, gender, race, and age. Throughout the late nineteenth and twentieth centuries, popular clothing trends emerged in Japan that were geared toward expressing modernity, a native past, or cosmopolitan identity. Reinvention of European and American styles and the recuperation of native ones led to hybridization. As well, foreign appropriations of Japanese styles, whether the kimono in the early twentieth century or Harajuku Girl mash-ups in the new millennium, have fueled Japanophilia abroad. The study of fashion takes on all these topics and, most interestingly, opens discussion on Japanese popular culture in ways that complicate the lines between high and low culture, revealing as well the vibrancy of intertextuality and transmedia flows.

This chapter suggests ways to teach Japanese popular culture by offering perspectives for analyzing key moments in modern fashion history. Rather than a comprehensive survey, this course on Japanese fashion emphasizes critical issues that give students a new appreciation of Japan and its material culture and Japan as an imagined place in global culture. As well, students gain "fashion literacy," that is, the ability to observe and analyze fashion from an academic standpoint. This extends the practice students have in interpreting literary and graphic images by asking them to think of garments in terms of such issues as the material (fabric, construction, and shape), manufacturing (designers, garment makers, merchandising, and point of sales), the symbolic (advertising, aspirational consumption, and the appeal of class, gender, and national identities), and location (global trends and local experiments). The course guides students to think about popular culture in terms of such fundamental issues as authenticity, appropriation, invented traditions, orientalism, and the recent construction of Cool Japan. Through regularly writing short essays, organizing information and ideas for exams, conducting research, and imagining their own museum exhibit, students develop ways of speaking about fashion as popular culture that relate to many of the questions animating Japanese studies today. What role does Japan play in the global imaginary? How does Japan domesticate cultural forms from abroad and how have people abroad reinvented Japanese styles and clothing? How are concepts of gender, class, and race in Japan constructed, muted, and reinvented through fashion?

Although this chapter provides a plan for teaching an entire class on Japanese fashion, incorporation of even one of the units suggested here would work well in a course devoted to Japanese popular culture or, even more broadly, to Japanese history and literature. The course is divided into six major units: (1) developing fashion literacy through reading images,

(2) kimono cultures, (3) the Japanese avant-garde and popular culture, (4) the Modern Girl as icon of global/local fashion, (5) masculinity and modernity—and the politics of transgendered dressing, and (6) Cool Japan—from street fashion to global style and tourist campaigns. I begin this chapter by introducing the academic literature on fashion, particularly Japanese fashion, and suggest ways to frame the initial aims and methods of the class in the first week of the semester. I follow with descriptions of the main issues, texts, and student essay assignments for each unit of the course. I give the most detail for the first unit to show how class and homework exercises work to actively engage student learning and creativity. Ideas for students' research projects and their final-exam project—a plan for a museum exhibit—conclude the chapter. The course includes frequent short writing assignments and in-class objective midterm and final examinations. This syllabus draws on an advanced Japanese-language course that I have taught a few times and units on fashion incorporated in my other courses on Japanese literature and culture in English translation. I should note that my classes tend to be enviably small in size (twenty-five to thirty-five students), students are well-prepared academically, and my institution encourages faculty to incorporate opportunities for students' original research and active learning into syllabi.

Fashion as an Academic Topic

Academic writing has set fashion studies on firm ground, making it one of the most compelling new fields of inquiry. Parsons The New School for Design has initiated a masters program in fashion studies, emphasizing an interdisciplinary approach "to advance the research and analysis of fashion as a cultural phenomenon."[2] Scholarly literature on fashion has burgeoned in recent decades, leading to classroom texts that compile excerpts from influential essays in the history of fashion theory, edited volumes related to wide-ranging topics such as fashion in film and popular culture, and book-length studies of particular garments such as swimsuits, commercial aspects of the fashion industry, overviews of designers' careers, and fashion history.[3] Most useful as an online source is the Berg Fashion Library, which offers excellent lesson plans complete with suggested readings and discussion questions.

The sheer size of the scholarly literature on fashion makes entering the field daunting. This is complicated by the fact that most of the theory and much of the historical study rely on Euro-American experience. A welcome exception to this focus, *The Fashion History Reader: Global*

Perspectives (2010), edited by Giorgio Riello and Peter McNeil, offers approaches to fashion created outside the Euro-American experience with attention to historical and spatial contexts.[4] As a Japanese studies scholar, I have developed this course mainly by using sources directly related to Japanese fashion and expanding beyond these by incorporating well-known texts in Japanese cultural history, fiction, and film. I select from the literature in fashion theory and history what best relates to a specific Japanese topic at hand. I use this method for guiding student research as well.

English-language publications on Japanese fashion are modest in number and approachable in style. The field has two major types of books: large pictorials and academic studies of fashion history. The large pictorials, sometimes catalogs associated with museum exhibits, are useful for their striking color plates and array of diverse fashions, and often include insightful essays. The 2010 pictorial and exhibition catalog, available in paperback, *Japan Fashion Now!* offers essays by major figures in fashion studies; photographs of diverse fashions from street to runway visually expand the arguments made in the essays.[5] *Future Beauty: 30 Years of Japanese Fashion*, another exhibition catalog, covers some of the same ground and also includes contributions from major scholars, but it gives much greater emphasis to photographs and elite fashions.[6] Academic studies include works on the history of particular garments, modernity in fashion, influential designers, and subcultural styles and beautification practices. To anchor the class, one can assign Masafumi Monden's *Japanese Fashion Cultures: Dress and Gender in Contemporary Japan*, which explores questions about gender and transnational circulation of fashion through an analysis of youth styles that pique student curiosity.[7]

Throughout this chapter, I will introduce other academic work on Japan that is relevant to particular course units. Japanese fiction and film included in each unit further enhance students' understanding of the cultural context and symbolic weight of various fashions and also helps them make connections with other classes on Japan.

Despite the enormous academic literature produced in fashion studies, I have found no publication devoted to teaching a course on the topic. Fashion scholar and sociologist Yuniya Kawamura, who has authored books and articles on Japanese fashion, however, published a helpful guide in 2011 for students embarking on various kinds of qualitative research in the field. *Doing Research in Fashion and Dress* offers an introductory overview of all the steps necessary in designing, executing, and completing a research project.[8] Kawamura gives a brief overview of the most influential theories and the various methodologies (ethnography, surveys, semiology, object-based research, and other methods) commonly employed. A special 1998 issue on methodology of *Fashion Theory: The Journal of Dress, Body, and Culture* includes authors' experiences training students in the analysis of dress; the issue is also eye-opening for tracing the controversies about methods over past decades in this field.[9] Instructors considering teaching a unit or class on fashion may find these resources, as well as the Berg Fashion Library website mentioned above, handy for thinking about how to divide the broad field of Japanese fashion into manageable segments that emphasize student participation and make students aware of methodology itself.

A word about terminology is in order here. Shifting definitions of *fashion* and its potential difference from terms such as *dress, style,* and *clothing* emerge throughout this literature, and when reading various articles, students should take note of the classifications authors employ. The journal *Fashion Theory*, for example, takes a broad purview, adopting "as its starting point a definition of fashion as the cultural construction of the embodied identity."[10] "Dress and Identity" (1992), an influential article by Mary-Ellen Roach-Higgins and Joanne B. Eicher, on the other hand, argues for separating *dress* from *fashion*, providing a theoretical framework that aids in discussing dress in terms of function, communication, and identity construction.[11]

Unit 1: Developing Fashion Literacy

Clarifying the learning goals of the course and explaining the methods, texts, and means of assessing student achievement are the critical first steps for teaching this or any class, for bridging students' different interests, and for creating a learning community. The aura of superficiality attached to fashion, however, means that one must begin the class by making the case for taking fashion studies seriously and assigning Monden's initial chapter, "Introducing Japanese Fashion, Past and Present," in *Japanese Fashion Cultures* can open this conversation. Discussion of this chapter and our project as a whole underscores the fact that for our purposes studying fashion encompasses the examination of diverse texts, aesthetic codes, historical context, and critical theory.

Hands-on activities guide students toward understanding these abstract issues in concrete ways. The following exercises show how students learn analytical methods and the politics of fashion in the first week of class. In keeping with Henry A. Giroux's call for a critical pedagogy of popular culture that actively involves students in understanding patterns of authority and power, these exercises guide students to learn by doing.[12]

Asking students to interpret the famous 1945 photograph that captures General Douglas MacArthur's first meeting with Emperor Hirohito following the defeat of Japan and at the outset of the Allied occupation (1945–52) works well to show the politics of dress (fig. 5.1). The exercise also trains students to develop a critical eye for images and to verbalize what they see. They do not need any introduction to the photograph, as the stark contrast between the two men easily stimulates discussion. Here having students work in pairs and with a time limit can push them to produce many descriptive phrases that, in the class discussion that follows, highlight the function of fashion. Students can conclude the exercise by posing their own questions. What additional information do they need to interpret the photograph? What information might be part of the backstory operating here and not visible within the frame? What are the histories and significations of the two different kinds of menswear deployed in the photograph?

The students learn to view the photograph from various points of view. In brief the photograph shows a tall, older Anglo-American commander dressed in informal military clothing and assuming a casual posture and an air of aloofness, even boredom, as he towers over a smaller and younger Asian man standing stiffly and dressed in the height of formal men's fashion. The photograph, which was MacArthur's idea and something he ensured was widely distributed in Japan, communicates the power differential between the two men, but it also reveals that there will likely be a place for the emperor in the new regime.[13] Some have called this an *omiai* (arranged marriage) shot, which depicts a masculine United States newly partnered with a feminized Japan. One can ask students to imagine why MacArthur wanted this photo distributed and why it has been described in gendered terms. Much has also been made of Hirohito's transformation from wartime divinity to symbol of democracy through his donning of an ordinary business suit rather than imperial raiment as he traveled among the public in postwar Japan. Extending the exercise by asking students to describe the difference between images of Hirohito on his white horse commanding the troops during the war and those of

Figure 5.1. General Douglas MacArthur and Emperor Hirohito
photographed on September 27, 1945. Their respective postures
and degrees of sartorial formality signal a new power dynamic.
(Courtesy of the US Library of Congress)

his stoop-shouldered figure in an ordinary business suit after the defeat
underscores the differences in fashioning the monarch as awe-inspiring
divinity and "man of the people."

Making this discussion relevant to students' lives following Giroux's
suggestion, one can segue into showing images, also easily available on the
Internet, instructing young people in how to dress for a job interview at a
conservative corporation. A productive question to ask is if one came into a
room where a job interview was being conducted and saw two people, one
formally attired and sitting at attention and one less formally dressed and
appearing more relaxed, whom would one guess is the interviewee? This
elicits discussion of appearance management and power in the workplace,
drawing connections between the 1945 photograph and contemporary

fashion politics. Although the contexts differ radically, the visual cues bear similarity.

These initial exercises drive home the key issues and methods that frame the class and actively involve students from the start. Students understand that the course will investigate how fashion is used to construct national identities and international relations, status hierarchies, gender, and polarizing concepts of East and West. They know that each class session will include exercises asking students to attend to the visual cues of fashion, the frame that isolates and guides interpretation, and the means of disseminating (or censoring) images. The examples selected for study will tend to emphasize transformation—both broad shifts in fashion trends and changes in an individual's appearance—since focusing on change builds one's agility in visual analysis and also demonstrates the power of fashion as a means of communication. As well, students will look beyond the image to consider clothing, hairstyles, and accessories in their historical context, understanding them as responses to broader conversations of propriety and expression. Since most of our investigation relies on textual images, it is difficult to take full account of fashion artifacts as material culture, so bringing in supplemental reading on materiality, when available, is useful.

Students quickly learn that writing, oral presentation, and reading compose an essential part of the class. The course introduction proceeds to writing and presentation exercises by elaborating on the fashion politics of contemporary national leaders' costumes. For their first short assignment, students choose an image of a leader of their choice from the Internet and write 250 words analyzing what the leader's appearance communicates about his or her role as a leader and the nation he or she represents. In a small-group exercise in the next class, students briefly present their images and analysis orally. Each group recommends one for the class as a whole to consider. In discussion and later written comments on each student's paper, the instructor needs to guide students in two ways: (1) to describe an image in detail and (2) to use these observations as evidence with which to interpret the image. For example, returning to the 1945 photograph, it is not enough to say that "MacArthur is more casual and Hirohito is more formal, and MacArthur looks more powerful," although that may be the initial reaction. What are the specific cues about each man's posture, facial expression, style of dress, and placement in the photograph standing side by side that suggest difference in formality and authority? This kind of emphasis on "close readings" of images builds on skills students will likely have developed in literature classes.

As we turn to fashions for women in leadership in the next week, class discussions explore sartorial constructions of gender as well as nation. Taking students through examples from a variety of time periods launches major questions that link the examples through fashion. How are messages about "feminine virtue," high status, and tradition and modernity shaped by fashion? How does fashion highlight features that can be understood as particularly Japanese or cosmopolitan? We begin with Sally A. Hastings's 1993 article "The Empress' New Clothes and Japanese Women, 1868–1912," which introduces students to nineteenth-century instances of deliberation about Japanese imperial costume.[14] Hastings explains the new clothes adopted by both the Meiji emperor and empress, how the empress required other women in Japan to assume this modern fashion, and the role photography and public spectacle played in establishing new codes of propriety and gender in fashion (fig. 5.2). As well, students read my 1998 article on the royal wedding of 1993 and the fashion makeover that controversially transformed diplomat Owada Masako, known for her somber career-woman suits, into Crown Princess Masako, attired in pastel, ladylike dresses and kimono.[15] Concluding this discussion by connecting it to fashion theory, one can use Fred Davis's *Fashion, Culture, and Identity* (1992), particularly chapter 4, "Ambivalences of Status: Flaunts and Feints," to think more broadly about sartorial markers of elite and populist style.[16]

Figure 5.2. Empress Shōken and Emperor Meiji as styled in the late 1880s in the manner of European royalty, symbols of Japan as a modern nation. (Courtesy of the US Library of Congress)

The final in-class exercise for this unit makes methodology explicit. Presented with an image of two different leaders in Japan, the students take ten minutes to describe ten steps they would need to take in interpreting each image as "fashioning nation." These can include such tasks as making a list of every element in the photograph; investigating the time, place, and occasion when the image was crafted; the significance of the individual's clothing at that point in Japan; and, if known, who designed and made the clothing. Class discussion following the exercise builds a shared sense of the methods and goals of the course. Observing news reports of world leaders thereafter, students become acutely aware of the deployment of fashion.

Unit 2: Kimono Cultures

Exploring the kimono works perfectly to open our study of Japanese fashion as popular culture. It may be the only garment studied in the class that the students can actually experience in material form since often one can be obtained in the local community. Moreover, many English-language texts, from large pictorial books and documentary films to histories and anthropological studies, provide abundant information on the kimono.[17] The study of the kimono lends well to asking the kinds of intellectual questions that frame the class, guiding students to understand fashion as embedded in material and symbolic culture. The unit employs Japanese film and fiction to enhance students' appreciation of the kimono as an artistic form and a fashion interwoven with a sense of national, and often gender and class, identity. Questions can begin with the life of the kimono in contemporary Japan, expand to its long and colorful history, and move on to considering the kimono as a transnational garment—one that became defined as a "national costume" and even "quintessentially Japanese" yet inspired designs in the Euro-American West. The kimono inspiration leads into questions of orientalism and appropriation as students consider issues such as the Internet debate about American pop star Katy Perry in her geisha getup at the 2013 American Music Awards, as Melanie King also discusses in chapter 6 in this volume.[18]

Study of the kimono—particularly when it is opened flat in pictorials or museum exhibits—also raises a question for the class much discussed in fashion studies: Is clothing only fully animated when worn? Elizabeth Wilson, author of the influential *Adorned in Dreams: Fashion and Modernity* (1985), writes, for example, that articles of clothing "frozen in the mausoleums of culture" are "like souls in limbo," cut off from the vitality of those wearing them and their social lives.[19] Yet in Japan the kimono is often appreciated as a work of art separated from the wearer and even used to decorate a space. As former geisha Mineko Iwasaki writes, one-of-a-kind kimono "are given names, like paintings, and are treasured as such."[20] These ideas challenge students anew about how to define fashion and dress, as well as how to stage exhibits, questions to which they return in their own museum projects at the end of the course.

Explaining the main texts for this unit on the kimono gives the best idea of how to develop these questions. Terry Satsuki Milhaupt's *Kimono: A Modern History* promises to be an excellent textbook.[21] Published in 2014 in tandem with the New York Metropolitan Museum's exhibit on the kimono, it offers a comprehensive, accessible view of 150 years of the material, aesthetic, and social life of the kimono and includes many colorful images from diverse sources.[22] Milhaupt discusses the modernization of the kimono, its textile history, how it "migrated to the West," kimono designers, and the kimono "then and now." I have also found two older books useful for studying kimono culture: Liza Dalby's 1995 *Kimono: Fashioning Culture* and Rebecca Stevens and Yoshiko Iwamoto Wada's 1996 *The Kimono Inspiration: Art and Art-to-Wear in America*.[23] Dalby's accessible book has numerous illustrations and takes readers from the earliest days of the kimono in Japan to the spectacular design trends and fabric innovations of the Edo era and, with relish, to the Meiji era, when the kimono became fixed as *wafuku* (Japanese clothing) as opposed to *yōfuku* (western clothing) and cartoons in Tokyo newspapers satirized Japanese who mixed both in hopes of devising a smart, "modern" look—a section that harks back to our initial discussion of Meiji imperial clothing. Stevens and Wada's exhibition catalog, replete with many photographs of kimonolike garments, Anglo people dressed in them, and replications of artwork featuring the kimono, presents a similarly dynamic view of the kimono but examines it as fashion appropriated and reinvented by the Euro-American West. They display kimono made over for modern ladies' wear: new designs, especially long-sleeved, straight-torso gowns, inspired by the kimono, and kimono refashioned as afternoon tea gowns and costumes for stage performances of modern dance. Stevens and Wada bring in Edward Said's theories of orientalism, making this an effective point at which to introduce this concept.[24] Asking students to compare and contrast photographs of opera stars Frances Alda and Miura Tamaki underscores how the kimono took on different meanings when worn by Australian and Japanese divas in the early 1900s (figs. 5.3 and 5.4). For

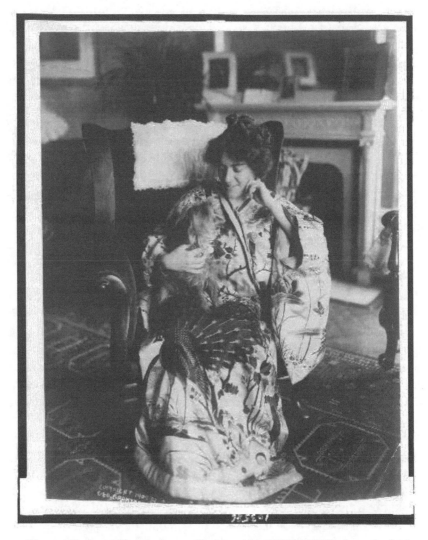

Figure 5.3. Australian opera star Frances Alda (1879–1952) photographed
relaxing in a kimono, a fashion favored by New Women in Europe and the
United States. (Courtesy of the US Library of Congress)

Figure 5.4. Japanese opera star Miura Tamaki (1884–1946) making up for
her role as Madama Butterfly circa 1901–1915. Known as a New Woman
in Japan, where she cut a modish figure in western-style clothing, Miura
typically wore a kimono on her travels abroad, reinforcing audiences'
perceptions of the authenticity of her performances of Cio-Cio-San.
(Courtesy of US Library of Congress)

Alda the kimono likely signaled her status as a fashionable "New Woman" whose Asian "dressing gown" departed as radically from proper Victorian notions of femininity as did her achievements in the public arena. In contrast, the sight of Miura sporting western-style clothing in Japan enhanced her reputation as one of the nation's own New Women (*atarashii onna*). Yet, as Mari Yoshihara has observed, when traveling abroad for her role as Madama Butterfly, Miura typically dressed in a kimono to meet foreign audiences' perceptions of a Japanese performer of this role.[25]

Studying the kimono across time and continents provokes discussion about authenticity and popular appropriation in fashion that will be expanded throughout the course. This also provides ways to discuss contemporary controversy fruitfully. Both Edo era Japanese experiments, often with Chinese materials, and Euro-American innovations raise the question of whether any original exists or if, like much fashion itself, all these kimono and "kimono" are intertextual references to each other. Through study of the kimono, students can place the controversy over Katy Perry's geisha performance in historical perspective. Students can search the Internet for the disparate comments that formed the debate analyzing the basis for arguments in support of and against her appropriation of the kimono. Assigning Melanie King's chapter in this volume, wherein she uses Said's views of orientalism to critique the Perry performance, will work well to stimulate conversation. Considering whether Perry's costume functioned as a nod from this global star to her numerous fans in Japan, whose responses may have differed from those of American critics, explores the connection between orientalism and geographic location. The topic of orientalism in fashion is not settled here but reemerges throughout the course.

Fiction and film introduce some Japanese ideas about the kimono. One of Japan's most popular modern writers, Tanizaki Jun'ichirō, employs fashion to delineate characters and their worlds. His 1929 novel *Tade kū mushi* (Some Prefer Nettles) tells the tale of a man feeling caught between the challenges of modernity and the apparent security of old Japan as styled in the puppet theater, older food fashions, and male privilege. Fashion emphasizes the "double life" experienced by the main character, who wears western clothes at work and kimono at home, whose modern wife favors bright red nail polish, and whose father-in-law's young mistress dresses in old-style kimono and outdated hairstyles to suit the old man's tastes. Discussing this book near the end of the unit gives students a sense of how *wafuku* and *yōfuku* point to new directions in gender roles as men in kimono miss the comfort of being in charge of their world while young women seek to escape that world, in part through suiting up in western clothing. The 1983 film *Sasameyuki* (The Makioka Sisters), based on a Tanizaki novel of the same name, fits well in this unit for the sensuality of the kimono that animate the screen.

Two essay assignments work well for this unit, building students' verbal agility and making them think about writing for different audiences—blog readers and academic readers. The first assignment (250 words) asks students to briefly explain the kimono in terms of some aspect of its materiality; they choose and research the topic (e.g., the association of kimono design with the seasons, used kimono for sale at contemporary flea markets, and kimono for the bride and groom). Students tailor their essays as a short blog post for travelers to Japan—interesting information presented in a concise and entertaining manner. The second, longer, and more academic essay (750 words) asks the students to think more deeply about fashion culture as exemplified in *Some Prefer Nettles*. Using passages from the novel, students examine how tradition and modernity are framed through fashions in the kimono and other clothing, cosmetics and hair, and matters of taste. These assignments give students practice in writing for different audiences about the materiality and culture of fashion. This unit on kimono cultures gives students a thorough introduction to the kimono as domestic and transnational fashion; as a particular kind of garment with conventions for making, cleaning, and wearing; and as a garment historically rich with multivalent symbolism.

Unit 3: The Japanese Avant-Garde and Popular Culture

Moving from the unit on kimono cultures to one on avant-garde fashion of the 1980s might seem a radical shift at first glance. But, as we shall see, this unit, too, continues the discussion of orientalism and the often blurred lines dividing elite culture from popular practice. For one thing, avant-garde designers reputedly took inspiration from the kimono and sought out designs and materials once common in clothing worn by Japanese peasants. They have sought ways to leave their clothing open to completion by the individual consumer. As well as exploring these ideas, this unit introduces students to one of the most famous chapters in modern Japanese fashion history and truly startling fashions.

Scholarship on Japanese fashion, whether pictorial book or history, regularly includes chapters on three late-twentieth-century avant-garde Japanese designers—Rei Kawakubo, Issey Miyake, and Yohji Yamamoto—all of whom achieved international fame through success in Paris. The academic literature on their designs and careers takes students into the world of haute couture and the importance of the French fashion system in creating a global brand. Questions about orientalism arise as scholarly and journalistic writing about the avant-garde designers strives to locate their work in Japanese aesthetic traditions. The uniqueness of the designs, their display on runways and in fashion magazines, however, raises a new question critical to our discussion of fashion as popular culture: if few ever wear this fashion and most admire it only in museums, what relation does it have to popular fashion? If fans of these designers buy their T-shirts and fragrances and adapt aspects of their elite work such as flat shoes, asymmetrical shapes, and black, is this popular fashion?

After their study of kimono cultures, students are aware of arguments about orientalism and primed to debate the effectiveness of interpreting the avant-garde designers in terms of Japanese aesthetic codes. This line of inquiry also raises the issue of how such codes have been shaped and reshaped in Japan to create a sense of cultural continuity that aspires to encompass popular and refined tastes.[26] To engage with this topic, students will benefit from reading Lise Skov's 1996 essay on the reception of Rei Kawakubo's work, "Fashion Trends, Japonisme, and Postmodernism; or, What Is So Japanese about *Comme des Garçons*?" Viewing this reception from multiple perspectives, Skov situates so-called Japanese fashion of the 1980s within global flows of fashion manufacturing, promotion, and appreciation.[27] Her references to the Japonisme of the late nineteenth century circle back to our previous discussion of the kimono "migrating to the West" while her thoughts on Kawakubo fans in the late twentieth century push us to avoid reductively equating clothing and Japaneseness. To return to one of the themes of this volume stated in the Introduction—to use Japan to explain the text rather than using the text to explain Japan—we understand the importance of *not* interpreting this call as a strategy for essentializing Japan or overstating its difference from other nations. Rather, we need to tack back and forth between reading Japanese texts and locating relevant contexts in Japan and abroad to produce complex interpretations of both the text and Japan.

For hands-on experience with this reflection of fashion criticism, students can search the Internet for journalistic writing on these three designers and bring examples to class for discussion. Building on their reading of Skov's article, they can read Patricia Mears's essay "Formalism and Revolution" in *Japan Fashion Now!,* which explicitly takes up the issue of orientalism in fashion writing but also elucidates the designers' remarkable innovations in tailoring and fabric design and how they established new ground on which other designers, such as Martin Margiela, have built.[28] Looking to a Japanese source, students can also read Tanizaki's short tongue-in-cheek tract on Japanese aesthetics, *In'ei raisan* (In Praise of Shadows, 1933), since it is often quoted in fashion writing on the avant-garde, and see for themselves to what extent it is effective as a means of interpreting contemporary fashion.[29] Viewing Wim Wenders's imaginative 1993 documentary *Notebook on Cities and Clothes*, which appreciates the work of Yohji Yamamoto and situates it within the vibrancy of urban Tokyo, and reading a critique of the film by anthropologist Dorinne Kondo continues the discussion of orientalism, the boundaries of popular and elite cultures, and authenticity in fashion.[30]

Students' essay assignments for this unit help them make links to the previous unit on kimono cultures. One short essay (500 words) in the blog post format requires students to select one of the designers' works and compare it to aspects of kimono design in formal terms that attend to cut, cloth, and convention for wearing. In the following class, students share their strategies for writing about these fashions in formal ways and read each other's posts. In a longer academic essay (750 words) at the end of the unit, students write a movie review of *Notebook on Cities and Clothes*, concentrating on how the film interprets Yamamoto's fashion, taking account of Kondo's critique and Mears's appreciation of the film. Writing this analysis gives the students further hands-on experience with fashion criticism.

Unit 4: The Modern Girl as Icon of Global/Local Fashion

To give students a richer sense of the popular and fashion in historical perspective, we move from discussions of the kimono and the avant-garde to the 1920s mode of the Modern Girl (*modan gāru*) as the target of investigation. Known for her bobbed hair, red lips, and short skirts, the Modern Girl was the darling of the media and an object of educator and parental concern. Her look signaled that she threatened to cross gender, class, and national boundaries in bold and visible ways. Studies such as the influential 2008 edited volume *The Modern Girl Around the World* show that the Modern Girl emerged in many locales, often with the same trademark fashion, exemplifying an interplay between transnational commerce and local gender politics.[31] Interpreting the Modern Girl from the perspective of fashion studies, students can explore literature, film, magazine culture, and history, asking what was "popular" about this fashion moment and questioning how the Modern Girl's unique style incited allure and anxiety. One can also ask how women may have selected aspects of this look to produce more individualized identities, raising the issue of personal creativity at work within popular trends.

English-language sources on the Modern Girl, including translations of fiction by 1920s and 1930s women writers, are abundant.[32] I offer texts here that all engage with constructing the Modern Girl through fashion and modernized spaces (new homes, cafés, shopping areas, and modes of transportation). Tanizaki's 1924 best-selling novel *Chijin no ai* (translated into English as *Naomi*), a popular classroom text, draws attention to fashion through attempts to make over café girl Naomi as the Hollywood star Mary Pickford and by Naomi's habit of littering her home with modern clothing.[33] Filling out the culture of the Modern Girl from a historical perspective, articles by Elise Tipton and Barbara Hartley, available in the online journal *Intersections*, illuminate new representations—patriotic and risqué—of urban Japanese women. Hartley attends to the visual by exploring popular magazine images and Tipton through descriptions of café spaces.[34] Using Rebecca L. Copeland's 1995 essay on the writer Uno Chiyo's strategic use of makeup as creating one identity and masking another opens up discussion of cosmetics in the 1920s as an increasingly acceptable technology of femininity and a metaphor for modernity.[35] The 2012 edited volume *Modern Girls on the Go* takes on the uniform as modern fashion in Japan, considering the attire of bus girls, elevator girls, and department store clerks as evocative of fresh modes of labor, sexuality, and consumption.[36]

This unit, too, engages with visual texts, particularly fashion in film. Mizoguchi Kenji's 1936 film *Gion no kyōdai* (Sisters of the Gion) uses kimono and modern dress to distinguish two sisters working in Kyoto's geisha district known as the Gion. The younger geisha's Modern Girl looks—cloche hats, bobbed hair, cosmetics, and belted skirts—reinforces her assertive self-interest and her brash (and ultimately failed) attempts to manipulate men rather than be exploited by them. The elder sister's consistent appearance in kimono and older hair fashions codes her as conventional. Considering films such as this within the broader field of early film extends our view of the Modern Girl and the Japanese version as an innovation within a globally circulating fashion vocabulary. Here students can read Deborah Shamoon's article on the vamp in early Euro-American film and fiction.[37] This article works particularly well if one also includes Tanizaki's *Naomi* since Shamoon traces the novel's many references to film stars in Europe and the United States, pointing to their links to icons of the vamp, a figure with origins in vampire fantasies connected to fears of racial and ethnic mixing.

Student assignments again include two essays. The first, a short assignment, calls for students to find images of the Modern Girl in Japan on the Internet and write a short blog post (500 words) that attends to its visual cues as markers of a Modern Girl look. The longer essay (750 words) analyzes the Modern Girl in either a film or a fictional work, tracing how the use of fashion and space frames her character as modern. This assignment challenges students to reflect on definitions of *modernity* in our readings and to consider how fashion articulated the modern in gendered terms.

Unit 5: Masculinity and Modernity and the Politics of Transgendered Dressing

The production of masculinity in Japanese fashion can encompass a host of modes, from the samurai to the salaryman, with much diversity in between. By exploring masculinity via military uniforms and business suits in the twentieth century and then moving to new forms of male beauty in the twenty-first, this unit provides a transition from the Modern Girl to the last unit on Cool Japan. By concluding the unit with thoughts on transgendered dressing, especially male-to-female transformation, we can better understand fashion's role in reinforcing gender norms.

Although the literature in fashion studies has focused most on women's fashion, the history of men's styles is receiving increasing attention, opening a conversation on the sartorial constructions of masculinity. Most broadly, *The Men's Fashion Reader* (2009) offers a host of short articles on topics such as the evolution of men's wear, subcultural style, and sexuality.[38] Turning specifically to Japanese fashion, Jason G. Karlin's research examines how young political activists in Japan known as *sōshi* deployed tough-looking dress—"long hair and tattered clothing"—to make their opposition to the government visible.[39] Toby Slade's 2009 *Japanese Fashion: A Cultural History* contributes to the field with a lengthy chapter on military uniforms and the advent of the business suit in Japan.[40] Our anchor text, Masafumi Monden's *Japanese Fashion Cultures: Dress and Gender in Contemporary Japan,* extends investigation of men's dress to the twenty-first century.[41]

Films can play a vital role in this unit. Viewing Kurosawa Akira's 1947 *Subarashiki nichiyōbi* (One Wonderful Sunday) brings attention to a man's ordinary suit as tangible proof of his impoverishment and struggles to survive in early postwar Japan. As the man and his date spend a Sunday together trying to have fun despite their poverty, the camera zooms in on his torn shoes, his increasingly wet and ragged clothes, and the coat he must pawn simply to pay for coffee. Rather than burnishing his masculinity, the old suit depicts his hopelessness. A later film that serves as a counterpoint to this, Nakahira Kō's 1956 *Kurutta kajitsu* (Crazed Fruit), based on Ishihara Shintarō's famous 1955 novel *Taiyō no kisetsu* (Season of the Sun), shows the youth fashions that captured the imagination of young people in Japan. Carefree and reckless, the teens in this film seem to be untouched by the war, and their relaxed fashion communicates leisure and privilege. Here Hiroshi Narumi's essay "Japanese Street Style: Its History and Identity" in *Japan Fashion Now!* is useful, offering photographs, such as those of motorcycle gangs, and deepening our understanding of men's fashion in occupied and early postwar Japan.[42]

Jumping decades ahead, we discover completely different views of male beauty and masculinity that speak to new cultural contexts and media platforms. The 2005 film *Densha otoko* (Train Man) draws sympathetic attention to a nerdy geek who transforms himself into an attractive young man through a complete style makeover. Here Alisa Freedman's article on the Train Man phenomenon, which got its start on the Internet and morphed into a print novel, manga, and TV show, as well as a film, gives a context to the appeal of the sweet nerd, particularly to women.[43] As well, Laura Miller's writing on contemporary male beauty work and my essay on men's etiquette guides serve to expand the context, distinguishing the masculinities embodied by the postwar salaryman and twenty-first-century beautiful boys and exploring contemporary faith in the transformative power of the makeover.[44]

The distinction between the salaryman as corporate warrior and images of beautiful boys in Japan today, from boy band members to manga characters, points to a continuum of gender. At this point, thinking about codes for transgendered dressing expands discussion. Vera Mackie's 2008 article, "How to Be a Girl: Mainstream Media Portrayals of Transgendered Lives in Japan," intertwines evidence from law and popular culture.[45] Most interesting for this class, Mackie observes how the male-to-female transgendered individual is costumed in highly feminine dress. This relates to transgendered fantasies on the Japanese stage, in both the all-female Takarazuka Revue and the all-male Kabuki theater, which leave no middle ground but hyperperform one gender or another. Bringing in the work of artist Morimura Yasumasa, who transforms himself across gender, race, and time, can extend the discussion on the power of dress to disrupt conventional displays of social location and personal identity.[46]

As we near the end of the course, students are busy with their semester projects, so only one short reflective essay is due. For this essay, the student chooses one instance of transformation, such as the makeover scene in *Train Man* or one in the life of a transgendered figure, and asks how the transformation is visually constructed and what is *lost* and *gained* in the process. We might also ask about the creative potential of a third term, one not perfectly crossed from one gender to another but displaying another subject position.[47]

Unit 6: Cool Japan—from Street Fashion to Global Style and Tourist Campaigns

An examination of the playful street fashions emerging in late-twentieth- and early-twenty-first-century Japan concludes the class, reviewing its major themes: the blurred divide between high and popular culture, fantasies of East and West, constructions of gender and class, and representations of Japan. In contrast to the unit on the Modern Girl, which emphasized Japanese adaptations of a globally circulating model of womanhood, this unit explores how fanciful fashions developed in Japan, such as frilly "Lolita" looks that depict a quasi-Victorian fantasy, and the street-costume phenomenon known as cosplay (*kosupure* in Japanese) have won fans across the world.[48] This unit highlights questions about appropriation and intertextuality. How have Japanese young people, influenced by fanciful depictions of European youth circulating in manga, created their own romantic fashions? How do their constructions speak to others popular in Japan such as the unique costume of the apprentice geisha (*maiko*) and the edgier teenage *ko-gyaru* look of the late 1990s? Is appropriation of these looks abroad by pop stars such as Gwen Stefani and her Harajuku Girls, which captured attention in 2005, a new orientalism or appreciative participation? What do we make of the Japanese government's promotion of subcultural urban fashion fantasies as a way to stimulate tourism to Japan?

Discussion of the Japanese concept of *kawaii*, typically translated in English as "cute" but having broader meanings in Japanese, is essential to this unit. Using the chapter "Glacé Wonderland: Cuteness, Sexuality, and Young Women" in Monden's *Japanese Fashion Cultures,* works well here. Reading this chapter and viewing the music videos online, students can define and debate *kawaii*, once again linking it to our discussion of Japanese aesthetic codes used to critique avant-garde fashion in the 1980s. How can one effectively employ terms such as *kawaii* and *wabi* to pinpoint cultural context while avoiding cultural essentialism?

The transmedial reach of contemporary youth fashions forms an indispensable part of this unit, encouraging some use of manga, fiction, and film. Here Takemoto Novala's 2002 novel *Shimotsuma monogatari*, later adapted as a manga and film and translated into English as *Kamikaze Girls*, works well for gaining an understanding of how fashion can inspire a fantastic world of characters delineated by sartorial choice. Historian Vera Mackie's 2010 essay "Reading Lolita in Japan" interprets Takemoto's fiction and other iterations of Lolita expression as a "case study of the cultural logic of the figure of 'Lolita'" in Japan.[49]

Student Research Projects

Students' major projects include an eight-page research paper and a final examination project. Together these assignments call on the students to bring the semester's training in fashion studies to bear in original ways and requires them to communicate to different audiences—academic conversations that focus on research and the public conversation of the museum exhibit.

The final examination project asks students to respond creatively— visually and verbally— to the course by imagining how they would curate a modest museum exhibit related to Japanese fashion for the general public. I ask students to assume that the museum space for the project is relatively small, allowing for only eight pieces (photographs, fashion artifacts, paintings, etc.). The assignment is virtual, and the students use PowerPoint slides to curate an exhibit of eight images. Since we have considered museum exhibits and exhibit catalogs as evidence throughout the course, this assignment flows well from our work, giving each student an opportunity to use this medium.

The museum project requires students to confront the challenge of presenting Japanese fashion in a compelling, highly visual way. They are instructed to assume that the viewer should not be expected to know about Japan or fashion. They may use themes from the course such as orientalism or focus on a specific kind of clothing such as school uniforms. Students have five specific questions to consider in designing their projects: (1) what are my goals for the exhibit?, (2) How do the images I have selected forward these goals?, (3) How will my exhibit labels guide viewers?, (4) How do I want viewers to understand the exhibit as a whole?, and (5) What questions do I want viewers to take away from the exhibit? Since the project is completed using PowerPoint, it can be turned in via the online course site, enabling students to use visual material without the expense of printing. Students make one slide that titles and explains the exhibit and then compose eight slides, each with an image and a short description in the style of a wall label in a museum. The assignment is graded on three measures. Do the exhibit title and overview make a clear, compelling argument? Do the wall labels guide the reader in viewing the image in the context of the exhibit and as a unique image? Is all the writing ready for public view (no typos, misspelled words, etc.)?

In small classes, I have used the museum exhibit project as the basis for a final oral exam. Students meet with me for sixty to ninety minutes in small groups, each presenting his or her exhibit to the others. As a group, we discuss how the exhibits relate to the major themes, texts, and methods of the class and ways in which we might define *Japanese fashion*. I also include an in-class final examination of short answers and objective questions that tests students' knowledge of the materials covered in the second half of the class. Doing this ensures that students will keep up with the work throughout the class and approach their final projects from an informed perspective.

Conclusion

Teaching Japanese popular culture through fashion gives students a complex view of popular culture itself. They develop fashion literacy and critical acuity as they interpret fashions in shifting historical and cultural contexts and locales. Although this course emphasizes the semiotics of fashion over the materiality of artifacts, it provides a good foundation for students wishing to pursue this or other methods of inquiry. Questions of authenticity and appropriation, conventional and subcultural styles, and orientalism are thoroughly discussed but ultimately left open for students to continue pondering them. Students' regular writing assignments, research papers, and museum exhibits encourage original thought and stimulate class discussion. Students come away from the class with new ways of looking at Japan and critical tools for analyzing fashion.

Notes

I wish to thank Laura Miller for her comments and Masafumi Monden, too, for his suggestions and references to fashion studies literature.

[1] See Elizabeth L. Cline, *Overdressed: The Shockingly High Cost of Cheap Fashion* (New York: Portfolio, 2012). Cline's book connects the proliferation of inexpensive clothing to exploitation of workers and the environment around the world.

[2] For more on this program, see Parsons The New School for Design, http://www.newschool.edu/parsons/ma-fashion-studies

[3] Compilations of excerpts from essays in fashion theory have been published for classroom use; among the most approachable and enjoyable is Linda Welters and Abby Lillethun's *The Fashion Reader,* 2nd ed. (London: Bloomsbury Academic, 2011), which offers a wide range of essays from diverse sources on provocative topics. This is a good place to start reading in fashion studies. For more specific work, see books in the Berg Fashion Library's Dress, Body, and Culture series and the peer-reviewed academic journal *Fashion Theory: The Journal of Dress, Body, and Culture.*

[4] Giorgio Riello and Peter McNeil, eds., *The Fashion History Reader: Global Perspectives* (New York: Routledge, 2010).

[5] Valerie Steele, ed., *Japan Fashion Now!* (New Haven, CT: Yale University Press, 2010).

[6] Catherine Ince and Rie Nii, eds., *Future Beauty: 30 Years of Japanese Fashion* (London: Merrell Publishers, 2010).

[7] Masafumi Monden, *Japanese Fashion Cultures: Dress and Gender in Contemporary Japan* (London: Bloomsbury, 2014).

[8] Yuniya Kawamura, *Doing Research in Fashion and Dress: An Introduction to Qualitative Methods* (New York: Berg Publishers, 2010).

[9] Valerie Steele, ed., "Methodology," special issue, *Fashion Theory: The Journal of Dress, Body, and Culture* 2, no. 4 (1998).

[10] Quoted from Bloomsbury website for *Fashion Theory* at http://www.bloomsbury.com/us/fashion-theory-volume-1-issue-1-9781859739662/. Valerie Steele, "Letter from the Editor," *Fashion Theory: The Journal of Dress, Body & Culture* 1 (1997): 1.

[11] Mary-Ellen Roach-Higgins and Joanne B. Eicher, "Dress and Identity," *Clothing and Textiles Research Journal* 10, no. 1 (1992): 1–8.

[12] Henry A. Giroux, *Disturbing Pleasures: Learning Popular Culture* (New York: Routledge, 1994), 121.

[13] John W. Dower, *Embracing Defeat: Japan in the Wake of World War II* (New York: W. W. Norton, 1999), 292–93.

[14] Sally A. Hastings, "The Empress' New Clothes and Japanese Women, 1868–1912," *Historian* 55, no. 4 (1993): 677–92.

[15] Jan Bardsley, "Japanese Feminism, Nationalism, and the Royal Wedding of 1993," *Journal of Popular Culture* 31, no. 2 (1998):189–205.

[16] Fred Davis, *Fashion, Culture, and Identity* (Chicago: University of Chicago Press, 1992).

[17] See, for example, Stefano Ember, *Fashioning Kimono: Dress and Modernity in Early 20th-Century Japan* (Milan: 5 Continents, 2005); Yori Suzuki, *The Kimono: History and Style* (Tokyo: PIE International, 2011); and instructional videos such as *Kimono: Symbol of a Nation* (New York: Films Media Group, 2008).

[18] Katy Perry, dressed as a kind of geisha, performed the song "Unconditionally" at the American Music Awards live on November 24, 2013, in Los Angeles. Backup singers costumed and made up to look "oriental" performed with Perry in front of a cherry-blossom-themed backdrop. Debate ensued over the Internet about racial insensitivity. See also Melanie King's discussion of this episode in chapter 6 of this volume.

[19] Elizabeth Wilson, *Adorned in Dreams: Fashion and Modernity* (New Brunswick, NJ: Rutgers University Press, 1985), 1.

[20] Mineko Iwasaki and Rande Brown, *Geisha: A Life* (New York: Atria Books, 2002), 234.

[21] Terry Satsuki Milhaupt, *Kimono: A Modern History* (London: Reaktion Books, 2014).

[22] The exhibit *Kimono: A Modern History* ran from September 27, 2014, through January 19, 2015. See Metropolitan Museum of Art, http://www.metmuseum.org/about-the-museum/press-room/exhibitions/2014/kimono.

[23] Liza Dalby, *Kimono: Fashioning Culture* (Seattle: University of Washington Press, 1995); Rebecca Stevens and Yoshiko Iwamoto Wada, *The Kimono Inspiration: Art and Art-to-Wear in America* (Washington, DC: Textile Museum, 1996).

[24] Edward W. Said, *Orientalism* (New York: Pantheon Books, 1978). Useful here, too, is the special double issue "Fashion and Orientalism" edited by Nandia Bhatia and Nirmal Puwar, in *Fashion Theory: The Journal of Dress, Body, and Culture* 7, nos. 3–4 (2003): 249–423. Ann Marie Leshkowich and Carla Jones's article in this issue, "What Happens When Asian Chic Becomes Chic in Asia?" (281–300) takes discussions of orientalism past a simple East-West binary, showing the multivalent meanings and multiple locations that give

rise to (self-)orientalizing fantasies, and suggests ways of interpreting fashion by "viewing dress choices as performance practices" (294) for specific audiences. For further discussion of orientalism in fashion, see Adam Geczy, *Fashion and Orientalism: Dress, Textiles, and Culture from the 17th to the 21st Century* (Oxford: Berg, 2013).

[25] Mari Yoshihara, "The Flight of the Japanese Butterfly: Orientalism, Nationalism, and Performances of Japanese Womanhood," *American Quarterly* 56, no. 4 (December 2004): 975–1001.

[26] For more on this topic, see Michael F. Marra, ed., *Modern Japanese Aesthetics: A Reader* (Honolulu: University of Hawai'i Press, 1999).

[27] Lise Skov, "Fashion Trends, Japonisme, and Postmodernism; or, What Is So Japanese about *Comme des Garçons?,*" *Theory, Culture, and Society* 13 (August 1996): 113–28.

[28] Patricia Mears, "Formalism and Revolution," in *Japan Fashion Now!*, ed. Valerie Steele (New Haven, CT: Yale University Press, 2010), 141–207.

[29] Tanizaki Jun'ichirō, *In Praise of Shadows,* trans. Thomas J. Harper and Edward G. Seidensticker (New Haven, CT: Leete's Island Books, [1933] 1977).

[30] Dorinne K. Kondo, "Part Two: Consuming Gender, Race, and Nation," in *About Face: Performing Race in Fashion and Theater* (New York: Routledge, 1997), 103–189.

[31] Modern Girl Around the World Research Group, *The Modern Girl Around the World: Consumption, Modernity, and Globalization* (Durham, NC: Duke University Press, 2008). This volume includes two introductory essays useful for analyzing fashion trends as interactions between the global and the local. See "The Modern Girl as Heuristic Device: Collaboration, Connective Comparison, Multidirectional Citation" and "The Modern Girl Around the World: Cosmetics Advertising and the Politics of Race and Style." The book also includes two chapters, by Barbara Sato and Ruri Ito respectively, specific to Japan as well as commentary by Miriam Silverberg, who did much to bring the topic of the Modern Girl to the forefront of Japanese Studies.

[32] Short stories by Nakamoto Takako, Okamoto Kanoko, and Uno Chiyo in the collection *To Live and to Write* work well in class as examples of Modern Girl fiction. See Yukiko Tanaka, ed., *To Live and to Write: Selections by Japanese Women Writers, 1913–1938* (Seattle: Seal Press, 1987).

[33] Tanizaki Jun'ichirō, *Naomi [Chijin no ai]*, translated by Anthony H. Chambers (New York: Random House, [1924] 1985).

[34] See Barbara Hartley, "Performing the Nation: Magazine Images of Women and Girls in the Illustrations of Takabatake Kashō, 1925–1937," *Intersections: Gender and Sexuality in Asia and the Pacific*, no. 16 (2008), http://intersections.anu.edu.au/issue16/hartley.htm; and Elise Tipton, "Pink

Collar Work: The Café Waitress in Early 20th Century Japan," *Intersections: Gender, History, and Culture in the Asian Context,* no. 7 (2002), http://intersections.anu.edu.au/issue7/tipton.html.

[35] Rebecca L. Copeland, "The Made-Up Author: Writer as Woman in the Works of Uno Chiyo," *Journal of the Association of Teachers of Japanese* 29, no. 1 (1995): 3–25.

[36] Alisa Freedman, Laura Miller, and Christine Yano, eds., *Modern Girls on the Go: Gender, Mobility, and Labor in Japan* (Stanford, CA: Stanford University Press, 2013).

[37] Deborah Shamoon, "The Modern Girl and the Vamp: Hollywood Film in Tanizaki Jun'ichirō's Early Novels," *positions: east asia cultures critique* 20, no. 4 (2012):1067–93.

[38] Peter McNeil and Vicki Karaminas, eds., *The Men's Fashion Reader.* New York: Berg, 2009.

[39] Jason G. Karlin, *Gender and Nation in Meiji Japan: Modernity, Loss, and the Doing of History* (Honolulu: University of Hawai'i Press, 2014), 44.

[40] Toby Slade, "Japanese Menswear: Masculinity and Sartorial Statecraft," in *Japanese Fashion: A Cultural History* (Oxford: Berg, 2009), 65–97.

[41] Monden, *Japanese Fashion Cultures.*

[42] Hiroshi Narumi, "Japanese Street Style: Its History and Identity," in *Japan Fashion Now!,* ed. Valerie Steele (New Haven, CT: Yale University Press, 2010), 229–52.

[43] Alisa Freedman, "*Train Man* and the Gender Politics of Japanese '*otaku*' Culture: The Rise of New Media, Nerd Heroes, and Fan Communities," *Intersections: Gender and Sexuality in Asia and the Pacific,* no. 20 (2009), http://intersections.anu.edu.au/issue20/freedman.html.

[44] See the chapter "Male Beauty Work" in Laura Miller, *Beauty Up: Exploring Contemporary Japanese Body Aesthetics* (Berkeley: University of California Press, 2006), 125–158; and Jan Bardsley, "The *Oyaji* Gets a Makeover: Guides for Japanese Men in the New Millennium," in *Manners and Mischief: Gender, Power, and Etiquette in Japan,* ed. Jan Bardsley and Laura Miller (Berkeley: University of California Press, 2011), 114–35.

[45] Vera Mackie, "How to Be a Girl: Mainstream Media Portrayals of Transgendered Lives in Japan," *Asian Studies Review* 32, no. 3 (2008): 411–23.

[46] Vera Mackie, "Understanding through the Body: The Masquerades of Morimura Yasumasa and Mishima Yukio," in *Genders, Transgenders, and Sexualities in Japan,* ed. Mark McLelland and Romit Dasgupta (London: Routledge, 2005), 126–44.

[47] For more on interpreting cross-dressing, see Marjorie Garber, *Vested Interests: Cross-Dressing and Cultural Anxiety* (London: Routledge, 1991).

[48] Lolita fashions have inspired several academic essays, including Brian Bergstrom, "Girliness Next to Godliness: Lolita Fandom as Sacred Criminality in the Novels of Takemoto Novala," *Mechademia* 6, no. 1 (2011): 21–37; Isaac Gangné, "Urban Princesses: Performance and 'Women's Language' in Japan's Gothic/Lolita Subculture," *Journal of Linguistic Anthropology* 18, no. 1 (2008): 130–55; K. A. Hardy Bernal, "Japanese Lolita: Challenging Sexualized Style and the Little-Girl Look," in *Fashion Talks: Undressing the Power of Style,* ed. Shira Tarrant and Marjorie Jolles (New York: State University of New York Press, 2011), 117–32; and Theresa Winge, "Undressing and Dressing Loli: A Search for the Identity of the Japanese Lolita," *Mechademia* 3, no. 1 (2008): 47–63.

[49] Vera Mackie, "Reading Lolita in Japan," in *Girl Reading Girl in Japan,* ed. Tomoko Aoyama and Barbara Hartley (London: Routledge, 2010), 187.

Works Cited

Bardsley, Jan. "Japanese Feminism, Nationalism, and the Royal Wedding of 1993." *Journal of Popular Culture* 31, no. 2 (1998): 189–205.

———. "The *Oyaji* Gets a Makeover: Guides for Japanese Men in the New Millennium." In *Manners and Mischief: Gender, Power, and Etiquette in Japan*, edited by Jan Bardsley and Laura Miller, 114–35. Berkeley: University of California Press, 2011.

Bergstrom, Brian. "Girliness Next to Godliness: Lolita Fandom as Sacred Criminality in the Novels of Takemoto Novala." *Mechademia* 6, no. 1 (2011): 21–37.

Bhatia, Nandia, and Nirmal Puwar, eds. "Fashion and Orientalism." Special issue. *Fashion Theory: The Journal of Dress, Body, and Culture* 7, nos. 3–4 (2003): 249–423.

Cline, Elizabeth L. *Overdressed: The Shockingly High Cost of Cheap Fashion*. New York: Portfolio, 2012.

Copeland, Rebecca L. "The Made-Up Author: Writer as Woman in the Works of Uno Chiyo." *Journal of the Association of Teachers of Japanese* 29, no. 1 (1995): 3–25.

Dalby, Liza. *Kimono: Fashioning Culture*. Seattle: University of Washington Press, 1995.

Davis, Fred. *Fashion, Culture, and Identity*. Chicago: University of Chicago Press, 1992.

Dower, John W. *Embracing Defeat: Japan in the Wake of World War II*. New York: W. W. Norton, 1999.

Ember, Stefano. *Fashioning Kimono: Dress and Modernity in Early 20th-Century Japan*. Milan: 5 Continents, 2005.

Freedman, Alisa. "*Train Man* and the Gender Politics of Japanese '*Otaku*' Culture: The Rise of New Media, Nerd Heroes, and Fan Communities." *Intersections: Gender and Sexuality in Asia and the Pacific*, no. 20 (2009). http://intersections.anu.edu.au/issue20/freedman.html.

Freedman, Alisa, Laura Miller, and Christine Yano, eds. *Modern Girls on the Go: Gender, Mobility, and Labor in Japan*. Stanford, CA: Stanford University Press, 2013.

Gangné, Isaac. "Urban Princesses: Performance and 'Women's Language' in Japan's Gothic/Lolita Subculture." *Journal of Linguistic Anthropology* 18, no. 1 (2008): 130–55.

Garber, Marjorie. *Vested Interests: Cross-Dressing and Cultural Anxiety*. London: Routledge, 1991.

Geczy, Adam. *Fashion and Orientalism: Dress, Textiles, and Culture from the 17th to the 21st Century*. Oxford: Berg, 2013.

Giroux, Henry A. *Disturbing Pleasures: Learning Popular Culture*. New York: Routledge, 1994.

Hardy Bernal, K. A.. "Japanese Lolita: Challenging Sexualized Style and the Little-Girl Look." In *Fashion Talks: Undressing the Power of Style*, edited by Shira Tarrant and Marjorie Jolles, 117–32. New York: State University of New York Press, 2011.

Hartley, Barbara. "Performing the Nation: Magazine Images of Women and Girls in the Illustrations of Takabatake Kashō, 1925–1937." *Intersections: Gender, History, and Culture in the Asian Context*, no. 16 (March 2008). http://intersections.anu.edu.au/issue16/hartley.htm.

Hastings, Sally A. "The Empress' New Clothes and Japanese Women, 1868–1912." *Historian* 55, no. 4 (1993): 677–92.

Ichikawa Kon, director. *The Makioka Sisters* [Sasameyuki]. Tokyo: Toho Company Ltd., 1983.

Ince, Catherine, and Rie Nii, eds. *Future Beauty: 30 Years of Japanese Fashion*. London: Merrell Publishers, 2010.

Ishihara Shintarō. *Season of the Sun* [Taiyō no kisetsu]. Tokyo: Shinchōsha, 1957.

Iwasaki, Mineko, and Rande Brown. *Geisha: A Life*. New York: Atria Books, 2002.

Karlin, Jason G. *Gender and Nation in Meiji Japan: Modernity, Loss, and the Doing of History*. Honolulu: University of Hawai'i Press, 2014.

Kawamura, Yuniya. *Doing Research in Fashion and Dress: An Introduction to Qualitative Methods*. New York: Berg, 2010.

Kimono: Symbol of a Nation. New York: Films Media Group, 2008.

Kondo, Dorinne. "Part Two: Consuming Gender, Race, and Nation," in *About Face: Performing Race in Fashion and Theater*, 103–189. New York: Routledge, 1997.

Kurosawa Akira, director. *One Wonderful Sunday* [Subarashiki nichiyōbi]. Tōhō Co., Ltd., 1947.

Leshkowich, Ann Marie, and Carla Jones. "What Happens When Asian Chic Becomes Chic in Asia?" *Fashion Theory* 7, nos. 3–4 (2003): 281–300.

Mackie, Vera. "How to Be a Girl: Mainstream Media Portrayals of Transgendered Lives in Japan." *Asian Studies Review* 32, no. 3 (2008): 411–23.

———. "Reading Lolita in Japan." In *Girl Reading Girl in Japan*, edited by Tomoko Aoyama and Barbara Hartley, 187–201. London: Routledge, 2010.

———. "Understanding through the Body: The Masquerades of Morimura Yasumasa and Mishima Yukio." In *Genders, Transgenders, and Sexualities in Japan*, edited by Mark McLelland and Romit Dasgupta, 126–44. London: Routledge, 2005.

Marra, Michael F., ed. *Modern Japanese Aesthetics: A Reader*. Honolulu: University of Hawai'i Press, 1999.

McNeil, Peter, and Vicki Karaminas, eds. *The Men's Fashion Reader*. New York: Berg, 2009.

Mears, Patricia. "Formalism and Revolution." In *Japan Fashion Now!*, edited by Valerie Steele, 141–207. New Haven, CT: Yale University Press, 2010.

Milhaupt, Terry Satsuki. *Kimono: A Modern History*. London: Reaktion Books, 2014.

Miller, Laura. *Beauty Up: Exploring Contemporary Japanese Body Aesthetics*. Berkeley: University of California Press, 2006.

Modern Girl Around the World Research Group. *The Modern Girl Around the World: Consumption, Modernity, and Globalization*. Durham, NC: Duke University Press, 2008.

Monden, Masafumi. *Japanese Fashion Cultures: Dress and Gender in Contemporary Japan*. London: Bloomsbury, 2014.

Murakami Shosuke, director. *Train Man* [Densha otoko]. Tokyo: Toho Co., Ltd., 2005.

Nakahira Kō, director. *Crazed Fruit* [Kurutta kajitsu]. Tokyo: Nikkatsu, 1956.

Nakashima Tetsuya, director. *Kamikaze Girls* [Shimotsuma monogatari]. Tokyo: Tōhō Co., Ltd., 2004.

Narumi, Hiroshi. "Japanese Street Style: Its History and Identity." In *Japan Fashion Now!*, edited by Valerie Steele, 229–52. New Haven, CT: Yale University Press, 2010.

Riello, Giorgio, and Peter McNeil, eds. *The Fashion History Reader: Global Perspectives*. New York: Routledge, 2010.

Roach-Higgins, Mary-Ellen, and Joanne B. Eicher. "Dress and Identity." *Clothing and Textiles Research Journal* 10, no. 1 (1992): 1–8.

Said, Edward W. *Orientalism*. New York: Pantheon Books, 1978.

Shamoon, Deborah. "The Modern Girl and the Vamp: Hollywood Film in Tanizaki Jun'ichirō's Early Novels." *positions: east asia cultures critique* 20, no. 4 (2012): 1067–93.

Skov, Lise. "Fashion Trends, Japonisme, and Postmodernism; or, What Is So Japanese about *Comme des Garçons?*" *Theory, Culture & Society* 13 (August 1996): 113–28.

Slade, Toby. "Japanese Menswear: Masculinity and Sartorial Statecraft." In *Japanese Fashion: A Cultural History*, 65–97. Oxford: Berg, 2009.

Steele, Valerie, ed. *Japan Fashion Now!* New Haven, CT: Yale University Press, 2010. Exhibition catalog.

———, "Letter from the Editor." *Fashion Theory: The Journal of Dress, Body and Culture* 1, no. 1 (1997): 1-2.

———, ed. "Methodology." Special issue. *Fashion Theory: The Journal of Dress, Body, and Culture* 2, no. 4 (1998).

Stevens, Rebecca, and Yoshiko Iwamoto Wada. *The Kimono Inspiration: Art and Art-to-Wear in America*. Washington, DC: Textile Museum, 1996.

Suzuki, Yori. *The Kimono: History and Style*. Tokyo: PIE International, 2011.

Tanaka, Yukiko, ed. *To Live and to Write: Selections by Japanese Women Writers, 1913–1938*. Seattle: Seal Press, 1987.

Tanizaki Jun'ichirō. *In Praise of Shadows* (In'ei raisan). Translated by Thomas J. Harper and Edward G. Seidensticker. New Haven, CT: Leete's Island Books, (1933) 1977.

———. *Naomi* (Chijin no ai). Translated by Anthony H. Chambers. New York: Random House, [1924] 1985.

———. *Some Prefer Nettles* [Tade ku mushi]. New York: Vintage Books, [1929] 1995.

Tipton, Elise. "Pink Collar Work: The Café Waitress in Early 20th Century Japan." *Intersections: Gender, History, and Culture in the Asian Context,* no. 7 (2002). http://intersections.anu.edu.au.

Welter, Linda, and Abby Lillethun. *The Fashion Reader*. 2nd ed. London: Bloomsbury Academic, 2011.

Wenders, Wim, director, with Yohji Yamamoto. *Notebook on Cities and Clothes*. Berlin : Road Movies Filmproduktion GmBH, 1993.

Wilson, Elizabeth. *Adorned in Dreams: Fashion and Modernity*. New Brunswick, NJ: Rutgers University Press, 1985.

Winge, Theresa. "Undressing and Dressing Loli: A Search for the Identity of the Japanese Lolita." *Mechademia* 3, no. 1 (2008): 47–63.

Yoshihara, Mari. "The Flight of the Japanese Butterfly: Orientalism, Nationalism, and Performances of Japanese Womanhood." *American Quarterly* 56, no. 4 (December 2004): 975–1001.

PART III

USING POPULAR CULTURE IN TEACHING

6

Confessions of an Anime and Manga Ignoramus

Approaches to Japanese Contemporary Popular Culture for the K-12 Classroom

Melanie King

Introduction

As an undergraduate studying art history and Japanese language and literature, I was often at a loss as to how to connect with those students whose entrée into Japanese studies was through anime and manga. I came to Japanese studies as a heritage learner, looking to learn about my ancestry vis-à-vis the language, literature, history, and artistic expressions of Japan. For the most part, my fellow students were either heritage learners or studying Japanese in preparation for a career in international business. Japan was a leading economic power, not the cultural powerhouse exporter we know it to be today. Twenty years later I find myself encountering the same roadblock with my own students. However, their awareness and access to the world far exceed anything I can fathom, so I find myself in the same position of knowing very little not only about anime and manga but also about video games, J-pop, Pokémon, and more. In a nutshell, I lack any serious street cred when it comes to teaching the Japan that brings many students to our classrooms. I maintain a distant relationship with anime, my closest connection being Studio Ghibli productions, and I only think about manga as it relates to its antecedents. I must confess I am not interested in delving into the latest manga series, and my interest in gaming is nonexistent. I am aware of and embrace my lack of any "cool factor" necessary to teach about contemporary Japanese popular culture and to relate to many of the millennials who enter our classrooms. I teach art history at an urban college and work with K–12 educators, helping them to teach about East Asia through the visual arts, so it is important that I am not entirely dismissive of these expressions of popular culture. From twenty years ago to today, I have come to respect the broad reach and deep artistic roots of these expressions and see them as a vehicle through which I can make deeper, more meaningful connections to the past, societal shifts, historical artistic expressions, and contemporary events.

In this chapter I will discuss how I engage Japanese popular culture as a means of connecting students to deeper artistic, religious, and historical traditions while complicating their understanding of Japan. To this end, we will consider the well-known and at times controversial work of artist Murakami Takashi (b. 1962). I strive to expose my students to many examples of contemporary culture but believe that a close examination of a single artist creates an opportunity for students to enhance their understanding of popular culture within the context of a deeper exploration of Japanese art history. Following a multilayered discussion of Murakami Takashi, I will highlight a few ways in which K–12 teachers can incorporate his work and other aspects of Japanese popular culture into their curricula. We all face the challenge of keeping our students engaged, which can seem even more difficult within the ever-changing landscape of educational standards, and it is my hope that this examination of Japanese popular culture can provide a jumping-off point for others.

One of my goals in teaching art history is for students to leave class with a deeper understanding and appreciation of the cultural icons they consume on a daily basis, and I believe this requires us to confront the lens through which we (especially my American-based college students) appreciate and/or fetishize Japanese culture. We do not have to look too far to see popular artists adopting elements of Japanese culture with little regard for the origins of what they borrow and strip from their original context. In this vein, I discuss pop singer Katy Perry's 2013 American Music Awards performance as one example drawn from the many that serve as examples of cultural appropriation. Considering the access the Internet provides, left unchecked our students receive their education of visual culture through their consumption of Japanese popular culture and the bastardization of an imagined "Other." I want to honor and validate what my students are passionate about, yet my responsibility is to further their understanding of what they consume lest we find ourselves regressing toward an antiquated understanding of an "exotic Orient." I have a responsibility to provide my students with the tools to appreciate the cultures we study but also to give them an understanding of the history of colonialism, cultural exchange, and orientalism, which underlies this larger discussion. In the twenty-fifth anniversary edition of *Orientalism* (2003), Edward W. Said reminded us that "history is made by men and women, just as it can also be unmade and rewritten, always with various silences and elisions, always with shapes imposed and disfigurements tolerated, so that 'our' East, 'our' Orient becomes 'ours' to possess and direct."[1] Just over a decade later we appear to have lost sight of the lessons left by Said and others; thus, we are tasked with creating a more meaningful and authentic discussion of Japan while challenging our cultural unconscious in an effort to educate more civically minded global citizens.

Each of the essays in this volume engages the manner in which we as educators are responding to our students who grew up watching anime, living in a time when cartoons from around the world were broadcast twenty-four hours a day and playing video games with cheat codes available online. In the end, it probably does not matter how my fellow authors or I came to this point; the reality is that many of us are working in a time of reduced resources, declining enrollments, an almost single-minded focus on STEM fields (science, technology, engineering, math), and for K–12 teachers in the United States the controversial implementation of Common Core Standards. The task we all face is figuring out how to best connect with students who have grown up in a decidedly different world.

Useful in this discussion is chapter 1, by Sally McLaren and Alwyn Spies, in this volume, which outlines five approaches to discussing Japanese popular culture in an academic setting. Whether it is "pop to prop," "proper pop," "pop as propaganda," postcolonial popular culture "poco pop," or "pop to prep," each approach or rationale behind our use of popular culture speaks to a student-focused approach. Whether we are trying to entice students back to a waning field in "pop to prop," celebrating popular culture as in "pop as propaganda," or viewing Japanese popular culture through a postcolonial lens as in "poco pop," each approach has merit, and I believe that, depending on the audience, where we are in the world, and recent events, our approach will continually be in flux.

For example, each time I introduce the fundamentals of Shintō to my students, inevitably there is one who has heard of Amaterasu, star of the 2006 video game Ōkami. While I still have little idea what the goal of this game is, I do know that Amaterasu is represented as a white wolf with a paintbrush for a tail whose footsteps give life to flowers and grass. The last time someone mentioned this game in class, we went online to explore the game further and immediately noticed that Amaterasu has a bronze mirror strapped to her back. We had just discussed the Three Imperial Regalia, and my students were thrilled to understand that this is why she rides on a bronze sword with a bronze disc (mirror) strapped to her back. This is just scratching the surface of this game, and yet in this singular, rather shallow example I see students understanding video games within an academic framework ("proper pop"), which can also be a hook ("pop as propaganda"). This inevitably leads to a deeper conversation as we discuss State Shintō and think about Japanese popular culture from a postcolonial perspective ("poco pop"). This also opens the door for our students to see their interests and hours spent watching anime, reading manga, or playing video games as a key to understanding twenty-first-century visual culture ("pop to prep"). This game serves as a powerful example of popular culture as a place to meet our students—where they can teach us and we can engage their interests in a manner that validates their knowledge and helps them question the use of cultural references seemingly devoid of context or relevance.

Case Study: Murakami Takashi and Superflat as Popular Culture

Ōkami is just one of many examples that remind me that my students and I are two ships passing in the night with regard to our cultural references; however, I have found visual artist Murakami Takashi to be an especially compelling individual for introducing students to another perspective on Japanese popular culture. Murakami serves as a useful case study for engaging contemporary popular culture because he works from images and concepts familiar to our students while also rooting his work in a deeper intellectual and cultural tradition. And who would not be intrigued with someone who provokes this headline? "Takashi Murakami Takes on Critics With Provocative Versailles Exhibition: Art Bad Boy's Sculptures Clash with Formal French Palace Setting As Show Goes Ahead."[2] While not all of Murakami's works are suitable for the K-12 classroom, the intention behind his work is certainly a solid starting place.

Perhaps without our knowing it, Murakami's works have come into our consciousness. Most widely seen is the multicolored Louis Vuitton monogram on a white and black background or his camouflage Louis Vuitton line, also known as his "monogramouflage,"[3] widely photographed and touted by celebrities such as Kanye West, Rhianna, Jim Jones, John Mayer, and Fabolous.[4] With the omnipresent image of celebrity, Murakami's genius has also transcended the boundaries of high art as consumer product. While his work is predicated on a generation of "pampered" two-dimensional individuals, he lays claim to his art not just as political, societal, or generational commentary but as grounded in a much larger Japanese art historical context.

Japanese art critic Midori Matsui sees Murakami as "[t]aking the American category of Pop and inverting its meaning with resources from his own culture . . . making it a vehicle for a postcolonial redefinition of Japanese cultural identity and turning the tables against modern Western cultural authority."[5] This is where the genius of Murakami is to be found. Trained in the study of Japanese visual culture, with a PhD in *Nihonga* (Japanese-style paintings of the modern era), visually Murakami extends his definition of two-dimensionality to Japanese art as seen in the woodblock prints of the Tokugawa era (1603–1868) and other artists whose influence can be traced to the origins of a uniquely Japanese style of art that began to emerge during the Heian era (794–1185). There is a flatness to this earlier art (*yamato-e*) which sees the emergence of the bird's-eye view or blown-off roof (*fukunuki yatai*) perspective. This is in contrast to the one-point or vanishing-point perspective seen in western art, which creates a sense of three-dimensionality on a two-dimensional surface. In traditional Japanese art, there is no attempt to create an illusion of depth; the objects located higher on the picture plane are read as being farther away. Additionally, in Japanese art of this era, emphasis was given to a subtle communication of emotions, a slight tilt of the head, a curtain quietly blowing, or sharp diagonals, all of which created a sense of tension or heightened emotion. Due to complex and well-known societal rules, a court member of this era would immediately recognize the complexity and subtle message encoded in these images, aspects of which can be seen in current artistic productions. Most significant to the discussion regarding Murakami is the manner in which he extends this two-dimensionality to the present, rooting it in a tradition largely foreign to a western audience lacking the social acumen to situate the image let alone interpret the subtle cues.

Murakami's 2005 international exhibition *Little Boy: The Arts of Japan's Exploding Subculture* provides additional context for his work as a result of postwar occupation and rebuilding.

> Japan has been a testing ground for an American-style capitalist economy, protected in a greenhouse, nurtured and bloated to the point of explosion. The results are so bizarre, they're perfect. ... [W]e Japanese are truly, deeply, pampered children. And as pampered children, we throw constant tantrums while enthralled with our own cuteness. It's the denouement of a culture, nourished by trauma, smugly raised in the incubator of a society gone slack.[6]

As a by-product of this reality, Murakami draws from the saccharine sweetness pervading Japanese popular culture, profiting from the *kawaii* (cute) obsessed.[7] Through partnerships with Louis Vuitton and Kanye West, Murakami lays claim to a Japanese cultural identity that has been reinterpreted and re-presented by the West since its first encounter with Japan.

Louis Vuitton and Murakami have mutually benefitted from their collaborative efforts. However, this does not mean we can stray too far from an analysis of Murakami's work that reinforces Said's constructed Orient. From Louis Vuitton's "Friends of the House":

> Painter. Sculptor. Prolific digital artist and Japanese icon. In his relatively short career, this joyfully off-kilter visionary has earned many accolades, solo shows and a cult following around the world. Like Andy Warhol a generation before him, Takashi Murakami has the impressive knack for turning mass culture into high art.

> Inspired by the bold yet lighthearted vision he saw in Murakami's art, Marc Jacobs, Louis Vuitton's Creative Director, first approached the artist in 2003 with the idea of collaborating. From the initial Monogram Multicolore bags to the most recent Cosmic Blossom collection, Murakami has continued to bring an unexpected and whimsical touch to the House of Vuitton.[8]

"Joyfully off-kilter," "bold yet lighthearted vision," "unexpected," "whimsical." A deeper analysis of his Louis Vuitton bags or any of Murakami's work challenges these blithe interpretations. At the outset of *Disturbing Pleasures: Learning Popular Culture*, Henry A. Giroux provides a framework for considering this collaboration: "[C]onsumer postmodernism produces meanings mediated through claims to truth represented in images that circulate in an electronic informational hyperspace which disassociates itself from history, context, and struggle."[9] The "whimsical" brings people to Murakami's work, and from there we are given the opportunity to challenge our students' understanding of his work as it is fed to them through popular imagery, stripped of any connection to its original context or history. In Murakami's work and the House of Louis Vuitton's reflection on his work, the promotion of his work "disguises the political nature of everyday life and appropriates the vulnerable new terrain of insurgent differences in the interests of crass consumerism."[10] Outside of reinforcing these stripped down, whitewashed presentations of mass culture, we return to my original goal of using Murakami Takashi and his productions with students as a valuable introduction for disrupting this singular, shallow reading of his work.

Murakami Takashi in a Post-Apocalyptic Japan

Absent from this reading of Murakami's work is any trace of what media theorist Dick Hebdige terms "Murakami's redemption war machine." Wrapped up in this redemption war machine is the mass destruction of World War II in the form of fire bombings, Hiroshima and Nagasaki, Article 9 of Japan's constitution, which strips the country of the right to use force except in self-defense, and the humiliation of the postwar occupation by US forces.[11] There is no hint of this in any of the marketing of Murakami's work. For those unable to afford a Louis Vuitton bag, we see a separation of class status, not a postwar reassertion of Japanese cultural identity. For those able to afford the luxury brand, there is no need to distinguish between aesthetic beauty and the deeper motivation driving the creator. If there was any question as to what extent we have lost cultural and historical context, we simply need to look to Louis Vuitton's creative director, Marc Jacobs, who writes, "When I first saw Takashi's work I smiled and I wondered: Where did this explosion come from? I thought I would love it if the mind that imagined this dizzy-making world of jellyfish, singing moss, magic mushrooms, morphing creatures, would be willing to give a go at the iconic Louis Vuitton monogram."[12] And thus these colorful monogram handbags intrinsically exist not only for commercial consumerism but also as markers of a past to be known only by a deeper investigation of Murakami's work.

Murakami Takashi and Hip-Hop

A second inquiry of Japanese popular culture vis-à-vis Murakami's work is possible through his artistic relationship with hip-hop artist Kanye West. The 2008 Murakami/Kaikai Kiki Co. animated video *Good Morning* serves as a locus for navigating contemporary Japanese culture, visual culture, and the politics of our time in a meaningful manner.[13] Students may have a preconceived notion of what they will learn in class, but it is unlikely they are thinking about how what they will learn pertains to them. Within the first two weeks of class, whether it is modern art, art appreciation, or a survey of Asian art history, I show my students Kanye West's *Good Morning* music video, which is in the style of Murakami's imagined postapocalyptic world. We watch as an adorable wide-eyed bear, decked out in the latest Kanye-inspired fashion, remains undeterred despite a broken down DeLorean, excessively long bus lines, and subway doors slamming shut in his face as he makes his way to receive his diploma on graduation day. The words are compelling: "But you graduate when you make it up outta the streets. From the moments of pain, look how far we done came. Haters saying you changed, no you doing your thang."[14] But perhaps even more enchanting and obviously relatable for students is the animated video. The analysis of Kanye West could occupy us for days, but my goal is for students to think about the greater impact of the collaboration between these two artists. Providing historical context for the malformed, brightly colored creations of Murakami encourages students to think beyond their surface reading of a text or image. As Matsui writes, "Murakami's uniqueness lay in his dialectical thinking, which inspired him to turn negative conditions of postmodern society into new methods of creating and interpreting a uniquely Japanese art."[15]

Assessing Student Learning and Engagement

While this discussion of Louis Vuitton and hip-hop music is interesting, it is necessary that we are able to articulate how and why these concepts are connected to educational standards. At my institution, they are called Course Level Outcomes, which must align with Program Level Outcomes and College Level Outcomes. Packaged like this, they seem fairly benign, but my colleagues and I are already stretched too thin, and it is hard to not see these standards as an elusive target imposed from outside. My colleagues are resentful, as they feel the needs of our students fall in priority to the seemingly inane task of ensuring that our outcomes are written using the "approved" verbiage and that all instruction aligns with abstract concepts.

Across the United States this discussion has intensified at the K–12 level with the introduction of the Common Core State Standards Initiative. Debating its merits, while important, is not my intention in raising this issue. What I do see within Common Core that I value is the push to incite more critical thinking.

> As a natural outgrowth of meeting the charge to define college and career readiness, the Standards also lay out a vision of what it means to be a literate person in the twenty-first century. Students who meet the Standards ... habitually perform the critical reading necessary to pick carefully through the staggering amount of information available today in print and digitally. They actively seek the wide, deep, and thoughtful engagement with high-quality literary and informational texts that builds knowledge, enlarges experience, and broadens worldviews.[16]

By no means do I claim to have any deep connection to or understanding of Common Core, but within these standards, and in many regards with all that has come before, I see efforts to elevate our students and transfer the skills needed for them to be successful. I want my students to think critically, to question sources, question me, and make deeper connections beyond rote memorization. I am saddened when I encounter students who do not know how to respond when I ask them, "What do you think?" Students who have the ability to think for themselves will be better situated to engage the world beyond. Wherever we may stand on the Common Core debate, I can appreciate *New York Times* visual op-ed columnist Charles M. Blow's reflections on Common Core.

> [W]e need a national standard for the kind of education that we want our children to receive. Our educational system has become so tangled in experiments and exams and excuses that we've drifted away from the basis of what makes education great: learning to think critically and solve problems.

> We have drifted away from the fundamentals of what makes a great teacher: the ability to light a fire in a child, to develop in him or her a level of intellectual curiosity, the grit to persevere and the capacity to expand.[17]

I love having students who are excited to learn, ask thought-provoking questions, challenge the dominant narrative, and possess the drive to learn.

I have found that the best means to this end is to make what I teach relevant to them. We look to the millennials to right the wrongs of the past, we ask them to engage in their community, respect others, and be open, but are we giving them the skills they need? This generation gets a bad rap. I have lamented the shortcomings of this generation, just as I am certain those who came before me claimed a certain downfall with the coming of my generation. However, what never fails to impress me is that this generation asks questions. When given the opportunity, when shown respect, they rise to the occasion. Trivial as it might seem, beginning a course with popular culture validates them and what they bring to the table. This generation has grown up virtually connected. They are more diverse, more open to change and same-sex marriage, and will become the most educated generation.[18] For these reasons, I love this generation, and I hope they enjoy learning about the underpinnings of the popular culture they have grown up with just as much as I enjoy learning about popular culture from them.

Murakami Takashi and Common Core

The fact remains that we are educating a different generation, and I see in Common Core the possibility of responding to the needs of our students. For example, within the "Key Ideas and Details" grouping, CCS.ELA-Literacy.RH.6.8.1 (for those unfamiliar with Common Core speak, this means English Language Arts—Literacy in Reading and History, grades 6–8, standard 1).[19] Here students are expected to "Cite specific textual evidence to support analysis of primary and secondary sources."[20] And in "Integration of Knowledge and Ideas," CCSS.ELA-Literacy.RH.6–8.9 (English Language Arts—Literacy in Reading and History, grades 6–8, standard 9), students should be able to "Analyze the relationship between a primary and secondary source on the same topic."[21] These tasks can be addressed with a close examination of Murakami's work. For example, according to Murakami's "Superflat Manifesto":

> The world of the future might be like Japan is today—super flat. Society, customs, art, culture: all are extremely two-dimensional. It is particularly apparent in the arts that this sensibility has been flowing steadily beneath the surface of Japanese history. Today, the sensibility is most present in Japanese games and anime, which have become parts of world culture.[22]

This excerpt lends itself to an examination of what "two-dimensionality" is. What does it look like? How can society or customs be two-dimensional? Analysis of this text extends to a consideration of Murakami's work and other Superflat-influenced artists to identify two-dimensionality and visual connections to anime and manga. For older students this can lead to a discussion of the deeper meaning behind Murakami's critique of Japanese society and what he means by two-dimensionality in this context.

As for ninth and tenth graders, under "Craft and Structure," Standard 4, CCSS.ELA-Literacy.RH.9–10.4 (English Language Arts—Literacy in Reading and History, grades 9–10, standard 4), they should be able to "Determine the meaning of words and phrases as they are used in a text, including vocabulary describing political, social, or economic aspects of history/social science."[23] Murakami's work leads to a discussion of the history of Japan and the constant reminder he had growing up from his mother, who lived in Kokura, the city that was clouded over, leaving Fat Man to be dropped instead on Nagasaki.[24] This also prompts students to think about how growing up in postwar US-occupied Japan might have impacted Murakami and others of his generation. Thinking about the economic situation in Japan in the postwar era, leading up to the present day, lends itself to a discussion of where Murakami, his works, and consumers of his works play a significant role. There are many other connections to be made. These are just a handful of ideas for building a rationale for including contemporary Japanese popular culture in our curricula.

Murakami Takashi Post-3.11

Before we leave the world of Murakami to explore other points of intersection with Japanese culture, it is vitally important that we consider his response to the triple disaster of March 11, 2011 when a magnitude 9.0 earthquake struck off the coast of northern Japan, leading to a devastating tsunami and the meltdown of the Fukushima Daiichi nuclear power plant. His critique of the millennials has been harsh, and yet the tenor of his work has changed since 2011 as revealed in his exhibition at the Qatar Museums Authority in Doha when he installed *Murakami–Ego* (February 9–June 24, 2012). From the exhibition catalogue and the Qatar Museums Authority:

> A portrait of the artist as a cartoon, *Murakami–Ego* will illuminate the role of the artist as a cipher and critic of pop phenomena, as well as a mirror of global networks of consumerism, interpretation, and exchange. The exhibition pays special attention to the diverse strands of contemporary culture and art history that inform and inspire Murakami's paintings and sculptures, while also highlighting both the joyful and obsessive qualities

of his work. The provocative title is drawn from Murakami's desire to create an exhibition that is "a dialogue with one's own ego," reflecting the artist's struggle to create a private fictional universe in response to a growing information overload.[25]

His productions continue to evolve and speak to the issues we face and the challenges to which our students are particularly sensitive. With regard to our larger discussion, what is notable for me is his installation *The 500 Arhats*, inspired by Kanō Kazunobu's *500 Arhats,* created in response to the 1855 Edo earthquake.[26] Writer, collector, and art critic Adam Lindemann traveled to Qatar for the exhibition and responded to this massive installation.

> *The 500 Arhats* relates not only to the tragedy but also his pride in Japan and its cultural strength. Implicit in that pride has long been his carefully disguised animosity toward the West, including bitter feelings about a castrating defeat in World War II and the devastation caused by two atomic bombs. But that anger had run its course in Mr. Murakami's work and the tsunami gave him new inspiration for a great painting that represented the four elements—fire, earth, air, and water—and Japan's long tradition of proudly overcoming natural disaster.[27]

Reflecting on this work, Murakami said, "In the old days, where there was a disaster, the monks had paintings made that they used to promote religion among the people who were suffering. I consider *The 500 Arhats* to be an equivalent of those historical works. It's a consolatory painting—it's my *Guernica*, perhaps."[28] Over the course of a decade, Murakami's work and responses to his popular creations have served as an entrée to a variety of topics that ultimately help us achieve our goals as educators. His work is complex and controversial, and, as a self-professed otaku,[29] perhaps his identity and approach speak to our students in a manner of which those of us unfamiliar with other popular productions are unaware.

Cultural Appropriation or Appreciation?

At the outset of this chapter, I mentioned Katy Perry's November 24, 2013, performance at the American Music Awards and the issue of cultural appropriation. I first learned about this performance from news sources, which led me to discover a billboard.com headline: "Katy Perry Goes Full Geisha for 'Unconditionally' at AMAs: Watch."[30] I had to read the article because I was unsure exactly what going "full geisha" might entail: "Draped in geisha-inspired clothing—which she kept on, completely,

Perry and her cadre of background dancers made good use of strobes, confetti, and gigantic stage-enveloping screens playing colorful scenes of the Orient."[31] This performance has served as an important reminder for me to continue to stay connected to popular culture, in part to be familiar with what my students are consuming.

It was painful to watch and write about, but this performance highlights the importance of continuing to engage in a dialogue about how we consume Japan and Japanese popular culture vis-à-vis misappropriated notions of the exotic "Orient" courtesy of purveyors of popular culture. As we study and teach about other cultures, it is important to keep the words of Henry A. Giroux in mind.

> As new cultural boundaries and spaces emerge crisscrossed with a diversity of otherness, dominant strategies of representation are abrogated and struggled over through an ongoing process of negotiation, translation, and transformation. The sensibility that informs the relationship between cultural borders reorders the codes of reference for engaging cultural differences and their related networks of hierarchy, power, and struggle.[32]

In this Katy Perry production, we see Said's constructed and directed western version of the "Orient" reflected through the consumption and power of western cultural authority.

I think the best way to characterize Perry's American Music Awards performance is as a menagerie of Otherness. There was a *shōji* screen, *taiko* drums, a shamisen, a vermillion torii gate, Japanese lanterns floating in air, large red fans inscribed with the character 愛 (love), cherry blossoms, maple trees, images of a castle, temple lanterns, Mount Fuji, and an arched bridge, all set against the background of a monochromatic Chinese-inspired sumi painting. Katy Perry, who performed in a Japanese kimono/Vietnamese ao dai/traditional Chinese dress at one point is handed an umbrella, which she takes and spins around in a dramatic fashion and falls to the ground as cherry blossoms also fall to the stage. In four minutes of this mildly entertaining and simultaneously horrifying performance, Ms. Perry and her production crew put on display anything that could be seen as "exotic," which resulted in the obliteration of any distinction of difference. Watching it most recently with my Asian Art class, one student connected the spinning umbrella scene to the final performance in the film *Memoirs of a Geisha*.

It is worth asking what we can learn about contemporary Japan from this performance. Or are we so stunted in our understanding of Japanese culture, past and present, that the general public is unable to interpret these cultural miscues? Perhaps the better questions concern where we start to challenge this narrative and why have we not progressed beyond it? Furthermore, how do we address these issues with our students, as they are the target audience? Viewing a performance on this stage reminds me that we need to provide our students with the cultural competency to decipher the multitude of issues presented here.

In discussions of the power of Japanese culture, Joseph S. Nye, Jr.'s well-known "Soft Power" essay, can provide a lens through which to view this performance. Nye explores the move towards valuing technology, education, and economic growth over military power.[33] Douglas McGray (2002) extends this idea in his piece "Japan's Gross National Cool," by discussing the increasing cultural influence of Japan via its soft power.[34] Katy Perry's performance is a consequence of the power of Cool Japan and an example of "co-optive power," which Nye asserts is equally important as "command power": "If a state can make its power seem legitimate in the eyes of others, it will encounter less resistance to its wishes. If its culture and ideology are attractive, others will more willingly follow."[35] The exportation of cultural power leads us to performances such as Katy Perry's bastardized interpretation of "Japan." In some ways, we might consider Murakami to be the counterpoint to Katy Perry's performance, as they speak to two sides of the same coin. Murakami is a producer of Japanese popular culture, criticizing the two-dimensionality of society, while Katy Perry is the flip side: consumer of this popular culture, playing out her "flat" understanding of what she thinks it means to be Japanese.

So the question remains, as educators how do we engage our students and challenge their understanding of Japan? How do we convince them that the Orient doesn't exist when this image is presented? How do we convince them that the appropriation of other cultures is not an indicator of progress, and that learning about the history of Japan and its lengthy cultural traditions can help us to navigate these bigoted presentations of Otherness? Giroux reminds us that "educators need to understand and develop in their pedagogies how identities are produced differently, how they take up the narratives of the past through the stories and experience of the present."[36] Undoubtedly, what we have witnessed is cultural appropriation, and we know that no two people will have the same response. Some might consider Perry's performance an homage to Japan, while to others it was blatantly racist. Headlines in the days following her performance reflect this dialogue. The *New York Post*'s was "American Music Awards 2013: Katy Perry's Opening Act Called Out as Racist."[37] The *Huffington Post* wrote, "Katy Perry's AMAs Performance Of 'Unconditionally' Sparks Controversy."[38] And cosmpolitan.com asked, "Was Katy Perry's AMAs Performance Racist?"[39] While the Perry camp remained silent on the subject, Lady Gaga came to her defense. "Maybe it's because 'Unconditionally' means you're supposed to love no matter what geishas are paid?" Gaga joked in an interview with Carson Daly, adding, "I think people are generally too sensitive and they should just leave her be, but you know, I'm not really the person to ask."[40] Certainly, Lady Gaga does not help assuage any misgivings regarding Perry's performance, as she asserts her cultural privilege while further reinforcing stereotypes of geisha and continuing to play out an overdone postcolonial interpretation of the "exotic Other."

Cultural Appropriation as "Profound Offense"

The philosopher James O. Young elucidates how we define profound offense with regard to cultural appropriation in the *Journal of Aesthetics and Art Criticism*. In assessing the value of a production such as Katy Perry's performance of "Unconditionally," Young posits that one should consider the social value of an offensive performance. He also reminds us:

> We need to know how offensive the members of some cultures find a given act of cultural appropriation. . . . Sometimes I expect, an artwork will have a degree of social value that can counterbalance the offense felt by the members of a culture whose culture has been appropriated.[41]

Offensive as I found Perry's performance, theoretically I can understand Young's reflection on freedom of expression as it pertains to artistic productions. Even when an act of cultural appropriation has limited social value, it may not be wrong. Under certain circumstances, I am extremely reluctant to say that an act of free artistic expression is wrong, even when it is profoundly offensive and does not result in particularly good art.[42]

This is where my opinion differs from Young's. This speaks to a larger discussion of what exactly constitutes art, which the art historian in me appreciates and values. However, I cannot help but ask, if a work is "profoundly offensive" and does not result in "particularly good art," what is the point? Regardless of artistic expression, this performance was offensive, added little to no value to the meaning of the song, and reified an imagined Orient. If we subscribe to Young's premise, then we would have to take Ms. Perry's performance as an unintentional violation of our moral code. This brings us back to Lady Gaga's conciliatory remarks. Processed by our students, they may initially respond with the feeling that something was not quite right about the performance, but once told they are "too sensitive" their moral values are negated. Ultimately, I believe that we need to be cognizant and respectful of other perspectives, and I hope that students will approach visual culture and especially cultural appropriation critically.

From Peggy McIntosh, we have "White Privilege: Unpacking the Invisible Knapsack" (1989), which is a requisite lens through which we can help our students view their reading of other cultures—in this case, Japanese popular culture and its producers, both insiders and outsiders.[43] As a feminist, McIntosh is well versed in male privilege.

> After I realized the extent to which men work from a base of unacknowledged privilege, I understood that much of their oppressiveness was unconscious. Then I remembered the frequent charges from women of color that white women whom they encounter are oppressive. I began to understand why we are justly seen as oppressive, even when we don't see ourselves that way. I began to count the ways in which I enjoyed unearned skin privilege and have been conditioned into oblivion about its existence.[44]

While I am thankful for the James O. Youngs of the world who are tackling the issue of cultural appropriation, we also have to consider points of perspective and privilege employed, intentionally or unintentionally. Lady Gaga saying that people are "too sensitive" is a reminder that we are not too sensitive—she is unaware of her position of privilege, as is Katy Perry who apparently saw nothing culturally insensitive or offensive about her performance. While seemingly separate from our discussion of teaching Japanese popular culture, I believe that it is not enough to merely expose our students to other cultures; we also have to give them the proper tools for understanding how and why they respond to events, history, society, and artistic expression the way they do. It is not enough to teach students not to be racist; they have grown up with this awareness. They need to understand the perspective with which they are approaching the material. In this case, they need to realize that, while they may not find Katy Perry's performance offensive, there are others who just might and their response needs to be respected. Students need to be able to think critically as we prepare them for the twenty-first century. Not only do they need to know about the cultures and traditions of others, but they need to understand that their perspective, whatever it may be, is not the only perspective.

While I would like to believe that this is just a one-off misstep, these instances happen more than I would like to admit. We only need to look back to the tragic July 6, 2013, Asiana Flight 214 crash at San Francisco International Airport and the prank of a National Transportation Safety Board summer intern, who reported the cockpit crew as comprised of Captain Sum Ting Wong, Wi Tu Lo, Ho Lee Fuk, and Bang Ding Ow.[45] And as if I needed further evidence, I was waiting in line at a local drug store recently when my ten-year-old nephew recognized Daruma sitting in full lotus position in a setting inspired by Hokusai's *Thirty-Six Views of Mount Fuji* on the cover of a birthday card. It warmed my heart that he recognized the first patriarch of Chan Buddhism and even could recite the story of how Daruma lost his arms and legs. The card read, "Your 40th Birthday reminds me of that great oriental philosopher," and inside the card, "Yung No Mo." It is clear we have a long way to go.

Our students have access to a great number of resources, images, and pieces of information, but how many different stories do they know? I am reminded of writer Chimamanda Ngozi Adichie and "The Danger of a Single Story," which can:

> show a people as one thing, as only one thing, over and over again, and that is what they become. It is impossible to talk about the single story without talking about power. . . . Power is the ability not just to tell the story of another person, but to make it the definitive story of that person.[46]

Do our students have the tools to understand that there are many other stories that need to be explored? We are but one step on that journey, helping them to be aware of other narratives, of their own place in this world, and why they matter. Anime, manga, J-pop, Pokémon, Murakami Takashi, Louis Vuitton, and Kanye West may be a hook for some, but each can serve as a bridge on which to build our students' knowledge and validate their interests, while simultaneously debunking misconceptions and expanding their worldview so that they may go on to tell multiple stories.

Notes

[1] Edward W. Said, *Orientalism* (London: Vintage Books, 2003), xviii.

[2] Lizzy Davies, "Takashi Murakami Takes on Critics with Provocative Versailles Exhibition: Art Bad Boy's Sculptures Clash with Formal French Palace Setting as Show Goes Ahead," *Guardian*, September 10, 2010, http://www.theguardian.com/world/2010/sep/10/takashi-murakami-versaillesexhibition.

[3] Jeanius, "Louis Vuitton Vampire Life: Jim Jones Vampin & Travelling in Louis Vuitton Monogramouflage Luggages," *Splashy Splash*, February 20, 2013, http://splashysplash.com/2013/02/jim-jones-vampin-travelling-in-louis-vuitton-monogramouflage-luggages/.

[4] Allen Onyia, "Star Watch: LV Camo Travel Bag," *UpscaleHype*, January 1, 2009, http://www.upscalehype.com/2009/01/star-watch-lv-camo-travel-bag/.

[5] Midori Matsui, "Murakami Matrix: Takashi Murakami's Instrumentalization of Japanese Postmodern Culture," in ©Murakami, ed. Mika Yoshitake, Paul Schimmel, and Lisa Gabrielle Mark (Los Angeles: Museum of Contemporary Art, 2007), 96.

[6] Takashi Murakami, *Little Boy: The Arts of Japan's Exploding Subculture* (New Haven, CT: Yale University Press, 2005), 141.

[7] For a discussion of the cult of *kawaii*, see Christine R. Yano, "Wink on Pink: Interpreting Japanese Cute as It Grabs the Global Headlines," *Journal of Asian Studies* 68, no. 3 (August 2009): 681–88.

[8] House of Louis Vuitton, "Friends of the House: Takashi Murakami," May 20, 2013, http://www.louisvuitton.com/front/#/eng_US/Journeys-section/Friends-of-the-House/Friends-of-the-House/Takashi-Murakami.

[9] Henry A. Giroux, *Disturbing Pleasures: Learning Popular Culture* (New York: Routledge, 1994), 4.

[10] Ibid, 6.

[11] Dick Hebdige, "Flat Boy vs. Skinny Boy: Takashi Murakami and the Battle for 'Japan,'" in ©*Murakami*, ed. Mika Yoshitake, Paul Schimmel, and Lisa Gabrielle Mark (Los Angeles: Museum of Contemporary Art, 2007), 24.

[12] Jill Gasparina et al., *Louis Vuitton: Art Fashion and Architecture* (New York: Rizzoli International Publications, 2009).

[13] Kanye West, *Good Morning*, Roc-A-Fella Records, LLC, 2008, YouTube video, 3:08, posted by KanyeWestVEVO. http://www.youtube.com/watch?v=6CHs4x2uqcQ.

[14] Ibid.

[15] Matsui, "Murakami Matrix," 84.

[16] "English Language Arts Standards," Common Core: State Standards Initiative, last modified 2012, http://www.corestandards.org/ELA-Literacy.

[17] Charles M. Blow, "The Common Core and the Common Good," *New York Times*, August 22, 2013, http://www.nytimes.com/2013/08/22/opinion/blow-the-common-core-and-the-common-good.html.

[18] Pew Research Center, "Millennials: Confident, Connected, Open to Change," February 24, 2010, http://www.pewsocialtrends.org/2010/02/24/millennials-confident-connected-open-to-change.

[19] "English Language Arts Standards: History/Social Studies, Grades 6–8," Common Core: State Standards Initiative, http://www.corestandards.org/ELA-Literacy/RH/6-8.

[20] National Governors Association Center for Best Practices, Council of Chief State School Officers. *Common Core State Standards English Language Arts and Literacy in History/Social Studies.* National Governors Association Center for Best Practices, Council of Chief State School Officers, Washington D.C., 2010. http://www.corestandards.org/ELA-Literacy/RH/6-8/1/.

[21] Ibid., http://www.corestandards.org/ELA-Literacy/RH/6-8/9/.

[22] Takashi Murakami, *Super Flat* (Tokyo: Madora Shuppan, 2000), 7.

[23] "English Language Arts Standards: History/Social Studies, Grades 9–10," Common Core: State Standards Initiative, http://www.corestandards.org/ELA-Literacy/RH/9-10/4.

[24] Peter Schjeldahl, "Buying It: A Takashi Murakami Retrospective," *New Yorker*, April 14, 2008, http://www.newyorker.com/magazine/2008/04/14/buying-it.

[25] "Qatar Museums Authority to Present Murakami–Ego: A New Exhibition by Japanese Artist Takashi Murakami," Qatar Museums Authority, http://www.qma.com.qa/en/news/news-archive/342-qatar-museums-authority-to-present-murakami-%E2%80%93-ego-a-new-exhibition-by-japanese-artist-takashi-murakami.

[26] "Sackler Gallery Premieres Visionary Works by Japanese Master Painter: Kazunobu's Epic Series Presents the Legendary Lives and Deeds of the Buddha's 500 Disciples," *Freer|Sackler: The Smithsonian's Museums of Asian Art*, , March 1, 2012, http://www.asia.si.edu/press/2012/masters-of-mercy.asp.

[27] Adam Lindemann, "Sushi in the Desert: Takashi Murakami Brings His 'Ego' to Qatar," *Observer Culture* February 21, 2012, http://observer.com/2012/02/sushi-in-the-desert-murakami-qatar-02212012/.

[28] Murakami Takashi and Massimiliano Gioni, *Murakami: Ego*. New York: Skira Rizzoli, 2012.

[29] Michael Darling, "Plumbing the Depths of Superflatness," *Art Journal* 60, no. 3 (Autumn 2001): 77.

[30] "Katy Perry Goes Full Geisha for 'Unconditionally' at AMAs: Watch," Billboard.com, November 24, 2013, http://www.billboard.com/articles/columns/pop-shop/5800692/katy-perry-goes-full-geisha-for-unconditionally-at-amas-watch.

[31] Ibid.

[32] Giroux, *Disturbing Pleasures*, 76.

[33] Joseph S. Nye, Jr., "Soft Power," *Foreign Policy* 80, (Autumn 1990): 154.

[34] Douglas McGray, "Japan's Gross National Cool," *Foreign Policy* 130 (May 2002): 44–54.

[35] Nye, Jr., "Soft Power," 167.

[36] While this discussion takes place in Giroux's *Disturbing Pleasures,* in the chapter "White Utopias and Nightmare Realities: Film and the New Cultural Racism," it is particularly useful in thinking that identity politics has been co-opted and does not give students the opportunity to recover their history. "[A] pedagogy of representation would give students the opportunity not simply to discover their hidden histories but to recover them." 89.

[37] Zayda Rivera, "American Music Awards 2013: Katy Perry's Opening Act Called Out as Racist," *New York Daily News*, November 25, 2013, http://www.nydailynews.com/entertainment/music-arts/katy-perry-amas-opening-act-called-racist-article-1.1528285.

[38] "Katy Perry's AMAs Performance of 'Unconditionally' Sparks Controversy," *huffingtonpost.com*, November 24, 2013, http://www.huffingtonpost.com/2013/11/24/katy-perry-amas unconditionally_n_4334677.html.

[39] Amy Odell, "Was Katy Perry's AMAs Performance Racist?," cosmopolitan.com, November 24, 2013, http://www.cosmopolitan.com/celebrity/news/katy-perry-amas-asian.

[40] "Lady Gaga Defends Katy Perry After Controversial AMA Performance," huffingtonpost.com, November 27, 2013, http://www.huffingtonpost.com/2013/11/27/lady-gaga-defends-katy-perry-ama_n_4349503.html.

[41] James O. Young, "Profound Offense and Cultural Appropriation," *Journal of Aesthetics and Art Criticism* 63, no. 2 (Spring 2005): 139.

[42] Ibid., 140.

[43] Peggy McIntosh, "White Privilege: Unpacking the Invisible Knapsack," *Peace and Freedom*, July–August 1989, 10–12.

[44] Ibid., 10.

[45] Mark Gibbs, "News Station KTVU Punk'd Over Asiana Aircraft Pilot's Names," forbes.com, July 12, 2013, http://www.forbes.com/sites/markgibbs/2013/07/12/news-station-ktuv-punkd-over-asiana-aircraft-pilots-names/.

[46] Chimamanda Ngozi Adichie, *Chimamanda Ngozi Adichie: The Danger of a Single Story*, filmed July 2009, TEDvideo, 18:46, posted October 2009, http://www.ted.com/talks/chimamanda_adichie_the_danger_of_a_single_story.hml.

Works Cited

Adichie, Chimamanda Ngozi. *Chimamanda Ngozi Adichie: The Danger of a Single Story.* Filmed July 2009. TEDvideo, 18:46. October 2009. http://www.ted.com/talks/chimamanda_adichie_the_danger_of_a_single_ story.hml.

Blow, Charles M. "The Common Core and the Common Good." *New York Times,* August 22, 2013. http://www.nytimes.com/2013/08/22/opinion/ blow-the-common-core-and-the-common-good.html.

Darling, Michael. "Plumbing the Depths of Superflatness." *Art Journal* 60, no. 3 (Autumn 2001): 76–89.

Davies, Lizzy. "Takashi Murakami takes on critics with provocative Versailles exhibition: Art Bad Boy's Sculptures Clash with Formal French Palace Setting as Show Goes Ahead." *Guardian,* September 10, 2010. http://www. theguardian.com/world/2010/sep/10/takashimurakami-versaillesexhibition.

Gasparina, Jill, Glenn O'Brien, Taro Igarashi, Ian Luna, and Valerie Steele. *Louis Vuitton: Art Fashion and Architecture.* New York: Rizzoli International Publications, 2009.

Gibbs, Mark. "News Station KTVU Punk'd Over Asiana Aircraft Pilot's Names." *forbes.com,* July 12, 2013. http://www.forbes.com/sites/ markgibbs/2013/07/12/news-station-ktuv-punkd-over-asiana-aircraft-pilots- names/.

Giroux, Henry A. *Disturbing Pleasures: Learning Popular Culture.* New York: Routledge, 1994.

Hebdige, Dick. "Flat Boy vs. Skinny Boy: Takashi Murakami and the Battle for 'Japan.'" In ©*Murakami*, eds. Mika Yoshitake, Paul Schimmel, and Lisa Gabrielle Mark, 14–51. Los Angeles: Museum of Contemporary Art, 2007.

House of Louis Vuitton. "Friends of the House: Takashi Murakami." May 20, 2013. http://www.louisvuitton.com/front/#/eng_US/Journeys-section/ Friends-of-the-House/Friends-of-the-House/Takashi-Murakami.

Jeanius. "Louis Vuitton Vampire Life: Jim Jones Vampin & Travelling in Louis Vuitton Monogramouflage Luggages." *Splashy Splash,* February 20, 2013. http://splashysplash.com/2013/02/jim-jones-vampin-travelling-in-louis- vuitton-monogramouflage-luggages/.

"Katy Perry Goes Full Geisha for 'Unconditionally' at AMAs: Watch." Billboard.com. 2013. http://www.billboard.com/articles/columns/pop- shop/5800692/katy-perry-goes-full-geisha-for-unconditionally-at-amas- watch.

"Katy Perry's AMAs Performance Of 'Unconditionally' Sparks Controversy." huffingtonpost.com, November 24, 2013. http://www.huffingtonpost. com/2013/11/24/katy-perry-amas unconditionally_n_4334677.html.

"Lady Gaga Defends Katy Perry After Controversial AMA Performance." huffingtonpost.com, November 27, 2013. http://www.huffingtonpost. com/2013/11/27/lady-gaga-defends-katy-perryama_n_4349503.html.

Lindemann, Adam. "Sushi in the Desert: Takashi Murakami Brings His 'Ego' to Qatar." *Observer*, February 21, 2012. http://observer.com/2012/02/sushi-in-the-desert-murakami-qatar-02212012/.

Matsui, Midori. "Murakami Matrix: Takashi Murakami's Instrumentalization of Japanese Postmodern Culture." In ©Murakami, edited by Mika Yoshitake, Paul Schimmel, and Lisa Gabrielle Mark, 80–127. Los Angeles: Museum of Contemporary Art, 2007.

McGray, Douglas. "Japan's Gross National Cool." *Foreign Policy*, 130 (May 2002): 44–54.

McIntosh, Peggy. "White Privilege: Unpacking the Invisible Knapsack." *Peace and Freedom,* July–August 1989, 10–12.

Murakami, Takashi. *Little Boy: The Arts of Japan's Exploding Subculture.* New Haven, CT: Yale University Press, 2005.

———. *Super Flat.* Tokyo: Madora Shuppan, 2000.

Murakami, Takashi, and Massimiliano Gioni. *Murakami: Ego.* New York: Skira Rizzoli, 2012.

National Governors Association Center for Best Practices, Council of Chief State School Officers. *Common Core State Standards English Language Arts and Literacy in History/Social Studies.* National Governors Association Center for Best Practices, Council of Chief State School Officers, Washington D.C., 2010.

Nye, Joseph S., Jr. "Soft Power." *Foreign Policy* 80 (Autumn 1990): 153–71.

Odell, Amy. "Was Katy Perry's AMAs Performance Racist?" *cosmopolitan.com*, November 24, 2013, http://www.cosmopolitan.com/celebrity/news/katy perry-amas-asian.

Onyia, Allen. "Star Watch: LV Camo Travel Bag." *UpscaleHype*, January 1, 2009. http://www.upscalehype.com/2009/01/star-watch-lv-camo-travel-bag/.

Pew Research Center. "Millennials: Confident, Connected, Open to Change," February 24, 2010. http://www.pewsocialtrends.org/2010/02/24/millennials-confident-connectedopen-to-change.

"Qatar Museums Authority to Present Murakami–Ego: A New Exhibition by
    Japanese Artist Takashi Murakami." Qatar Museums Authority.
    http://www.qma.com.qa/en/news/news-archive/342-qatar-museums
    authority-to-present-murakami-%E2%80%93-ego-a-new-exhibition-by-
    japaneseartist-takashi-murakami.

Rivera, Zayda. "American Music Awards 2013: Katy Perry's Opening Act
    Called Out as Racist." New York Daily News. November 25, 2103.
    http://www.nydailynews.com/entertainment/music-arts/katy-perry-amas-
    opening act-called-racist-article-1.1528285.

"Sackler Gallery Premieres Visionary Works by Japanese Master Painter:
    Kazunobu's epic series presents the legendary lives and deeds of the
    Buddha's 500 disciples." *Freer|Sackler: The Smithsonian's Museums of
    Asian Art.* March 1, 2012. http://www.asia.si.edu/press/2012/masters-of-
    mercy.asp.

Said, Edward W. *Orientalism.* London: Vintage Books, 2003.

Schjeldahl, Peter. "Buying It: A Takashi Murakami Retrospective." *New
    Yorker,* April 14, 2008. http://www.newyorker.com/arts/critics/
    artworld/2008/04/14/080414craw_artworld_schjeldahl.

West, Kanye. *Good Morning.* Roc-A-Fella Records, LLC, 2008. YouTube video,
    3:08. Posted by KanyeWestVEVO, December 31, 2009.
    http://www.youtube.com/watch?v=6CHs4x2uqcQ.

Yano, Christine R. "Wink on Pink: Interpreting Japanese Cute as It Grabs the
    Global Headlines." *Journal of Asian Studies* 68, no. 3 (August 2009):
    681–88.

Yoshitake, Mika, Paul Schimmel, and Lisa Gabrielle Mark, eds. ©Murakami.
    Los Angeles: Museum of Contemporary Art, 2007.

Young, James O. "Profound Offense and Cultural Appropriation." *Journal of
    Aesthetics and Art Criticism* 63, no. 2 (Spring 2005): 135–46.

7

Co-teaching and Foreign Language across the Curriculum

Using Japanese Popular Culture

Deborah Shamoon

Content-based instruction, that is, including critical thinking skills and analysis of culture along with grammar and vocabulary, has been an important topic in language-teaching pedagogy for many years. Fred Genesee, writing in 1994 on Canadian immersion programs, notes, "[S]econd language instruction that is integrated with instruction in academic or other content matter is a more effective approach to teaching second languages than methods that teach the second language in isolation."[1] Despite widespread acceptance of this long-standing pedagogical model, many programs have difficulty implementing content-based instruction in a comprehensive manner. While Japanese language courses at the university level have for many years used authentic materials such as newspaper and magazine articles, short stories, and TV shows, not all programs have a mechanism for direct integration of area studies courses taught in English with language courses. Many programs and individual faculty members are experimenting with various ways to implement content-based instruction.[2] In this volume, Marc Yamada (chapter 8) and James Dorsey (chapter 9) give two examples of using pop culture texts to integrate the discussion of gender roles in language courses. This essay introduces a different model, using co-teaching to integrate advanced language teaching into an existing pop culture course.

Japanese language, Japanese literature, and other area studies courses are usually taught in the same departments in universities in the United States, but it is only recently that there has been a concentrated effort to bridge the institutional and curricular gap between those courses. In 2009 Chikamatsu Nobuko and Matsugu Miho hosted a conference at DePaul University titled "Bridging Japanese Language and Japanese Studies in Higher Education." Among the best practices for achieving better integration between language and area studies, they list collaboration among instructors, use of content-based instruction (CBI), and foreign language across the curriculum (FLAC) courses.[3] In the same year, 2009, I collaborated with my colleague at the University of Notre Dame, Hanabusa Noriko, to create a new cotaught FLAC section as a supplement to my existing course on Japanese popular culture. This chapter is a reflection of our experiences in developing and teaching that course, with consideration of the utility of CBI and the FLAC model.

The Potential and Limits of CBI and FLAC

One example of the various possibilities for designing content-based language classes is provided by Myriam Met. Met describes a continuum with two poles: on one side a content-driven course in which students are evaluated on content mastery and second language (L2) teaching goals are secondary, and on the other side, a course that is language driven, where students are evaluated solely on language proficiency and content is used as material for language instruction.[4] Met also describes various courses along the middle of this continuum, which she calls the adjunct model: "Students are expected to learn content material while simultaneously acquiring academic language proficiency. Content instructors and language instructors share responsibility for student learning, with students evaluated by content instructors for subject matter mastery, and by language instructors for language skills."[5] This is the model we used in designing the FLAC section, although balancing both subject matter and teaching responsibilities is a challenge.

Foreign language across the curriculum courses, that is, second-language adjunct courses that supplement English-language courses, have existed since the 1970s in the United States,[6] and many follow the adjunct model that Met describes. In these programs, courses taught in English also offer an optional supplementary section in a second language for students with intermediate or advanced L2 skills. This can take the form of an extra section or weekly discussion in the second language, with some assignments and readings completed in that language.

David P. Sudermann and Mary A. Cisar offer an overview and critique of such programs at two of the first institutions to implement them, Earlham College and St. Olaf College. According to Sudermann and Cisar, the primary objectives of these programs are not so much large gains in L2 proficiency as broader institutional benefits: "While both FLAC programs seek to change student attitudes toward FL [foreign language] learning and to promote advanced FL study, neither aims explicitly to expand FL skills; for both, the general goal is not so much to develop the FL tool as to use it to increase liberal knowledge and critical skills."[7] More specifically, the benefit is greater integration between language and liberal arts, with regard to both students and faculty, who are called on to combine language teaching with other forms of discipline-specific pedagogy.

While the promise of the FLAC model is better curricular integration, as well as implementation of content-based instruction, there are pitfalls. Sudermann and Cisar are highly critical of the adjunct model, which they see as producing minimal gains in L2 proficiency and enforcing rather than bridging disciplinary divides. Some of their objections stem from the all-inclusive concept of FLAC as they describe it at Earlham and St. Olaf, where the programs appear to have been designed to reorganize the curriculum entirely; in that case, it is true that not many courses are appropriate for supplementary language study (such as courses that cover material from many languages) and that there are few students with the requisite language skills. Moreover, Sudermann and Cisar assume that all such courses will be reading intensive, hence their criticism that, as most foreign language programs emphasize speaking, few students will have the necessary reading skills. They describe one of the goals of these courses as "to read substantial portions of unedited masterworks in a FL," which they argue persuasively is not possible for students at the intermediate level, while also dismissing less tangible gains such as language maintenance or illustrating the value of foreign language competency, even if students have not yet reached proficiency.[8]

While Sudermann and Cisar question the purpose of introducing authentic reading materials at the intermediate level, others, such as Chikamatsu and Gisela Hoecherl-Alden, advocate it.[9] Rather than simply assigning students a difficult text with the help of a vocabulary list, Hoecherl-Alden views reading as a holistic activity that includes interactive reading strategies as well as critical thinking and community-building exercises. She writes, "A literature based program does not preclude structural practice. On the contrary, it contributes greatly to oral and written language acquisition, since literacy leans heavily on students' oral language development, and oral language in turn provides the foundation for reading and writing."[10] Furthermore, the model of a literature-based class that Hoecherl-Alder describes does not depend on the most difficult texts but begins with texts for children, which are linguistically simpler but still offer rich opportunities for discussions of culture.[11]

While the all-inclusive model of FLAC, such as the program at St. Olaf, is ambitious, there can be advantages in a program that is smaller in scope and avoids some of these pitfalls. Despite the small number of eligible students, there is no reason not to limit enrollment to advanced language majors, especially in small programs where advanced language courses are limited; in this way, such adjunct courses can help diversify course offerings and expose students to material they would not otherwise encounter. One reason we developed the FLAC course at Notre Dame was to provide a much-needed advanced course for fourth-year students returning from study abroad and a small number of heritage learners. These students were too few in number to justify creating a new stand-alone course, and the language faculty at the time was already stretched to capacity.

Moreover, the goal of reading "substantial portions of unedited masterworks" is not the only option for a FLAC course. The desire to have students read canonical works in the original seems more suited to Romance- or German-language programs; the example Sudermann and Cisar cite is Kant.[12] In the case of Japanese, however, undergraduates are not expected to read entire novels even in advanced classes, and reading unedited or unannotated classics written before the linguistic reforms of the late nineteenth century is difficult if not nearly impossible even for native speakers. This is not necessarily a case of what Sudermann and Cisar call "the downward adjustment of expectations to meet lesser skill levels,"[13] but an acknowledgment of linguistic features of the Japanese language: reading large sections of text, particularly of classic literature, is not a realistic expectation for even advanced undergraduates.

Furthermore, reading large amounts of weighty text should not be the only measure of rigor for advanced language study. Watching films or televisions shows without subtitles, practicing storytelling skills, learning specialized academic vocabulary, and comprehending conversational speech patterns are all appropriate activities for advanced Japanese-language students. While large programs can offer a range of advanced Japanese courses, such as Business Japanese or an advanced readings course, smaller programs do not always have that option. In this case, an adjunct FLAC section can offer students wider exposure to authentic materials and additional opportunities for L2 use than they encountered in the primary language course.

Another advantage of CBI, as Chikamatsu points out, is its potential to bridge the gap between language and area studies courses and between faculty members in those disciplines.[14] But, while the goal of encouraging integration within the liberal arts is an important one, it is not easily accomplished, and in some cases the opposite might occur inadvertently. Sudermann and Cisar criticize the programs at St. Olaf and Earlham for expecting instructors to teach the FLAC courses as an overload, and for a division of labor that reinforces disciplinary hierarchies, with foreign-language teachers responsible for creating vocabulary lists and grading student homework, while the nonlanguage faculty members have the (presumably less labor-intensive and more intellectually rewarding) task of running the discussion section.[15] They argue that if the integrative goals of FLAC are to be met, then faculty members must learn each other's disciplines, that is, foreign-language teachers must learn how to teach history, for instance, and historians must become more like language teachers.[16] While this is a worthy goal, there are significant institutional restrictions on achieving this end, which begin with the requirements leading toward narrow specialization in graduate school.

Nevertheless, the growing popularity of CBI has led some language instructors to bring other disciplines into the language class, such as the way Yamada and Dorsey use TV dramas and popular songs, respectively, to introduce students to cultural studies analysis. They were able to offer this content thanks to their graduate training and research profile in Japanese literature. Faculty members with a background in second-language acquisition may find creating content outside their area of expertise more difficult. Laurent Cammarata conducted a study of teachers' emotional and intellectual responses to an intensive training program in CBI and found that, while the participants were intellectually willing to implement new methods, emotionally they felt uncertain and lacking in the requisite experience.[17] Cammarata describes how the participants found the experience traumatic and demoralizing as they not only attempted to master a completely new pedagogy and work cycle but also confronted the limits of their own expertise. He quotes poignantly from one of the participants:

> As a language teacher, I am not an expert in economics, politics, history, or ... when I try to develop a lesson around the economy of [name of country], or around a company structure, or even key historical events, I feel kind of threatened ... as a teacher I cannot help feeling incompetent or even threatened, you know ... I think that it's a good idea to bring in the contexts to really support the language component, but, you know, sometimes I feel I am not qualified.[18]

Similarly, Mariko Wei, reflecting on her own experiment with content-based instruction in advanced Japanese at Purdue University, also expresses anxiety over the issue of expertise. She found that locating appropriate authentic materials was extremely time consuming; she spent a considerable amount of time doing research on the topic herself in order to gain some knowledge of terminology and current academic and popular discourse.[19] Furthermore, Chikamatsu and Matsugu cite lack of language teaching pedagogy training in area studies faculties as another impediment to implementing CBI, particularly in Japanese programs.[20] The issue of expertise on the part of both language and area studies instructors is a serious one.

Both Cammarata and Wei suggest team teaching as the solution to the problem of expertise. Ōshima Yayoi reports that students appreciate the plurality of viewpoints presented by having more than one instructor.[21] Team teaching can indeed be a successful part of CBI if it is implemented voluntarily and with mutual consideration. Sudermann and Cisar point out that the team-teaching environment must be carefully structured in order to avoid reinforcing unfair and exploitative tendencies within the academic hierarchy.[22] As Chihiro Kinoshita-Thomson writes, the majority of Japanese-language instructors are disadvantaged within academia in the United States (and in Australia, where she is located). They are predominantly Japanese women holding untenured lecturer positions, and, as native Japanese speakers, they are a linguistic and ethnic minority at their institutions.[23] Collaboration between language and area studies instructors must be negotiated with care to avoid the kind of unequal scenario Sudermann and Cisar describe, in which an area studies professor teaches the course while a language lecturer is relegated to supplying vocabulary lists and grading homework.[24]

Ideally, team teaching should reflect the strengths, as well as the research interests, of both instructors. However, when Hanabusa and I presented our experience collaborating on the FLAC course at various academic conferences, we found that our colleagues assumed an unequal division of labor between us, and assumed that Hanabusa, as the language instructor, had sole responsibility for the FLAC section. In other words, the term *team teaching* for most people seems to imply alternating teaching responsibilities rather than both instructors in the classroom at the same time, as was the case in our class. For this reason, we instead use the term *co-teaching* to indicate that we shared equally in lesson planning, assessment, and contact hours. If both instructors collaborate to share the pedagogical approaches of their respective disciplines, the result can indeed bridge divides not only across fields but within language and literature departments. The result is not only collaboration among faculty members but integration of course offerings for language majors. See figures 7.1 and 7.2 below.

Figure 7.1. Shamoon teaching Introduction to Japanese Popular Culture, the English language course.

Figure 7.2. Shamoon (right) and Hanabusa (left) co-teaching
the Japanese Popular Culture LAC adjunct section
for advanced Japanese language students.

Language across the Curriculum at Notre Dame

At the University of Notre Dame, the Language across the Curriculum (LAC) initiative began in the 2004–5 academic year, originating in the College of Arts and Letters but was later housed within the Center for the Study of Languages and Cultures (CSLC). The initiative was modeled in part on programs at the State University of New York, Binghamton; Auburn University; and Wake Forest University. Unlike the programs at Earlham and St. Olaf, it is not a central part of the curriculum but relies on members of the faculty to create adjunct sections on a voluntary basis.

The LAC initiative encourages faculty members teaching area studies courses to offer an optional section for supplemental instruction in a second language. According to the CSLC website, "The LAC Program provides foreign language mini-courses to accompany related humanities and social science coursework where study and discussion of foreign language source material significantly facilitates learning."[25] More specifically, the LAC course is an optional adjunct section in an English-language area studies course. It cannot be taken independently of the English-language-content course. The LAC course usually takes the form of an hour-long discussion in L2 once a week. The baseline of L2 proficiency is left to the instructor's discretion, but the assumption is that the LAC course is for advanced language students, primarily language majors. The course is graded on a pass/fail basis, and reading assignments are limited to ten to fifteen pages per week. Although the guidelines encourage proposals from any discipline, professors who teach literature in translation are particularly encouraged to participate.

In addition to ours in Japanese, there have been LAC sections offered in Spanish, German, and Chinese, among other languages, primarily in conjunction with literature courses. The university's stated guidelines for the LAC initiative encourage team teaching, but an informal poll of our colleagues revealed that this is not the norm in practice. Most LAC sections are taught by the same instructor who teaches the English-language course, most often members of language and literature departments who also have experience teaching language courses. The LAC section is taught as an overload without compensation, either monetary or otherwise, which may be one reason co-teaching is not more common. This extra course may not represent a hardship for tenured or tenure-track faculty at Notre Dame, who typically have lighter teaching loads, but it does present a significant hurdle for the participation of nontenured language instructors.

Creation of an LAC section in Japanese was a topic of discussion in the Department of East Asian Languages and Cultures for several years prior to implementation, but these early suggestions were discarded as impractical because they focused on the literature survey courses. In particular, an LAC section in conjunction with a survey course on modern Japanese literature seemed unworkable. The modern literature course began with texts from the late Edo and early Meiji eras, which students in a fourth-year Japanese-language class cannot easily read due to changes in orthography. The Japanese-language program at Notre Dame does not teach *kyū kanji* and *kyū kanazukai* (traditional characters and spelling), whereas most of the content in the literature class was written before 1947, before spelling reforms were implemented. Combined with the unfamiliar grammar and vocabulary in canonical novels of modern Japanese literature, it seemed that such a course would not be appropriate for our students. On the other hand, an LAC section seemed to be a natural fit with the course on Japanese popular culture I had already developed, which only covered the postwar period. All the primary material (novels, films, TV shows, and manga) use the contemporary colloquial language that students learn in Japanese class.

Japanese Popular Culture and the LAC Course

I developed the Japanese language LAC course jointly with Hanabusa as a supplement to the area studies course Introduction to Japanese Popular Culture, which I had previously developed on my own and taught solely in English. The LAC section was an optional supplement to the English-language course. Students who completed third-year Japanese or the equivalent were allowed to register for the optional Japanese-language section for one credit. We taught the LAC course twice, in 2009 and 2011.[26] Because the number of advanced Japanese students at Notre Dame was relatively limited, enrollment in the LAC course was small: three students each semester out of the larger class of twenty-five to thirty-five. To provide some background, the number of students in fourth-year Japanese at Notre Dame at the time was usually around fifteen, and there were forty Japanese majors and minors each year on average. The LAC course was not intended to substitute for a language-based advanced course (fourth- or fifth-year Japanese) but was designed as a supplement to diversify course offerings.

Before discussing the LAC section in more detail, it is worth explaining how I designed and taught the English-language course. In order to create a cohesive course with clear learning goals, I limited the scope of the course to narrative fiction, with an emphasis on formal and genre analysis, with units on novels, live-action film, animation, and manga but not music, video games, sports, martial arts, nonfiction television (such as game shows), or fashion, among other topics. Despite skipping over some important aspects of Japanese popular culture, I preferred to focus tightly on a few topics (genre studies and visual analysis) and emphasize mastery of analytic skills rather than attempting to cover a wide variety of topics shallowly. This approach provided a framework for the syllabus, which was divided into sections by medium, and allowed comparison of different genres across media. This approach also led to an emphasis on formal analysis of visual texts (manga, anime, and film), which is a concrete skill set students can learn in one semester.[27] Overall, this course received positive feedback from students, and many advanced Japanese majors went on to use the analytic skills learned in that class in writing honors theses on popular culture topics. This use of skills acquired in that course to continue on to more advanced independent work is a significant measure of a successful outcome.

Although Introduction to Japanese Popular Culture was an upper-division course, there were no prerequisites. Enrollment was usually divided more or less evenly between Japanese majors or minors, film studies majors or minors, and those with no background in either Japanese or film. For this reason, I assumed no prior specialized knowledge and devoted a significant amount of class time to providing background in Japanese history and culture and teaching students the basics of formal film analysis, as well as visual analysis of anime and manga. The other overarching topic of the course was critical reflection on the study of popular culture as a field. Two key questions were addressed throughout the course: what theories and methods are available for the study of popular media, particularly visual media; and what is the difference between high culture and popular culture?

To give a brief overview of the scope of the course, the semester began with two novels, so as to highlight the difference between high culture and pop culture. The first novel, *Norwegian Wood* (*Noruwei no mori*), by Murakami Haruki, encompasses both "pure literature" (*junbungaku*) and pop culture; although it is more dense and reflective than most popular fare, it was also a media sensation when it was first published, and it allows for discussion of the difference between highbrow and lowbrow entertainment, as well as how a mass culture phenomenon can exceed the content of the original text. The second book, *All She Was Worth* (*Kasha*), by Miyabe Miyuki, is clearly genre fiction, in this case a detective novel, which serves as an introduction to using genre, rather than symbolism or characterization, to analyze a work of fiction. Starting with these two novels allows students to see how analysis of popular culture is different from that used in the "great books" courses they may have taken previously. Having established genre as one means of analysis, the course then moved on to live-action film, and then to animated film and television shows. In discussing anime, we read Murakami Takashi's "Superflat Manifesto" and discussed how his theory of superflat art provides multiple paradigms for the analysis of anime. The final unit is on manga, and we used Scott McCloud's *Understanding Comics* as a model for visual analysis. Assignments included an oral presentation, a short paper and a ten-page paper written in two drafts.

Hanabusa and I developed the LAC section after I had already offered the English-language pop culture course for several years. Our collaboration arose from a mutual desire to find new methods for incorporating language- and content-based instruction beyond the courses we were currently offering. It was not required of us at the department or college level, and this was a crucial point. It is important that team teaching or co-teaching is undertaken voluntarily, both to avoid a clash of personalities or teaching styles and to avoid exacerbating unequal employment practices. We met once a week to plan the lesson together, and we taught each LAC class meeting together, taking joint responsibility for guiding class discussion and answering student questions. The fact that we were able to collaborate on devising lesson plans and running each class helped to mitigate some of the institutional inequality, as we could decide how to divide the workload ourselves.

In addition, we each made an effort to attend each other's classes and to read and discuss the secondary literature of each other's fields. In practical terms, however, the burden of preparation fell much more heavily on Hanabusa, especially in the first year, as she was unfamiliar with most of the content. Preparing for the LAC section meant that she had to read or watch all the primary and secondary assigned texts in the English-language course and attend my lectures in English twice weekly. In the second year in which we offered the LAC section, this was less necessary, as most of the content was repeated. I also sat in on a few fourth- and fifth-year Japanese language classes to get a sense of the students' abilities and attended the Japanese language table monthly, an extracurricular activity in which students meet for free, unstructured conversation in Japanese. However, this was a significantly lower time commitment. Moreover, I already had some pedagogical training and many years of experience teaching Japanese language in graduate school, while narrative and visual analysis of fiction was a new discipline for Hanabusa. Part of the reason our collaboration was successful despite these inequalities is that Hanabusa was strongly motivated to participate because of her prior interest in content-based instruction and had a strong desire to study and publish on innovative pedagogical practices.[28] This is another reason why both FLAC and co-teaching must be undertaken on a voluntary basis rather than imposed from above, as faculty members may have other incentives for taking on additional work.

In terms of our instructional goals for the LAC course, we emphasized the language and content equally. The goals of the English-language course, articulated in the syllabus, were to gain familiarity with some key texts in postwar Japan; to learn various methods for analyzing those texts, that is, in approaching each medium (novels, film, TV, manga, anime) to use film, animation, and comics theories to analyze them; and to gain proficiency in the academic analysis of popular culture through essay writing and oral presentation. The additional goals of the LAC course, which we developed jointly and wrote in the syllabus (in Japanese), were to become familiar with major postwar popular culture texts in Japanese; to learn various theories and methods for analyzing those texts and to be able to express them in Japanese; to be able to discuss the content of those texts more deeply; to learn specialized vocabulary necessary for the analysis, as well as other advanced-level vocabulary (such as *giseigo* and *gitaigo*); to increase recognition of kanji compounds; to acquire oral proficiency to precisely describe, explain, and summarize the content of texts; and to concisely state one's opinions on specific topics. Thus the course goals for the English-language section were (necessarily) wholly content driven, and the goals stated in the syllabus of the LAC section asked students to incorporate literary, visual, and film analysis with acquisition of new vocabulary, and to work on advanced oral and written proficiency. Instruction in the LAC section was not wholly language driven but asked students to perform the same kinds of critical analysis and critical thinking as in the English-language section.

Critical Thinking

One of the goals of content-based language instruction was to encourage students to develop critical thinking skills while expressing themselves in Japanese. This was also part of our larger goal of integrating language and area studies courses, to help dispel the negative assumption that language classes are primarily about rote memorization, while the more rigorous task of learning critical thinking only occurs in content courses. However, it is important to step back and consider the various meanings and implications of the term *critical thinking*.

Critical thinking, while a central part of the liberal arts education, is understood in markedly different ways across the curriculum, and instructors collaborating across different fields may not be aware of how widely their definitions diverge. For language instructors, critical thinking often means encouraging students to be self-critical, that is, to reflect on their own language production and self-correct errors. In a literature course, on the other hand, critical thinking can mean (among other things) reflecting on the cultural and historical context in which a novel was written, or using critical theory to analyze a text. These are only two limited, practical examples.

In a larger sense, critical thinking in the undergraduate classroom requires students to be reflective and to reason through complex issues or topics. A recent textbook designed to teach students critical thinking across the curriculum begins by stating that critical thinking has three parts: asking questions, reasoning out the answers to those questions, and believing the results.[29] Part of believing the results of reasoning, as the text explains later, derives from understanding the logic, vocabulary, and fundamental concepts of the respective field or discipline.[30] A. Suresh Canagarajah offers a more specific definition of critical thinking as part of critical pedagogy, which is not merely what he calls "detached rational thinking" but demands both the instructors and the students reflect on their own biases.[31] Some questions he suggests are "What are the interests served for the writing in making these claims? What in his or her social positioning explains the way this argument is made? What in your social status and experience makes you relate to this subject differently? What are other perspective/angles on this subject?"[32] In teaching the LAC section, we attempted to incorporate various approaches to critical thinking, asking students to reflect critically both on the course material and on their own performance in class and on assignments.

LAC Course Assignments

As the LAC section was a one-hour pass/fail course, we were very limited in the kinds of assignments and the amount of homework we could require. Assignments varied from week to week, depending on content. In most weeks students were asked to prepare a short reading in Japanese, sometimes three to five pages of a novel or essay or twenty pages of a manga assigned in full in the English-language course. Of course, students can handle many more pages of manga than of a novel; essays are the most difficult and necessarily the shortest. Occasionally students were given a short reading that had not been translated into English and was not assigned in the main course, such as Okada Toshio's *Otakugaku nyūmon* (*Introduction to Otakuology*).[33] In this way we gave students access to the original language of some texts, and expanded their knowledge of untranslated secondary texts.

In creating assignments and in-class discussions, our goal was to integrate the critical-thinking skills students learned in the English-language course with advanced language learning. Although students in third- and fourth-year Japanese at Notre Dame regularly read authentic materials, LAC students still had some difficulties with both the novels and the essays. We discovered that students tend to be more accustomed to reading newspaper and magazine articles, which are written in a very different style. In particular, they had difficulty with dialogue in the two novels, as well as sorting out which character uttered each line. In the first year in which we taught the LAC course, we did not anticipate enough how much of a problem this would be for students. It was only after talking to them in class that we realized how much they had misunderstood the original, even when they had access to an English translation. In the second year, we addressed this by asking the students to focus on the dialogue and distinguish who is speaking as they were preparing the text as homework. In class discussion, we reflected on different prose styles, specifically, the way English-language novels must repeat "he said" and "she said" (or some variation) to attribute dialogue, while Japanese often dispenses with these attributions because linguistic markers in the dialogue itself indicate the age, gender, and relative social position of the speaker. This is one example of the direct impact of reading even short sections of fiction in increasing proficiency for Japanese-language students, and it indicates the importance of including a variety of authentic materials in content-based instruction.

Written exercises also provided an opportunity for integration of CBI and critical-thinking skills. Students wrote several short essays over the course of the semester on topics related to course content. While students engage in writing exercises in all levels of Japanese-language courses, topics tend to be descriptive (e.g., what they did last weekend) rather than argumentative and analytic. While students are expected to know how to write an argumentative essay in English, they seemed to have difficulty transferring the most basic essay-writing skills they possess in English to Japanese; for instance, they had trouble formulating a clear thesis statement, as well as remembering to use transitional phrases and provide concrete examples from the text. This indicates how difficult it is to engage in high-level academic discourse in a foreign language and suggests that students need far more exposure to this integrated approach. Students also need instruction on grammatical features of formal academic writing specific to Japanese, for instance, using *de aru* rather than *da* and distinguishing statements of fact from opinion, by using *de arō*, for example.

While these examples all relate to reading and writing skills, we also used film viewings as an opportunity for students to practice oral storytelling skills. Students prepared a short presentation recounting the plot of a film viewed in class, using complete sentences and linking episodes using transitional words and phrases. This was an activity significantly different from the kinds of oral presentations students typically make in other language courses, where the emphasis tends to be on relating personal experience (what I did last weekend) or nonnarrative (e.g., summarizing an assigned newspaper article). We also required students to learn and use the language of film criticism in Japanese. As most of these terms (*close-up, cut,* etc.) are English loanwords, this was a skill they easily acquired, even within the limited parameters of the LAC course.

In teaching advanced vocabulary and grammar patterns, our intention was to encourage the students to engage in high-level academic discourse and analysis. We found that certain materials lend themselves to language instruction that students would not otherwise encounter in an advanced Japanese-language course. For instance, while the dialogue in manga tends to be fairly straightforward and easy for students to comprehend, the sound effects are not. *Shōjo* manga in particular lends itself to an extended lesson on *giseigo* and *gitaigo* (onomatopoeia), as many of the sound-effect words in *shōjo* manga are affective or symbolic rather than mimetic. *Shōjo* manga has a high incidence of *gitaigo* in order to convey the emotional state of the characters. We used this as an opportunity to discuss the importance of *gitaigo* in Japanese in general and to teach students the common meanings of certain sound clusters. We also discussed why *shōjo* manga uses more *gitaigo* than other manga genres, because it is more focused on the representation of emotion than on the progression of action. In this way, the focus was not only on language usage but on genre analysis as well.

Another example of integrating this kind of academic analysis with language study was in our reading of the novel *Norwegian Wood*. Students read and discussed the entire novel in English in the main course, then read a short excerpt in Japanese for the LAC section. One topic that we discussed in the LAC section is Murakami's use of the pronoun *boku*. First we reviewed gendered pronouns as a warmup, then we asked students to reflect on the difference between the male pronouns *boku* and *ore*. This is a fairly straightforward vocabulary point, and students who have spent time in Japan are generally aware of the implications of these pronouns.

We then asked them to consider why Murakami chose to use *boku* rather than any other pronoun, a task that required them to integrate vocabulary knowledge with literary analysis. We followed this up with a discussion of the importance of pronoun choice in Murakami's work and modern Japanese literature in general. In fact Murakami's use of the pronoun *boku* is consistent across many of his novels, to the extent that *"Boku"* has become a topic of analysis in Japanese literary criticism and something of a recurring character. Thus his choice of pronoun suggests a deeper meaning than simply an inevitable choice for a narrator who is young and male. In this way, we were able to incorporate a vocabulary lesson into a fairly sophisticated literary analysis, even without assigning extensive additional readings. This is a topic that would not normally be discussed in an undergraduate literature course taught in English, and it adds real-life context to a vocabulary lesson.

Reflections

Outcomes assessment has necessarily become a major component of pedagogy, particularly in language teaching. However, the emphasis on large amounts of quantifiable data poses a problem for those of us teaching very small classes or developing experimental courses, as is the case with many contributions to this volume. In our case, we taught our LAC course twice with enrollments of three students each time. Unfortunately, as I left the University of Notre Dame in 2012, we were not able to develop the course further. We must then leave the longitudinal studies on CBI and FLAC to others; presented here are reflections on the course as we designed it.

In one measure of outcomes, the student response was positive, both in university-administered anonymous feedback and surveys we presented directly to them. One student wrote in the anonymous feedback:

> Probably some of the hardest material that I've ever read in Japanese and I really appreciated that! It was really great to have the opportunity to discuss difficult topics in Japanese because we usually don't get to that in the language classes. Making us summarize the movie was a good exercise. Maybe you should also make students read their paper aloud and discuss it with their peers.

In the survey we gave to students at the end of the course in 2011, we asked them first to comment on class discussion. One student wrote:

> One of the most difficult components of the class but probably the most beneficial to my Japanese speaking skills because it forced me to think and respond analytically in Japanese. Usually I can focus more on using correct Japanese. But in this class, I had to think simultaneously about the content.

These comments indicate that students perceived very well the gap between the demands of language and area studies courses, and that they appreciated having a course that asked them to integrate skill sets, even if it was difficult.

In the same survey, we also asked students about the essay-writing assignments. Two students responded similarly:

> Loved having the chance to write such analytical papers in Japanese. It really was a challenge to articulate academic thoughts in Japanese. It made me feel like my Japanese had become more well-rounded.

> Writing persuasive essays in this format definitely helped. It was interesting I think because it was fairly unstructured, whereas often in language classes the essay writing is very structured in nature.

The first student responded to the challenge we explicitly set the participants in this course, to combine essay-writing skills with Japanese-language skills. This was a goal we frequently articulated in class and explained to students as part of the essay assignment. The second student, however, responded to an aspect we had not anticipated, one regarding the structure of the assignment. We left the students free to choose the topic and argument of the essay, as long as it related directly to assigned texts. The fact that students do this without comment in English-language courses but find it challenging in Japanese again reflects the need for a bridge between area studies and L2 skill sets. It was clear to us that students need more advance preparation for essay writing. Secondary readings assigned in class can also serve as models, but only if students' attention is focused specifically on the writing style in addition to the content of the reading. Since expressing critical thinking in an L2 essay is particularly challenging, it may also be helpful to have students do prewriting exercises in class to help them articulate their ideas orally first.

Another area that could be improved is integration between the English-language and Japanese-language sections. This means not only reviewing and extending in the LAC section the conversations begun in the English section but also making sure the flow of information and ideas goes in both directions. The students taking the LAC section gain more specialized and in-depth knowledge of the material, and this should be incorporated into the English-language section as well. This could be as simple as calling on students to recount discussions from the LAC section or to review material only available in Japanese. It could also be more directed, such as asking students to give short presentations in English.

While there are institutional hurdles to creating FLAC courses, continued experimentation can provide new opportunities for both faculty and students. In those institutions that already support FLAC, Japanese instructors should not use the difficulty of written texts as an excuse not to participate. Popular culture materials, if used as part of serious instruction and not merely for entertainment, can help bridge area studies and language courses. Team teaching or co-teaching between faculties in Japanese studies programs can also help to break down institutional inequalities, for instance, by implementing CBI at all levels and jointly creating an integrated curriculum. Finally, I would argue against the prejudice that small classes are not worth the effort of developing or reporting on. For those teaching at smaller institutions and in small fields such as Japanese popular culture, class size will be relatively small. But small classes such as ours could be the first step in implementing larger curricular or pedagogical changes.

Conclusion

Although the adjunct model necessarily provides less L2 exposure than the immersion model, there are advantages to conducting an L2 lesson in conjunction with an English-language course. Students can read a large amount of material quickly and analyze the material on a sophisticated level in the L1 course, far more than would be possible in an immersion course. For instance, undergraduates who have completed only three years, or six semesters, of instruction in Japanese will never be able to read all of *Norwegian Wood* in the original in a week or comprehend a science fiction film without subtitles. However, if they come to class having mastered this material in English, they will be prepared to conduct critical analysis that would not have been possible in a purely language-driven course. Furthermore, by co-teaching this course, we were able to combine the pedagogical strengths of language and literature instructors.

Hanabusa and I found the co-teaching approach to integrated CBI to be very successful, not only in terms of diversified course offerings but also in terms of our own professional development. Too often the pedagogy in content-directed and language-directed courses are separated, even at advanced language levels. Content-based language instruction can and should be more than just the use of authentic materials and should incorporate the kinds of critical-thinking skills required of students in content-directed courses. Team teaching can be one way to facilitate this kind of integrated approach without placing an additional burden on language-teaching instructors to master an entirely new pedagogy. This kind of course also creates a stronger integration between the language and area studies courses required for the Japanese major. Finally, by using Japanese popular culture as the topic for this course, we can take advantage of student interest, using the kinds of texts that motivated many of them to undertake Japanese study in the first place and challenging them to not only engage with the original language but to think more deeply about the meanings and interpretations of those texts.

Notes

[1] Fred Genesee, *Integrating Language and Content: Lessons from Immersion*, National Center for Research on Cultural Diversity and Second Language Learning Educational Practice Reports, no. 11 (Washington, DC: Center for Applied Linguistics, 1994), 2.

[2] For example, see Chikamatsu Nobuko and Matsugu Miho, *Bridging Japanese Language and Japanese Studies in Higher Education: Report on the Forum on Integrative Curriculum and Program Development*, 1–5. Association of Teachers of Japanese Occasional Papers, no. 9 (Fall 2009); and Kinoshita-Thomson Chihiro and Makino Seiichi, eds., *Nihongo kyōiku to Nihon kenkyū no renkei: Naiyō jūshigata gaikokugo kyōiku ni mukete* (Linking Japanese language education and Japanese studies: Towards content-oriented second language learning). (Tokyo: Koko Shuppan, 2010).

[3] Chikamatsu and Matsugu, "Bridging Japanese Language," 2–3.

[4] Myriam Met, *Content-Based Instruction: Defining Terms, Making Decisions*, (College Park, MD: National Foreign Language Center, 1999), 4.

[5] Ibid., 7–8.

[6] Stephen B. Stryker and Betty Lou Leaver, eds., *Content-Based Instruction in Foreign Language Education: Models and Methods* (Washington, DC: Georgetown University Press, 1997), 5.

[7] David P. Sudermann and Mary A. Cisar, "Foreign Language across the Curriculum: A Critical Appraisal," *Modern Language Journal* 76, no. 3 (Autumn 1992): 296.

[8] Ibid., 297.

[9] Chikamatsu Nobuko, "Nihon kenkyū to gengo kyōiku no hazama de: jōkyū nihongo kontento bēsu kōsu sengo nihonjin no kōsatsu (In the gap between Japanese studies and language education: A study of advanced Japanese contents-based courses)." In *Gaikokugo to shite no nihongo kyōiku: takakuteki shiya ni motozuku kokoromi* (*Japanese as a foreign language education: Multiple perspectives*), ed. Hatasa Yukiko (Tokyo: Kuroshio Shuppan, 2008), 119–34; Gisela Hoecherl-Alden, "Connecting Language to Content: Second Language Literature Instruction at the Intermediate Level," *Foreign Language Annals* 39, no. 2 (Summer 2006): 244–54.

[10] Hoecherl-Alden, "Connecting Language to Content," 246.

[11] Ibid., 249.

[12] Sudermann and Cisar, "Foreign Language across the Curriculum," 300.

[13] Ibid., 298.

[14] Chikamatsu, "Nihon kenkyū to gengo kyōiku no hazama de," 119–34.

[15] Sudermann and Cisar, "Foreign Language across the Curriculum," 301.

[16] Ibid.

[17] Laurent Cammarata, "Negotiating Curricular Transitions: Foreign Language Teachers' Learning Experience with Content-Based Instruction," *Canadian Modern Language Review* 65, no. 4 (June 2009): 572-73.

[18] Ibid., 576.

[19] Mariko Wei, "Content Based Instruction," *International Journal of the Humanities* 3, no. 1 (2005–6): 78.

[20] Chikamatsu and Matsugu, "Bridging Japanese Language," 3.

[21] Ōshima Yayoi, "Senmon kamoku no kyōin to gengo no kyōin to no chīmu tīchinguno naka de no shidō jogen (Suggestions for guiding team teaching between major subject instructors and language instructors)," *Nihongogaku* (Japanese langauge studies) 23, no. 1 (2004): 26–35.

[22] Sudermann and Cisar, "Foreign Language across the Curriculum," 301.

[23] Kinoshita-Thomson Chihiro, "'Nihongo kyōiku' to 'Nihon kenkyū' no renkei no shōrai" (Encouraging links between "Japanese language teaching" and "Japanese studies"), in *Nihongo kyōiku to Nihon kenkyū no renkei: Naiyō jūshigata gaikokugo kyōiku ni mukete* (*Linking Japanese language education and Japanese studies: Towards content-oriented second language learning*), ed. Kinoshita-Thomson Chihiro and Makino Seiichi (Tokyo: Koko Shuppan, 2010), 59.

[24] Sudermann and Cisar, "Foreign Language across the Curriculum," 301.

[25] Center for the Study of Languages and Cultures, University of Notre Dame, http://cslc.nd.edu/lac

[26] In 2012 I left Notre Dame to take up a position at the National University of Singapore.

[27] For more detail on this course, including a sample syllabus, see Deborah Shamoon, "Teaching Japanese Popular Culture," *ASIANetwork Exchange: A Journal for Asian Studies in the Liberal Arts* 17, no. 2 (Spring 2010): 9–22.

[28] For instance, see Hanabusa Noriko et al., "Shokyū reberu ni okeru 'naiyō jūshi kyōiku' o mezashite" (Towards "content-based instruction" at the introductory level), in *Gaikokugo to shite no nihongo kyōiku: Takakuteki shiya ni motozuku kokoromi* (*Japanese as a foreign language education: Multiple perspectives*), ed. Hatasa Yukiko (Tokyo: Kuroshio Shuppan, 2008). Fukamachi Hideki and Hanabusa Noriko, "Shokyū nihongo kurasu no buroguprojekuto ni okeru 3R no kanōsei," [The possibilities of 3R in blog projects in introductory level Japanese] in *Ibunka komyunikēshon nōryoku o tou: Chōbunka komyunikēshonryoku o mezashite* [Problematizing intercultural communicative competence: Toward

super-cultural communication], ed. Saitō Shinji and Kumagai Yuri (Tokyo: Koko Shuppan, 2013).

[29] Gerald M. Nosich, *Learning to Think Things Through: A Guide to Critical Thinking across the Curriculum*, 3rd ed. Upper Saddle River, NJ: Pearson, 2009), 5.

[30] Ibid., 97–128.

[31] A. Suresh Canagarajah, *Critical Academic Writing and Multilingual Students* (Ann Arbor: University of Michigan Press, 2002), 99.

[32] Ibid.

[33] Okada Toshio, *Otakugaku nyūmon* (*Introduction to Otakuology*). (Tokyo: Ōta Shuppan, 1996).

Works Cited

Cammarata, Laurent. "Negotiating Curricular Transitions: Foreign Language Teachers' Learning Experience with Content-Based Instruction." *Canadian Modern Language Review* 65, no. 4 (June 2009): 559–85.

Canagarajah, A. Suresh. *Critical Academic Writing and Multilingual Students.* Ann Arbor: University of Michigan Press, 2002.

Chikamatsu Nobuko. "Nihon kenkyū to gengo kyōiku no hazama de: Jōkyū nihongo kontento bēsu kōsu sengo nihonjin no kōsatsu" (In the gap between Japanese studies and language education: A study of advanced Japanese contents-based courses). In *Gaikokugo to shite no nihongo kyōiku: Takakuteki shiya ni motozuku kokoromi* (Japanese as a foreign language education: Multiple perspectives), edited by Hatasa Yukiko, 119–34. Tokyo: Kuroshio Shuppan, 2008.

Chikamatsu, Nobuko, and Miho Matsugu. *Bridging Japanese Language and Japanese Studies in Higher Education: Report on the Forum on Integrative Curriculum and Program Development*, 1–5. Association of Teachers of Japanese Occasional Papers, no. 9 (Fall 2009).

Fukamachi Hideki and Hanabusa Noriko. "Shokyū nihongo kurasu no buroguprojekuto ni okeru 3R no kanōsei." [The possibilities of 3R in blog projects in introductory level Japanese] in *Ibunka komyunikēshon nōryoku o tou: Chōbunka komyunikēshonryoku o mezashite* [Problematizing intercultural communicative competence: Toward super-cultural communication], edited by Saitō Shinji and Kumagai Yuri. Tokyo: Koko Shuppan, 2013.

Genesee, Fred. *Integrating Language and Content: Lessons from Immersion.* National Center for Research on Cultural Diversity and Second Language Learning Educational Practice Reports, no. 11. Washington, DC: Center for Applied Linguistics, 1994.

Hanabusa Noriko, Hasegawa Atsushi, Yasuda Mano, and Matsumoto Kazumi. "Shokyū reberu ni okeru 'naiyō jūshi kyōiku' o mezashite" (Towards "content-based instruction" at the introductory level). In *Gaikokugo to shite no nihongo kyōiku: Takakuteki shiya ni motozuku kokoromi,* edited by Hatasa Yukiko, 135–150. Tokyo: Kuroshio Shuppan, 2008.

Hoecherl-Alden, Gisela. "Connecting Language to Content: Second Language Literature Instruction at the Intermediate Level." *Foreign Language Annals* 39, no. 2 (Summer 2006): 244–54.

Kinoshita-Thomson Chihiro. "'Nihongo kyōiku' to 'Nihon kenkyū' no renkei no shōrai" (Encouraging links between "Japanese language teaching" and "Japanese studies"). In *Nihongo kyōiku to Nihon kenkyū no renkei:*

Naiyō jūshigata gaikokugo kyōiku ni mukete (Linking Japanese language education and Japanese studies: Towards content-oriented second language learning), edited by Chihiro Kinoshita-Thomson and Makino Seiichi, 53–66. Tokyo: Koko Shuppan, 2010.

Kinoshita-Thomson Chihiro, and Makino Seiichi, eds. *Nihongo kyōiku to Nihon kenkyū no renkei: Naiyō jūshigata gaikokugo kyōiku ni mukete.* Tokyo: Koko Shuppan, 2010.

McCloud, Scott. *Understanding Comics.* New York: HarperCollins, 1993.

Met, Myriam. *Content-Based Instruction: Defining Terms, Making Decisions.* College Park, MD: National Foreign Language Center, 1999.

Miyabe Miyuki. *All She Was Worth [Kasha].* Translated by Alfred Birnbaum. Boston: Houghton Mifflin, 1999.

Murakami Haruki. *Norwegian Wood [Noruwei no mori].* Translated by Jay Rubin. New York: Vintage International, 2000.

Murakami Takashi. "Super Flat Manifesto." In *Superflat*, 5. Tokyo: Madra, 2000.

Nosich, Gerald M. *Learning to Think Things Through: A Guide to Critical Thinking across the Curriculum.* 3rd ed. Upper Saddle River, NJ: Pearson, 2009.

Okada Toshio. *Otakugaku nyūmon (Introduction to Otakuology).* Tokyo: Ōta Shuppan, 1996.

Ōshima Yayoi. "Senmon kamoku no kyōin to gengo no kyōin to no chīmu tīchinguno naka de no shidō jogen" (Suggestions for guiding team teaching between major subject instructors and language instructors). *Nihongogaku (Japanese language studies)* 23, no. 1 (2004): 26–35.

Shamoon, Deborah. "Teaching Japanese Popular Culture." *ASIANetwork Exchange: A Journal for Asian Studies in the Liberal Arts* 17, no. 2 (Spring 2010): 9–22.

Stryker, Stephen B., and Betty Lou Leaver, eds. *Content-Based Instruction in Foreign Language Education: Models and Methods.* Washington, DC: Georgetown University Press, 1997.

Sudermann, David P., and Mary A. Cisar. "Foreign Language across the Curriculum: A Critical Appraisal." *Modern Language Journal* 76, no. 3 (Autumn 1992): 295–308.

Wei, Mariko. "Content Based Instruction." *International Journal of the Humanities* 3, no. 1 (2005–6): 73–79.

8

Using Japanese Television Media in Content-Based Language Learning

Marc Yamada

Introduction

This chapter examines the use of television media as part of an advanced content-based Japanese language course. Television programming not only provides a context for the elements of conversational Japanese that learners encounter, but it also helps them gain an understanding of cultural perspectives in a way that cannot be replicated in a course taught in translation. Through an analysis of two popular forms of television programming—serial dramas and quiz shows—this chapter will consider how language learning and the development of skills in cultural analysis can inform one another.

The effectiveness of using a medium such as television programming in language learning has been documented in a number of studies. Fred Genesee suggests that language is acquired most effectively when it is introduced in a concrete and meaningful context rather than as an abstract system of syntax and grammar.[1] Studies have shown that the proficiency of learners increases, moreover, when language is used as a medium through which they can engage material that is of interest and relevance to them.[2] This is certainly the case with students in Japanese college courses, who are often drawn to the Japanese language because of their interest in manga, anime, and television dramas among other popular forms.

Too often, however, popular media merely provides an appealing context in which to study language. Content-based approaches, Fredricka Stoller suggests, can easily become a "shell for language learning" without encouraging deeper levels of analytical thinking and cultural awareness.[3] Indeed, the significance of the cultural perspectives represented in media such as literature, film, and television often goes unexplored in language courses. Even when content learning is identified as a goal, instruction often fails to engage media with the critical depth of courses taught in translation. Instead, it relies on examples that merely propagate conventional and even stereotypical ways of thinking about Japanese culture.

Superficial treatments of popular media fail to take advantage of the synergetic relationship between language learning and the development of skills in cultural analysis. These treatments fail to recognize that, while media enhances language learning in ways that cannot be replicated through pedagogical methods that deal with Japanese in isolation, engaging texts in the original cultivates an understanding of the conventions of Japanese media and the cultural values they relay in ways that cannot be replicated in a course that does not treat original sources. Considering the abundance of research on the way content can enhance language learning, this chapter will instead focus on the other side of the coin—on ways to improve content learning in advanced Japanese courses. Similar to chapter 7, by Deborah Shamoon, in this volume, it will consider the way students can "learn content material while simultaneously acquiring academic language proficiency."[4] Yet, instead of describing the implementation of this model in a foreign language across the curriculum (FLAC) course involving two or more teachers working in tandem, this chapter will describe ways in which individual instructors, particularly those who have training in both cultural studies and language teaching, can apply this model in an intermediate or advanced language course when team teaching may not be an option.

In particular, this chapter will focus on improving students' critical cultural awareness, helping them gain the ability to decode the ideological effects of media and to understand their role in shaping worldviews and instructing audiences about their place in a particular sociocultural system. Because language is one of the most important vehicles through which Japanese media define social and cultural identities, analytical and critical skills are developed most effectively when practiced in conjunction with language learning. As James Dorsey convincingly argues in chapter 9 of this volume, studying Japanese culture and language together helps "students to reflect on the ways in which entry into that, or any, semiotic system inevitably inscribes on them a worldview as well."[5] For this reason, evaluating the treatment of language in popular media yields insights into the ideological impulse of these forms that are only available by examining original sources.

Television programming, in particular, provides an accessible resource for practicing skills in decoding the systems of authority present in media. As mentioned in the introduction to this volume, Henry A. Giroux, in *Disturbing Pleasures: Learning Popular Culture,* argues that media serve a more important function than just making learning interesting or entertaining; they allow students to engage firsthand with the structures of power that influence us on a daily basis.[6] In particular, critical analysis of television programming in the classroom, as Kevin Tavin suggests, helps students recognize the way media contribute "language, codes, and values that become the material milieu of everyday discursive formations."[7] In her study on content-based learning, moreover, Gisela Hoecherl-Alden argues that studying TV media increases students' ability to detect "overt and covert stereotyping in the narratives of the dominant culture."[8] This chapter will provide specific examples of ways to synthesize linguistic and cultural learning through two types of TV programming that play a central role in formulating sociocultural identities in Japan: TV dramas (*dorama*) and quiz shows (*kuizu bangumi*). Television dramas offer a vast resource of scenarios that model colloquial expression while providing examples of the role language plays in the construction of identity. Due to their focus on conversational Japanese, moreover, quiz shows delve into the specifics of idiomatic Japanese while helping students understand the role these expressions play in formulating a community of native speakers.

Specifically, this chapter will focus on ways to use TV dramas, quiz shows, and serialized language programs to enhance learning in advanced courses. It will discuss how these programs can complement content-based instruction in textbooks such as *Tobira: Gateway to Advanced Japanese Learning through Content and Media.* As a resource for intermediate to advanced learners, *Tobira* offers a nice backbone for content-based learning, integrating reading comprehension, grammar development, and vocabulary building within the context of cultural, political, and sociological topics. The chapters of *Tobira* consist of articles, short dialogues, grammar points, and vocabulary items. The advantage of a text like *Tobira* is that it provides a prepared set of reading samples, vocabulary lists, grammar lessons, and comprehension questions. The disadvantage is that it tends to present rather shallow views of Japanese culture and often suffers from a lack of relevant and useful media sources to complement individual lessons. Integrating examples of TV media in *Tobira* lessons allows instructors to engage students' abilities in cultural analysis. This chapter will focus specifically on ways to incorporate media into the presentation of chapter 2 of *Tobira*—"Japanese Speech Styles."

TV Dramas and Gender

Studying idiomatic Japanese in the context of serialized dramas helps students recognize the function language plays in constructing gender identity. Like the pedagogical function of Japanese popular music described by Dorsey in this volume, dramas provide an engaging and comprehensible "text" that can enrich and enliven any language-learning curriculum.[9] Chapter 2 of *Tobira* outlines the particulars of male and female speech patterns, providing examples of pronouns, interjections, suffixes, and other linguistic elements used in daily conversation. Using dramas to illustrate gendered speech in interactions between characters not only develops students' familiarity with these expressions but also helps them recognize the way television contributes to the propagation of gender conventions and expectations through language.

Television dramas, as many critics note, serve an ideological function. Louis Althusser uses the term *interpellate* to describe the process by which media assigns an identity to viewers by "hailing" them into subjectivity.[10] Indeed, TV dramas play a central role in the interpellation process. Elizabeth Lozano and Arvind Singhal describe TV dramas as instruments of education with the power to reaffirm traditional social identities due in part to a melodramatic format that invites viewers to closely identify with main characters who embody favorable values.[11] Barbara J. Newton and Elizabeth B. Buck, moreover, argue that TV dramas serve as a "significant other" against which viewers "develop, maintain, and revise their self-concepts," including perceptions of gender roles.[12]

This is certainly the case with Japanese dramas. Ever since the 1970s, TV dramas have played a central role in defining gender expectations in Japan in large part by privileging female characters who display attributes and patterns of behavior in line with favored views of womanhood. During the 1970s, two basic types of TV drama—the "home drama," which focused on the experiences of the "reliable mother" archetype, and the "dramatic drama," which focused on the experiences of the "suffering woman"— reinforced the belief that women should first and foremost be good homemakers.[13] As opposed to the reliable mother, who found happiness and fulfillment with her place in the home, the suffering woman was often punished for her ambition to succeed in the male-centered professional world. As women became more active in the workplace in the 1980s, the focus of dramas shifted as well, continuing to reinforce traditional gender views by suggesting that women may pursue a professional life as long as it does not compromise their work in the home.[14] Even as female protagonists of dramas produced in the 1990s regularly had occupations outside of the home, again conforming to changes in social views of women in society, they were also rewarded in serials like *Tokyo Love Story* (1991) for displaying the characteristics associated with traditional views of motherhood as they balanced the demands of family and career.

Particularly effective in highlighting these gender ideals are "post-trendy dramas." Post-trendy dramas are serials produced after the crash of Japan's bubble economy in the early 1990s and include timeless classics like *Long Vacation* (1996). The story line for these dramas generally involves romantic relationships among young urban singles. Close attention to trendy locales and fashionable clothing and accessories helped to make them popular with postbubble audiences, particularly female viewers, as Japanese men generally do not watch TV dramas.[15] Post-trendy dramas, however, do not just provide escapist entertainment; according to surveys, a majority of viewers also watch dramas to "learn about life."[16]

Plot structure and character development are integral to the way dramas reinforce gender ideals. According to the renowned television producer Ōta Tōru, the creative mind behind *Long Vacation* and other popular shows, the predominantly female viewership of dramas influences the narrative makeup of post-trendy serials. Because female viewers watch dramas to identify with particular characters, Ōta claims, character development is prioritized in the storytelling process. In particular, Ōta suggests that female viewers show interest in the subtle differences in personality and temperament that distinguish one character from another.[17] For this reason, plots generally focus on the interaction between a spectrum of different female personas and only a handful of male character types. Due to the narrative constraints of episodic television, however, only one character can emerge as the protagonist from among these various female personas—often the one who most closely embodies ideal characteristics.

According to Ōta, these ideal characters reflect traditional views of women as dignified and virtuous, traditional but not old-fashioned, and alluring but not overly flirtatious and aggressive.[18] Dramas invite viewers to emotionally support and even identify with protagonists by contrasting their ideal attributes with their less than ideal supporting female characters and their generic male counterparts.

Due to the emphasis placed on language in the development of ideal protagonists, Japanese dramas provide a useful resource for merging language and cultural learning. Because the subtle linguistic nuances often lost in translation are the very things that distinguish one character from another, engaging series in the original allows for closer analysis of the speech styles that contribute to character development and the propagation of gender expectations. This chapter discusses how two iconic series in particular—*Long Vacation* and *Summer Snow* (2000)—provide examples of the function dialogue plays in characterization. With the vast amount of new dramas airing each year, serials can quickly become outdated. Therefore, these two relatively old examples are presented with an understanding of the need to historicize the social perspectives they present. At the same time, the cultural relevance of *Long Vacation* and *Summer Snow* endures, I suggest, because they illustrate some archetypal themes and narrative patterns common to Japanese dramas that continue to be recycled in current shows. The lasting influence of these shows is evident in their rankings as the seventh and sixth most popular television dramas of all time, respectively, according to a well-known Japanese drama website.[19]

Summer Snow

Summer Snow reinforces gender ideals through a mode of character development that is based on differences in speech patterns. A popular post-trendy drama that aired in 2000 on the Tokyo Broadcast System (TBS), *Summer Snow* involves a star-crossed romance between Yuki (Hirosue Ryōko), a young bank clerk who suffers from a heart condition, and Natsuō (Dōmoto Tsuyoshi), the owner of a neighborhood bicycle store. As the center of the melodramatic story line, Yuki possesses all the characteristics of the ideal female protagonist that Ōta outlines, and her femininity and refinement are demonstrated through her speech patterns in conversations with the male lead and supporting characters.

Close attention to the dialogue of *Summer Snow* reveals the function that gendered speech plays in the representation of Yuki as an ideal protagonist. The first few episodes of any drama series provide salient illustrations of the construction of gender identity because of the emphasis placed on defining characters and relationships early in the narrative. Two important scenes from early episodes provide an opportunity for students to practice recognizing the elements of gendered speech presented in the *Tobira* chapter. In a scene from the second episode, Yuki and Natsuō chat on a park bench, getting to know one another. The conversation highlights Yuki's femininity by contrasting the obliqueness of her speech with Natsuō's bluntness. Students watch the three-minute clip and identify elements of gendered speech mentioned in the *Tobira* chapter that are used by the two characters, referring to a transcript of the conversation. Examples include the contrasting use of the masculine pronoun おれ (*ore*) and the feminine あたし (*atashi*), softer sentence endings like でしょう (*deshō*) and けど (*kedo*) as opposed to the more masculine だよ (*da yo*), as well as ellipses that highlight the indirectness of feminine speech patterns. Class discussion then turns to the effects of these contrasting styles, specifically, the way they contribute to characterization and the representation of gender identity in the scene (fig. 8.1).

Figure 8.1. Natsuō (Dōmoto Tsuyoshi) and Yuki
(Hirosue Ryōko) in *Summer Snow* (2000).

Moreover, a scene from the first episode accentuates Yuki's ideal features by contrasting her with other female characters. Dramas often present less than ideal counterparts as foils in love triangles and other scenarios to underscore the protagonist's virtue. The contrast between these character types is reinforced through dialogue. In this scene, Yuki speaks with her colleague Misa (Kuninaka Ryōko) in the break room of the bank at which both women are employed as tellers. Misa's sole function in the narrative is to accentuate Yuki's virtue by offering an example of opposing characteristics of flirtatiousness, promiscuity, and impertinence through her behavior and particularly her speech. Students watch the clip, referring to a printed transcript of the exchange, and evaluate the two characters based on Ōta's definition of an ideal protagonist. Apart from Misa's cavalier tone, students may identify contrasts in the use of pronouns, sentence endings, and overall tone. Activities like these expose students to the use of gendered speech in a context that will also allow them to develop skills in deciphering media messages.

While melodramas like *Summer Snow* accentuate the virtue of protagonists, even dramas that showcase more complex female personas demonstrate the emphasis that dramas place on conformity. Viewer demand for characters with greater depth than the one-dimensional figures exemplified by Yuki has led producers to create protagonists who seemingly defy traditional ideals. However, at the same time these characters play a role in defining gender expectations because they model the process by which characters mature in a normalized pattern that leads back to family and marriage—patterns that are revealed through language usage.

Long Vacation

Long Vacation, which aired in 1996 on Fuji TV, highlights the role language plays in demonstrating characters' conformity with social expectations. The drama tells of a romance between a struggling pianist, Sena (Kimura Takuya), and a struggling model, Minami (Yamaguchi Tomoko). The story opens with Minami showing up at Sena's apartment in a traditional Japanese wedding kimono after being jilted at the altar by Sena's roommate. Although she dominates screen time, Minami at first resists identification as an ideal role model, appearing as crass and unrefined. However, her acting out, which is depicted largely by her modeling of male behavior, is revealed to be a superficial posture. As the story develops, her language becomes more self-reflective, illustrating the way female characters often conform to gender expectations as part of the maturation process (fig. 8.2).

Figure 8.2. Minami (Yamaguchi Tomoko) and
Sena (Kimura Takuya) in *Long Vacation* (1996)

Like Yuki in *Summer Snow,* Minami is defined in relation to other female characters, providing the catalyst for her eventual transformation. She is paired with the virtuous Ryōko (Matsu Takako) in a love triangle with Sena, ostensibly to identify Ryōko as the protagonist. In an effort to move beyond a simplistic character study, however, *Long Vacation* suggests that initial impressions can be deceiving. While Ryōko eventually proves to be one-dimensional, Minami develops the self-awareness that marks her as the real protagonist and the best match for Sena. The beginning of Minami's evolution as a character is captured in an argument between her and Sena in the first episode. Students view a clip of the argument and its subsequent resolution, paying attention to the way both Minami and Ryōko are defined in relation to Ōta's view of an ideal protagonist. In particular, they identify the language used to contrast Minami's crassness with Ryōko's refinement and virtue.

Sena: 本当に分からない人だなぁって。こんなに無神経だから、男に捨てられるんだよ。がさつだから。人の気持とか状況、分からないんだよ。

Minami: どういうこと？

Sena: 涼子ちゃんはね、あんたと違うの。 心の中がね 繊細な
の。 降ったばっかりの 雪でできてんだよ。人の足跡だらけに
なってないの。

Sena: You really have no clue. This is why you're always getting
dumped—you're insensitive and crude. You're oblivious to what is
going on and how people feel.

Minami: What do you mean?

Sena: You know, Ryōko is completely different from you. She's pure and
undefiled—like freshly fallen snow. Not trampled over by men.

While the scene ostensibly serves to present Ryōko as the embodiment of
the characteristics that Ōta identifies, class discussion can also focus on the
way this argument functions as a narrative device to prepare the ground for
Minami's development, making her transformation all the more dramatic.

The beginning of this transformation is implied in the next scene, where
Minami reflects on Sena's criticism while speaking with her friend Momo,
who is spending the night in her apartment. I use this scene to illustrate
another aspect of conversational Japanese covered in chapter 2 of *Tobira*,
abbreviations (短縮形). While not central to character development in the
same way that gendered speech is, forms like *to iu no wa* (*tte*) (というの
は／って), in this particular context, facilitate Minami's self-reflection in
her conversation with Momo. Students watch the scene, paying particular
attention to the function that -*tte* serves in Minami's self-realization as she
takes Sena's words to heart.

Minami: モモちゃん、寝た。モモちゃん、あたしって、がさつ。
あたしって、無神経。あたしって、「あんた、女だろう」って
感じ。

Minami: Momo-chan, are you sleeping? Momo-chan, am I really
insensitive? Am I really *rough*? Do I really not act like a proper woman?

This exchange highlights the role that -*tte* serves in Minami's self-
reflection, demonstrating the way she considers Sena's criticism and how
this introspection identifies her as a rounded character that can eventually
take on the attributes of a more ideal protagonist.

This is indeed the case, as we discover at the conclusion of the drama,
when Minami demonstrates her readiness for marriage. She takes on
the virtues that Ōta describes, becoming more modest and reserved and

revealing a deeper level of humanity and sensitivity as she encourages Sena to continue his career as a pianist even after he grows frustrated with his lack of success. I illustrate this point by showing the drama's final scene. In a reversal of the opening, in which Minami runs through Tokyo in traditional wedding attire, this time a tuxedo-clad Sena pursues Minami, who is appropriately dressed in a demure white outfit that seems to suit her better than the kimono she ungracefully wore in the opening. This time Minami stands placidly in place, waiting for Sena to find *her*. Having renounced her sassy ways, she has become a dignified and even passive protagonist who is a better fit for marriage (fig. 8.3).

Figure 8.3. Sena pursues Minami in *Long Vacation* (1996)

Although Minami provides a variation on the ideal protagonist that Ōta defines, she ultimately comes to embody many of the traditional characteristics that she initially resists. The roundness of her character arc, as demonstrated in her behavior and various conversational styles, serves the interpellation process because it highlights for audiences the means by which she eventually conforms to gender ideals. Certainly, most protagonists in Japanese dramas defy stereotypes to a certain degree, displaying an idiosyncratic depth that humanizes them in viewers' eyes. The fact that social pressure to conform to gender ideals trumps expressions of individuality, however, demonstrates the homogenizing function of TV dramas.

Reading the messages of TV dramas allows students to both develop skills in cultural analysis and to internalize the nuances of language usage.

Just as the process of learning colloquial speech patterns is aided by the context provided by dramas, so, too, is the development of the knowledge of and skills in decoding media enhanced by closely examining the way language is used in the development of characters that embody particular social values. Of course, *Summer Snow* and *Long Vacation* are just two possible examples of dramas that can be used in the classroom; locating instances of gendered speech in other television dramas is not difficult. Scanning the first episode of any character-based series will certainly yield many usable examples that can help students understand the nuances and cultural implications of the linguistic utterances that they encounter in everyday life in Japan.

Quiz Shows and Cultural Identity

In addition to TV dramas, quiz shows provide another medium through which to introduce the role that language plays in the ideological impulse of Japanese television. Quiz shows illustrate examples of vernacular speech presented in *Tobira* and other texts while helping students understand the way media standardize the use of the national language to reinforce the foundations of a shared cultural identity. As with dramas, the conventions of quiz shows are constantly recycled, making the study of any one particular show relevant to the understanding of the larger langue of the genre.

The role that TV plays in simulating national unity has been well documented. In his work on Japanese television, Andrew Painter suggests that TV programs create an in-group, or *uchi*, that viewers are invited to join.[20] They do this by presenting a quasi-intimate atmosphere, emphasizing themes related to national, cultural, or racial cohesiveness.[21] Morning news shows broadcast from Tokyo, for instance, reinforce the perception of national unity by including a series of reports from correspondents throughout the country, who discuss the weather and local events in the various locales. The quick cuts between these reports collapse time and space, Painter suggests, linking the diverse regions of the country into a single whole.

Yet, if morning shows unify Japan by underscoring the temporal and spatial continuity that links viewers, quiz shows emphasize a common cultural basis in the national language. Although they are intended for native speakers, quiz shows can supplement textbook instruction in *Tobira* and other sources. Along with illustrating the proper use of abbreviations, neologisms, and idiomatic constructions, quiz shows reveal the function language plays in the formulation of an "imagined community" of Japanese speakers. Indeed, Andrew Roy Miller argues that the Japanese language has served a central function in the formulation of an identity for Japan in the postwar period because it was one of the few "innocuous" cultural elements to survive the democratization process.[22] Contemporary quiz shows, of which there are an abundant number on TV, reinforce the bonds of national unity by delving into the complexities of the national language and appropriating viewers as learners, even allowing them to participate in standardizing new developments in idiomatic expression.

Tamori's Japonica Logos, a quiz show that ran from 2005 to 2008, illustrates the way educational programming forms a community centered on the national language. The interactive format of the show provides a useful supplement for chapter 2 of *Tobira* and other texts that focus on colloquial Japanese. Although new episodes of the show are no longer airing, past installments are still readily available online and through other sources. The format of the show is similar to the format of all quiz shows. Each hour-long segment brings together a panel of celebrities, a pair of hosts, and a language specialist—all native speakers—who discuss different issues related to language usage. The well-known and ubiquitous Tamori—a *manzai* comedian who is famous for his daytime show *Waratte mo ii tomo* (*It's All Right to Laugh*)—is a permanent fixture on the celebrity panel. As with morning programming, the format of *Tamori's Japonica Logos* appropriates audience members in the learning process, utilizing celebrities as proxies for the larger national community. These celebrities include actors, singers, and more than a few comedians whose improvisational skills keep the mood light. Indeed, spontaneity is key to building a sense of camaraderie among participants. Playful banter in which contestants chide those who are unsuccessful in answering questions stimulates interaction and reinforces the bonds of the group. The friendly competition and self-deprecation of the contestants cut celebrities down to size, a process known as *tōshindai*, leveling the distinctions between audience and celebrity as all participate in the learning process together (fig. 8.4).

Figure 8.4. The set of *Tamori's Japonica Logos* (2005–08)

The key to building unity is the show's treatment of the national language. The interactivity of the program allows Japanese viewers to participate in the standardization of this central component of national identity. Audience members are recruited in the learning of idiomatic expressions that are frequently used in daily conversation yet are often difficult to master. Episodes focus on the origins of various aspects of the language—including proverbs (*kotowaza*) and maxims (*meigen*)—while indexing the evolution of the everyday vernacular through attention to abbreviations (*ryakugo*) and neologisms (*nyūgo*). The overall focus is on accentuating the uniqueness of the language and its role in defining a cultural identity.

The show's focus on idiomatic Japanese makes it a perfect resource to combine linguistic and cultural learning for non-native speakers. Students benefit from the instruction offered by the program while also learning to identify the way media regulates language usage. One particular episode elucidates two forms of speech that are covered in Chapter 2 of *Tobira*: abbreviations and neologisms. Focusing on new additions to the national language, the show helps students recognize the way media monitors linguistic trends and sets the bounds of the community of Japanese speakers by cataloguing new additions to the national lexicon.

Figure 8.5. A scene from *Tamori's Japonica Logos* in which
participants discuss the neologism SKY (sūpā kūki yomenai,
really can't read the scene) (2005–08)

The episode on abbreviations, for instance, showcases commonly used
ryakugo, introducing viewers to expressions like JK (*joshi kōsei*, a female
high school student), KY (*kūki yomenai*, can't read the scene), and SKY
(*sūpā kūki yomenai,* really can't read the scene), while discussing the role
they play in everyday communication (see fig. 8.5).

The episode on neologisms, moreover, introduces students to new
developments in idiomatic Japanese while allowing them to see the role
media play in its standardization. Audience participation provides viewers
with a sense of ownership of the national language, which is evaluated
and amended through their contributions. During the episode, panelists
consider words sent in by audience members and determine whether they
should be included in the lexicon. Audience members are invited to appear
on the show to introduce their entries, which are re-created in dramatic
renditions with actors playing the roles of the individuals responsible
for coining the terms. The renditions are easy to follow and invariably
include subtitles, which help students grasp the narrative. Following the
excerpt, the official definition and part of speech of the word is presented,
along with information about its everyday usage, as well as example
expressions. At this point, the linguistic expert comments on the term's

suitability in reference to similar Japanese expressions. For example, for the entry "_____ *teki na samusingu*" (something like_____) the expert cites the novelist Akutagawa Ryūnosuke's expression *bungeiteki na amari ni bungeiteki na* ("literary, all too literary") as a precedent in the Japanese language. To close the show, the celebrity panel votes to see if the expression should be officially recognized as a new word. In this way, *Tamori's Japaonica Logos* demonstrates the use of idiomatic expressions such as abbreviations and neologisms that are presented in *Tobira* and other texts, helping students develop sensitivity to trends in the everyday vernacular even though they might not be expected to use all these expressions in daily conversation. By watching these programs, students do not just learn idiomatic Japanese; they also study the process by which media regulate linguistic activity and reinforce the status of the national language as a central component of a Japanese identity.

Other Japanese Language Resources

Similarly, serialized language workshops on NHK provide a useful resource for content-based language courses. These shows can complement lesson plans in preexisting texts but also can be used as part of an original course that focuses on the function of the Japanese language in media. Part of the challenge of designing content-based courses from the ground up is creating original activities and assignments. Language workshops offer a variety of activities of varying lengths that engage student learning while providing examples of media's function in standardizing Japanese. The individual installments of programs provide the basis for regular activities to help students warm up at the start of class or to grab their attention between sections of the lesson plan. *Kotoba Ojisan no Nattoku Nihongo Juku* (Mr. Japanese's Language Course), a language series designed for native speakers, offers a number of concise lessons that correct common errors in usage while presenting tips on how to speak appropriately in particular contexts. Due to the interactive format of the show, these lessons are delivered in an engaging and accessible manner that advanced students can easily follow. Each five-minute installment of *Kotoba Ojisan* focuses on a specific idiomatic or grammatical concept, providing a skit that introduces the concept, a specialist who explains its correct usage, and opportunities to practice. Examples include the correct use of colloquial expressions like "I see" (*naru hodo*) in daily conversation (see fig. 8.6).

Figure 8.6. A scene from *Kotoba Ojisan no Nattoku Nihongo Juku* (2006)

Finally, *Nihongo De Kurasō* (Getting Along in Japanese) and *Shin-Nihongo De Kurasō* (All New Getting Along in Japanese), like *Kotoba Ojisan*, provide tutorials in Japanese conversation in a slightly longer format that are designed for nonnative learners. Together they offer dozens of twenty-minute episodes that instruct viewers on the appropriate way to ask questions, pay compliments, and express gratitude in daily conversation. Like *Kotoba Ojisan*, these programs explicate the correct use of the expression and provide opportunities for students to practice in an engaging and entertaining format. Excerpts from these programs can be used in advanced Japanese courses as a warmup exercise presenting one isolated language point before the class delves into the main part of the lesson.

Conclusion

As this chapter has argued, television media allow instructors to synthesize language and cultural learning in content-based courses. Dramas and quiz shows model the use of grammatical principles and idiomatic phrases while helping students develop a deeper appreciation for the way popular media influence social views of gender ideals and formulate a shared sense of Japaneseness. Because language plays a central role in reinforcing these messages, content-based courses that deal with the language of television media are able to provide greater insight into the ideological significance of popular media than courses in which the cultural effect of language is not considered.

However, when planning content-based courses centered on television programming, instructors must take into account the accessibility of these media forms. Japanese television—particularly TV dramas—is readily available online from sites that stream media or from a variety of vendors. The elephant in the room for any discussion of television media is the issue of copyright. The growth in Internet resources for downloading media has dramatically increased the accessibility of Japanese programming for audiences outside of Japan while raising questions about the legality of the practice. In 2012 the Japanese government passed stricter laws against downloading music and video in Japan, and in 2014 it began a campaign to limit the uploading of Japanese manga and anime on the Internet for public viewing overseas, a practice that is widespread throughout Asia.[23]

Gray areas emerge, however, in the question of Japanese television dramas and other programming, which are not mentioned as a concern of government officials mainly because they have been viewed widely in legal and semilegal forms for decades in South Korea, Hong Kong, Taiwan, and other countries. Many argue that television broadcasts are part of the public domain or at the very least available for consumption in accordance with fair use laws. The legality of sharing and distributing Japanese television has been debated at least since the 1990s, when video CD (VCD) technology—a forerunner to the DVD format—led to the rampant bootlegging of Hollywood movies, Japanese dramas, and other forms of media throughout Asia. Yet, even at that time, as Kelly Hu suggests, VCD marketing of Japanese dramas in Asia existed in an "ambivalent sphere" located between a "normalized industry" and an "underground industry" as Japanese government officials turned a blind eye to the issue.[24]

What is certain is that technology will continue to challenge and in some cases transform the way we understand copyright laws concerning media, as was the case with videocassette recorders (VCRs) in the 1980s and digital video recorders (DVRs) in the 2000s. Considering the numerous benefits of using Japanese programming in language and cultural learning, as well as the history of ambiguity surrounding the rightful use of television media, does the incorporation of programming downloaded or viewed online in an educational, nonprofit context constitute the ethical and fair use of these resources? In the end, this is a question that individual instructors will need to carefully consider as they plan their courses.

Notes

[1] Fred Genesee, *Integrating Language and Content: Lessons from Immersion*, National Center for Research on Cultural Diversity and Second Language Learning, Educational Practice Reports, no. 11 (Washington, DC: Center for Applied Linguistics, 1994), 1.

[2] Mariko Wei, "Content-Based Instruction: Teaching Japanese Business and Current Affairs to American Students," *International Journal of the Humanities* 3, no. 1 (2005–6): 73.

[3] Fredricka Stoller, "Content-Based Instruction: A Shell for Language Teaching or a Framework for Strategic Language and Content Learning?," plenary address delivered at TESOL (Teachers of English to Speakers of Other Languages) 2002, Salt Lake City, Utah, April 2002, 1.

[4] Myriam Met, *Content-Based Instruction: Defining Terms, Making Decisions* (College Park, MD: National Foreign Language Center, 1999), 7.

[5] James Dorsey, "Performing Gender in the Prisonhouse of a (Foreign) Language: Blending Japanese Language Learning and Cultural Studies," in this volume.

[6] Henry A. Giroux, *Disturbing Pleasures: Learning Popular Culture* (New York: Routledge, 1994), 121.

[7] Kevin Tavin, "Wrestling with Angels, Searching for Ghosts: Towards a Critical Pedagogy of Visual Culture," *Studies in Art Education* 44, no. 3 (2003): 197.

[8] Gisela Hoecherl-Alden, "Connecting Language to Content: Second Language Literature Instruction at the Intermediate Level," *Foreign Language Annals* 39, no. 2 (2006): 244.

[9] Dorsey, "Performing Gender in the Prisonhouse."

[10] Louis Althusser, *Essays on Ideology* (London: Verso, 1984), 11.

[11] Elizabeth Lozano and Arvind Singhal, "Melodramatic Television Serials: Mythical Narratives for Education," *Communications: The European Journal of Communication* 18, no. 1 (1993): 117–18.

[12] Barbara J. Newton and Elizabeth B. Buck, "Television as a Significant Other: Its Relationship to Self-Descriptors in Five Countries," *Journal of Cross-Cultural Psychology* 16, no. 3 (1985): 295.

[13] Hilaria Gössmann, "New Role Models for Men and Women: Gender in Japanese TV Dramas," in *Japan Pop! Inside the World of Japanese Popular Culture*, ed. Timothy J. Craig (London: M. E. Sharp, 2000), 208.

[14] Ibid.

[15] Ōta Tōru, "Producing (Post-)Trendy TV Dramas," trans. Nasu Madori, in *Feeling Asian Modernities: Transnational Consumption of Japanese TV Dramas,* ed. Kōichi Iwabuchi (Hong Kong: Hong Kong University Press, 2004), 69–86; Andrew Painter, "Japanese Daytime Television, Popular Culture, and Ideology," *Journal of Japanese Studies* 19, no. 2 (1993): pp. 295–325.

[16] Gössman, "New Role Models," 207.

[17] Ota, "Producing (Post-)Trendy TV Dramas," 71.

[18] Ibid., 72.

[19] See J-Drama.com, http://www.jdorama.com/topdramas.htm.

[20] Painter, "Japanese Daytime Television," 296.

[21] Ibid., 297.

[22] Andrew Roy Miller, *Japan's Modern Myth: The Language and Beyond* (New York: Weatherhill, 1982), 7.

[23] "Japan Plans Campaign to Curb Manga, Anime Copyright Violations Abroad," *Japan Times*, July 27, 2014, http://www.japantimes.co.jp/news/2014/07/28/national/crime-legal/japan-plans-campaign-curb-manga-anime-copyright-violations-abroad.

[24] Kelly Hu, "Chinese Re-makings of Pirated VCDs of Japanese TV Dramas," in *Feeling Asian Modernities: Transnational Consumption of Japanese TV Dramas,* ed. Kōichi Iwabuchi (Hong Kong: Hong Kong University Press, 2004), 213.

Works Cited

Althusser, Louis. *Essays on Ideology*. London: Verso, 1984.

Genesee, Fred. *Integrating Language and Content: Lessons from Immersion.* National Center for Research on Cultural Diversity and Second Language Learning, Educational Practice Reports, no 11. Washington, DC: Center for Applied Linguistics, 1994.

Giroux, Henry A. *Disturbing Pleasures: Learning Popular Culture*. New York: Routledge, 1994.

Gössmann, Hilaria. "New Role Models for Men and Women: Gender in Japanese TV Dramas." In *Japan Pop! Inside the World of Japanese Popular Culture*, edited by Timothy J. Craig, 207–21. London: M. E. Sharp, 2000.

Hoecherl-Alden, Gisela. "Connecting Language to Content: Second Language Literature Instruction at the Intermediate Level." *Foreign Language Annals* 39, no. 2 (2006): 244–54.

Hu, Kelly. "Chinese Re-makings of Pirated VCDs of Japanese TV Dramas." In *Feeling Asian Modernities: Transnational Consumption of Japanese TV Dramas,* edited by Kōichi Iwabuchi, 205–26. Hong Kong: Hong Kong University Press, 2004.

"Japan Plans Campaign to Curb Manga, Anime Copyright Violations Abroad." *Japan Times*, July 27, 2014, http://www.japantimes.co.jp/news/2014/07/28/national/crime-legal/japan-plans-campaign-curb-manga-anime-copyright-violations-abroad.

Long Vacation. Prod. Ōta Tōru. Perf. Kimura Takuya and Yamaguchi Tomoko. Fuji TV, 1996. DVD.

Lozano, Elizabeth, and Arvind Singhal. "Melodramatic Television Serials: Mythical Narratives for Education." *Communications: The European Journal of Communication* 18, no. 1 (1993): 115–27.

Met, Myriam. *Content-Based Instruction: Defining Terms, Making Decisions.* College Park, MD: National Foreign Language Center, 1999.

Miller, Andrew Roy. *Japan's Modern Myth: The Language and Beyond*. New York: Weatherhill, 1982.

Mr. Japanese's Language Course [*Kotoba Ojisan No Nattoku Nihongojuku*]. NHK, 2006. DVD.

Newton, Barbara J., and Elizabeth B. Buck. "Television as a Significant Other: Its Relationship to Self-Descriptors in Five Countries." *Journal of Cross-Cultural Psychology* 16, no. 3 (1985): 289–312.

Nihongo de Kurasō (Getting Along in Japanese). NHK, 1999.

Ōta Tōru. "Producing (Post-)Trendy TV Dramas," translated by Nasu Madori. In *Feeling Asian Modernities: Transnational Consumption of Japanese TV Dramas,* edited by Kōichi Iwabuchi, 69–86. Hong Kong: Hong Kong University Press, 2004.

Painter, Andrew. "Japanese Daytime Television, Popular Culture, and Ideology." *Journal of Japanese Studies* 19, no. 2 (1993): 295–325.

Shin Nihongo de Kurasō (All New Getting Along in Japanese). NHK, 2004.

Stoller, Fredricka. "Content-Based Instruction: A Shell for Language Teaching or a Framework for Strategic Language and Content Learning?" Plenary address delivered at TESOL (Teachers of English to Speakers of Other Languages) 2002, Salt Lake City, Utah, April 2002.

Summer Snow. Prod. Itō Kazuhiro. Perf. Dōmoto Tsuyoshi and Hirosue Ryōko. Tokyo Broadcasting Station, 2000. DVD.

Tamori's Japonica Logos. Perf. Tamori. Fuji TV, 2005. DVD.

Tavin, Kevin. "Wrestling with Angels, Searching for Ghosts: Towards a Critical Pedagogy of Visual Culture." *Studies in Art Education* 44, no. 3 (2003): 197–213.

Tobira: Gateway to Advanced Japanese Learning through Content and Media. Oxford: Kurosio Publishers, 2008.

Tokyo Love Story. Prod. Ōta Tōru. Perf. Oda Yuji and Suzuki Honami. Fuji TV, 1991. DVD.

Wei, Mariko. "Content-Based Instruction: Teaching Japanese Business and Current Affairs to American Students." *International Journal of the Humanities* 3, no. 1 (2005–6), 74–79.

9

Performing Gender in the Prisonhouse of a (Foreign) Language

Blending Japanese Language Learning and Cultural Studies

James Dorsey

The fundamental challenge facing progressive educators within the current age of neo-liberalism is to provide the conditions for students to address how knowledge is related to the power of both self-definition and social agency. Central to such a challenge is providing students with the skills, knowledge, and authority they need to inquire into and act upon what it means to live in a radical multicultural democracy, to recognize anti-democratic forms of power, and to fight deeply rooted injustices in a society and world founded on systemic economic, racial, and gender inequalities.

— Henry A. Giroux

Introduction

Most educators would associate Giroux's call for a radically progressive pedagogy with classes centered on critical theory, classes in which students strive to master the concepts of Marxist, feminist, postcolonial, or postmodernist discourse by reading about, discussing, and then applying the paradigms to historical, literary, or social phenomena.[1] While this approach is important in the quest for greater equality and social justice, I would like to explore here a format in which similar goals are pursued in a somewhat less analytical but far more experiential format, one in which class participants undergo a process of socialization while simultaneously reflecting critically on it. In an intermediate Japanese class conducted during a study abroad program in Japan, I have experimented with blending language acquisition and gender studies through an engagement with popular music. In learning to speak culturally appropriate Japanese, students are simultaneously socialized as gendered subjectivities in a new linguistic and cultural environment; this course attempts to prod students to reflect on the ways in which entry into that, or any, semiotic system inevitably inscribes on them a worldview as well. The assumption is that consciously monitoring the socialization process at work while acquiring a foreign language as an adult will make them more sensitive to the manner in which the acquisition of their native language as a child also shaped their subjectivity.

While Japanese popular culture is the realm in which this agenda is pursued, the goal is not so much to nurture understanding of Japanese culture per se (though students do learn to recognize archetypes and tropes unique to Japan). Rather, the purpose is to reexperience the way gendered subjectivities are constructed in the acquisition of language. As such it does not fall neatly into any single one of the paradigmatic approaches to the teaching of popular culture outlined by Sally McLaren and Alwyn Spies in their insightful analysis in this volume. Of the five approaches they outline, "'poco pop'—which takes a postcolonial view of the study of Japanese popular culture by including cultural studies theory," is perhaps closest.[2] My course, however, differs in two important respects: (1) it is designed to offer an *experience* of gender construction rather than a traditional study of it, and (2) it encourages some degree of introspection in hopes that students will understand something of the processes that have shaped them in their acquisition of their native tongues. Ultimately, the object of scrutiny is the self as fabricated by linguistic socialization.

Theoretical and Pedagogical Underpinnings

In order to highlight issues of gender, the course discussed here employs "authentic materials" (by which I mean simply texts, broadly conceived, *not* created explicitly for language learning). The material is drawn from popular culture, primarily popular music. The incorporation of such materials into a language class raises various issues, and a brief discussion of them will highlight the way theory and practice meet in the course in question. Foreign language acquisition scholar William S. Armour quite rightly warns against an acritical adoption of material from Japanese pop culture. In addition to the danger of inadvertently turning students into *consumers* entangled in the web of Japan's soft power, the use of "authentic" texts from popular culture also runs the risk of confusing students through the introduction of highly idiosyncratic locutions and vocabulary. Simply put, because an expression comes from "real Japanese," students are prone to privilege it above textbook Japanese, which they often perceive as stilted. Without careful coaching, Armour warns, students may adopt vocabulary or phrases more appropriate for *yakuza* gangsters or seventeenth-century samurai—and all because it appeared in "authentic" texts.[3]

Armour is careful, though, to guard against a militantly prescriptive approach to the Japanese language as taught to nonnative speakers. There is a tendency to "police" the language used by students, categorically rejecting the use of certain phrases or speech patterns simply because they are "not proper" (*tadashiku nai*). The phrase "proper Japanese," of course, most often indicates the somewhat sterile speech of the educated middle class residing in the greater Tokyo metropolitan area. In an attempt to replace this unnecessarily narrow and prescriptive conception of appropriate language use, Armour evokes a concept gaining acceptance in Japanese language teaching circles: *kyōsei gengo toshite no Nihongo*, "Japanese as a communal language."[4] The phrase represents a nuanced and strategic reconceptualization of the pedagogical endeavor. Miyo Junpei and Kyung Hee Chung explain the conceptual shift as follows: "Rather than adopt the conventional assumption that there exists some normative 'proper Japanese' that is to be taught to learners, 'Japanese as a communal language' sees language as something formed through use as a means of two-way communication between learners and Japanese nationals, both with equal standing as members of society."[5] In this conception of the target language, it is not the case that expert native speakers prescribe the parameters of acceptable speech, but rather a situation in which the target language is a matter of constant negotiation and adjustment by all engaged parties. Here there would, presumably, be room for a negotiated incorporation of idiosyncratic locutions discovered in the texts of popular culture.

The latter conception of Japanese is surely more democratic and accommodating of our multicultural world and thus in keeping with Giroux's vision of a progressive educational agenda. Still it is important to acknowledge that even with the abandonment of prescriptive conceptions in favor of communally built models of language, foreign-language learning continues to construct subjectivities inflected in very specific ways. Wherever rules or conventions hold sway—and they must hold sway for communication to take place—certain patterns of thinking and perception will dominate others. That is to say, even *kyōsei gengo to shite no Nihongo* (Japanese as a communal language) is, at some level, *kyōsei gengo to shite no Nihongo* ("Japanese as a coercive language," with the Chinese characters for *kyōsei* changed from 共生 to the homophonous 強制). This applies, of course, to all languages. As we have no choice but to accept the predispositions and tendencies of a language if we are to communicate in it, we are perhaps best served by striving to observe how that process works and what are its results. As our first languages are acquired while we are infants without the capacity for critical analysis, the process of learning a second language as an adult becomes an ideal opportunity to experience and reflect on the ways in which a linguistic medium shapes thought and subjectivity.

Gender, with the hierarchies and inequalities that too often are attached to it, is one dimension of subjectivity that language acquisition inscribes on its users. In "Performative Acts and Gender Constitution," the philosopher Judith Butler outlines a useful paradigm for conceiving of the construction and perpetuation of gendered subjectivities. In this seminal essay she posits that "the ground of gender identity is the stylized repetition of acts through time, and not a seemingly seamless identity."[6] Furthermore, as the very title of the essay suggests, to Butler that "stylized repetition of acts" is a type of performance in the sense of being both codified and nonreferential. Performance is a key word and concept for this study because it is an integral part of second language acquisition; learners embrace the "lines" of others, repeating them in regulated (codified) contexts. And, if we are to accept even in soft terms the paradigm established by Ferdinand de Saussure, words and language are nonreferential, functioning instead because of the conventions that have emerged for and through their use.[7] All of this is to say that second-language acquisition inscribes, or reinscribes, a gendered subjectivity in learners through the repeated performance of stylized (linguistic) acts. If we are to heed Giroux's call for educators to "provide the conditions for students to address how knowledge is related to the power of both self-definition and social agency," then we must interrogate the process.

Background for, and Context of, the Course

Such an interrogation is part of the intermediate-level Japanese language course I regularly teach. It is offered as part of Dartmouth College's language study abroad program based on the campus of the Kanda University of International Studies (Kanda Gaigo Daigaku) in Chiba Prefecture, thirty-five minutes by train from Tokyo station. The ten-week program offers a course load and credit opportunities equivalent to any academic quarter on the home campus. Students take three classes, with classroom instruction running at approximately eighteen to twenty hours per week. They live with Japanese host families. Prerequisites for participation in the program include one academic year of Japanese language study and a course titled Introduction to Japanese Culture, a broad overview of Japanese cultural history with a focus on canonical literary texts (taught in English).

The course introduced here takes place during that study abroad program. It runs simultaneously with, but independent of, a more conventional language class based on the second volume of the *Yookoso!* textbook series. In a typical week, students spend thirteen to fifteen classroom hours working through the material in that textbook, and an additional five hours per week in the course introduced here today. In terms of language acquisition goals, the course is intended to:

- Provide students with loosely structured opportunities to use the grammar and vocabulary they have learned (or are learning) in more conventional language classes and through daily life in Japan with Japanese-speaking families

- Offer structured practice for discussions and conversations that students later pursue both formally and informally with Japanese host families and/or college students on the campus of the host institution

- Acclimate students to "real" Japanese, coach them in listening through the "static" of unfamiliar grammar and vocabulary, and introduce them to techniques for keeping a conversation going

In terms of literary and cultural studies, the course attempts to:

- Introduce "texts" (broadly conceived) for literary, cultural, and linguistic analysis

- Provide "texture" to a cultural history of postwar Japan

- Introduce primary (i.e. Japanese language) sources for a consideration of love, gender, and marriage as they are represented in popular culture

- Prompt students to consider the linguistic roots of gender and romance

- Encourage students to think critically and creatively about the processes by which language constructs gendered identities

The course takes as its primary "texts" mainly Japanese popular songs dealing with love, marriage, sex, and gender. These are divided into four categories that represent, in a loose way, both a chronology of postwar Japanese cultural history and four distinct musical genres, each with a (linguistic, cultural, and emotional) "grammar" all its own: enka/"oldies" (1945–65), folk/"new music" (1965–72), J-pop/Idols (1972–present), and other. The time periods associated with these genres are, of course, open to debate and are probably more a reflection of the course's pedagogical goals than the actual evolution of popular music trends. The majority of time is spent on the folk and new music genres popular in the late 1960s and the early 1970s. The reasons for this include (1) the genre's emphasis on a message presented in the lyrics and sung in a style relatively easy to understand and (2) the political and ideological concerns of the postwar generation that came of age in those years (reservations about the US-Japan Joint Security Treaty, or Anpō, the opposition to Japan's complicity in the US war in Vietnam, increased awareness of the oppression of minorities and women, etc.) and prompted song themes conducive to lyrical analysis.

The course incorporates some activities from traditional language study, but it differs in its inclusion of English-language readings on cultural studies (particularly the use of popular music in it), historical context, performer careers, popular music theory, and so on. Approximately 20 percent of class meetings are conducted in English; here students synthesize the "raw material" encountered in Japanese with the supplementary English-language readings. Greatly simplified, these same ideas are later reviewed in target-language (i.e. Japanese) sessions.

Sample Unit 1: Izumiya Shigeru's "I Love Ya" ("Ai shite ru yo," 1971)

Izumiya Shigeru (b. 1948) is well known in contemporary Japan as a character actor specializing in roles reflecting his public persona: brash, hardheaded, and uninterested in social niceties. Those over the age of fifty, however, will remember him also as a folk singer famous for the 1972 hit "Shunka shūtō" (The Four Seasons), a song so beloved that Izumiya was invited to revive it for a performance on the 2013 *Kōhaku uta gassen* (New Year's Eve songfest), a popular show sponsored annually by the national broadcasting company NHK.

"I Love Ya" ("Ai shite ru yo," 1971) is not nearly as well known a song but, delivered in the inimitable Izumiya style, it is easily recognizable as being sung by him. As the title suggests, this is a love song, but with a twist. The male protagonist chooses to express his love by releasing the object of his affections from many of the duties and restrictions conventionally leveled on women. First he insists that she need not be a good cook or do much laundry; later in the song he gives her permission to snore, grind her teeth, and even pass wind. His willingness to make these concessions is offered as proof that he is "totally in love with her from the bottom of his heart."[8]

The song works well in this course because, first of all, it offers some useful language patterns for review and practice in the classroom. Clearly the pattern for granting permission (*~te mo ii*) is a useful one for students beginning life with a Japanese host family, and it is repeated five times in the song as the protagonist gives permission for his love to snore, pass wind, and so on. The repetition of this pattern lends itself also to review and practice of the related structures of prohibition and insistence: *~te wa ikenai* (one "must not do X") and *~nakute wa ikenai* (one "must do X"). These patterns are particularly helpful for students newly settled in Japanese households. There are other items to pick up for review: the contractions (*ai shichatte ru*), the form for expressing personal desire (*~tai*), and the potential form (*~rarenai*).

More important, the song provides an easily comprehensible "text" and opportunity for students to experience the ways in which gender conventions are perpetuated in the process by which we acquire language, whether it be our first or second. In the guise of practicing the pattern for giving permission, apparent in the lyrics, I invite students to compose a few additional verses for the male protagonist to sing to his love. Their contributions often overlap extensively, and they offer in Japanese sentences that, in English, would read "It is okay if you use the credit card a lot," "It is okay if you don't do much cleaning," and "It is okay if you don't wash the dishes." As a follow-up activity students compose a similar song from a woman's perspective. Again, student contributions are often identical; their female protagonists grant permission to make only a mediocre salary, to watch sports on TV, and to go days without a shower. "Performing" the persona of this forgiving woman they even claim indifference to their male counterpart's loss of hair, and all as testaments to their enduring love. These sentences are composed in Japanese, in keeping with the language acquisition goals of the class.

In this phase of the unit students "perform" according to conventions with which they are intimately familiar, though they may never have been conscious of that fact. In the process of struggling to master the Japanese vocabulary and grammar new to them, and intensely aware that they do not fully understand their cultural context, their critical faculties are temporarily short-circuited and they rely heavily on the clues in the material before them. It is for these reasons, I believe, that they fall easily into a regurgitation of gender stereotypes, albeit negated (i.e. their song-writing alter egos offer their imagined partners permission to act in contradiction to the stereotypes). At some point after these exercises, and usually in one of the class sessions conducted in English, I point out to them how utterly unaware we are of our absorption of the "social code," or conventions, that we rely on when we improvise according to the models offered in Izumiya's song. I suggest to them that they have surely embraced, unconsciously, many other ideologically significant ideas as they acquired their first languages.

Lest students then categorically denounce the song as reliant on sexist stereotypes, I remind them that without the existence of such a code the protagonist would be unable to express his emotions. That is to say, the protagonist of the song can present himself as "progressive" and his love as genuine only because there are very clear gender rules in society that are available for the breaking. It is in this sense that any "communal language" (*kyōsei gengo*) is also a "coercive language" (again a *kyōsei gengo*). A speaker is coerced by the community into accepting certain social and linguistic conventions in order to communicate.

The societal rules, or conventions, that underpin the protagonist's expression can be extrapolated by reading between the lines. The third verse's granting of permission for his partner to grind her teeth, snore, and pass wind makes sense only in the context of societal conventions that frown on such behavior, particularly in women. The extraction of those social conventions from the utterances in the song does not usually require much coaching, and the basic idea of it can even be articulated in Japanese that intermediate-level students can understand. That articulation may take the primitive form of sentences such as "The 'I' in the song says that it is okay if she passes wind. Behind that statement exists the belief that women should generally not pass wind" (*uta no naka no "boku" wa "onara o shite mo ii" to iimasu. Sono kotoba no ura ni onna no hito wa onara o shite wa ikenai, to iu kangaekata ga arimasu*). Though not particularly subtle or eloquent, students understand the point and are then able to express a similar analysis concerning other gender conventions that underpin the song.

There is one final dimension of the song that similarly reveals language as a double-edged sword, one both empowering and coercive. This point revolves around the central grammatical point of the unit: the granting of permission. The class approaches the issue through a very simple question: "Is the protagonist of the song a kind person?" Most students will immediately answer in the affirmative. He does, after all, indicate that the object of his affection need not behave as society might dictate. With some prodding, however, a few will attempt to object on the grounds that granting permission implies that the bestower has that authority. We hold this discussion in Japanese, and therefore the articulation is never terribly sophisticated. Nevertheless, the point is eventually made in sentences like "The protagonist in the song said that she didn't have to do the laundry, but even if he did not say that, she doesn't have to do the laundry." Granted, this is not the same as stating the underlying abstract point: the song assumes it is a man's prerogative to delegate his partner's household responsibilities or to dictate what social conventions his partner may ignore. Nevertheless, the specific objection to the man's granting of permission is sufficient to reveal that the gender hierarchy remains in place even in this song's apparent attempt to question it. In an English-language class at some later point in the course the class discusses both what the widely acknowledged (if not necessarily accepted) social conventions are that make this expression of love possible and how even the rejection of one set of stereotypically gendered actions (cooking, cleaning, etc.)

requires the acceptance of another (men decide who has responsibility for household duties). Language is a double-edged sword, empowering but coercive, too.

Sample Unit 2: Souvenir Hand Towels for Husbands and Wives

A second unit in the course builds on these themes using a set of hand towels (*tenugui*) sold in the souvenir shop at the Kegon Falls in Tochigi Prefecture. They are clearly meant to be purchased by either husbands or wives as a gift to bring back from a vacation to the spouse left at home. In the first stage of this unit we read and discuss the hand towel designed to please the wife left at home. Covered with a small image and lots of print, the theme is declared in the title: "I have a hard time saying it to your face, but … 'thanks' to my wife." What follows are five statements of gratitude issued by the husband to his wife. These include: "Thank you for waking me up every morning at the same time and for waiting up for me even when it gets late," "Thank you for letting me play golf on my days off and for keeping in mind my bosses and colleagues," and "Thank you for keeping the house clean and for putting a fine shine on my shoes."

In terms of language acquisition, the hand towel provides an opportunity to learn or review many words related to everyday life in a Japanese household. It also includes numerous examples of both verbs of receiving and verbal gerunds employed to form a compound sentence. More specifically, here it uses the gerund to combine the act with the word of thanks: *konna ore ni tsuite kite kurete arigatō* (Thank you for coming along with [i.e. marrying] me). Living with Japanese host families that tend to pamper them, our exchange students find many opportunities to express their thanks with these sentence patterns.

Having recently completed the unit centered on the song "I Love Ya," described above, students would be cautious not to again fall prey to the temptation to allude to stereotypical gendered roles in a household. For this reason the assignment here is to ask their homestay family members to compose a parallel set of statements of gratitude, this time spoken by a wife to her husband. Students are instructed to withhold all details on the sample they had previously studied in class, and to offer nothing more than a vague description of the assignment.

The sentences collected are shared with the class as a whole. While the grammatical structures chosen vary slightly, much of the gratitude expressed to imaginary husbands falls neatly into several categories:

providing monetarily for the family, enduring a trying commute, persevering at some particularly challenging dimension of the job, and so on. It turns out that these correspond closely to those printed on the other handtowel, titled "Though I think about it all the time I have a hard time saying it . . . 'thanks' to my husband." These items are similar to those collected by the students and include: "Thanks for making the bumpy commute on a packed train and for your monthly salary" and "Thanks for groveling to your nasty bosses and for all the late night overtime." Here, too, the vocabulary is useful in everyday life, and the grammar reinforces the use of the verbal gerund for compound sentences.

With these sentences as "data," students then describe the life led by these imaginary husbands and wives represented on the hand towels. It is quite clear that both the sentences on the towels and the vast majority of the expressions offered by the host family assume as normative a middle-class nuclear family living in the suburbs, supported by a father employed as a salaried worker, and with a stay-at-home mother. This uniformity in the assumptions made is not surprising given the fact that the vast majority of the families hosting our students are themselves structured very much like the families imagined. The same might be said for the individuals targeted by the souvenir hand towels. Nevertheless, the extensive degree of overlap in the sentences gathered and examined in this unit is striking. As in the unit described above, students become aware of the existence of a shared ideology of the gendered subjectivities. In an English language session we discuss the rise of the salaried worker during Japan's postwar economic miracle, and the historical conditions that produced this family model as a national ideal.

For contrast to what strikes students as an ubiquitous and oppressive ideology dictating gender roles, the class then considers a number of *senryū* (short, comic haiku poems). They are all in a genre called "Salaried Worker Senryū," made popular by the reader contributions featured in the *Asahi* newspaper. These particular examples were drawn from a contest run by the Dai-ichi Seimei Insurance Company.[9]

ryōdoken,	Territorial rights,
tsuma wa ribingu,	My wife holds the living room,
ore toire	Me, the toilet

"meshi" "furo" ni,	To "Dinner!" and "My bath!"
kudasai tsuite,	With a "please" attached,
tsuma ugoku	The wife moves
"otsukare-sama,"	"You've had a long day"
tsuma no kawari ni,	In place of my wife,
nabi ga iu	The [car's] navigation system thanks me.

All three examples are easily understood, and all clearly depend for their humor on an awareness of the social conventions associated with the middle-class salaried worker's life. As in the humorous love song by Izumiya Shigeru, these poems shatter the myth of the man as "lord of the manor" (*teishu kanpaku*) or "master (of the household)" (*shujin*), as a husband may be called. To appreciate the poems one must have acquired the very "communal language" (in the broad sense of the phrase) that they undermine to humorous effect.

The final component of this unit is an assignment in which students compose sentences expressing appreciation. Rather than adopting the personas of the middle-class nuclear families we have been discussing, students are asked to imagine themselves as members of the "Kimura family." Based on actual acquaintances of mine, I describe the family as composed of a grandfather, a husband and wife, and two children in elementary school. The family business is a convenience store; the margin of profit is rather tight, so both husband and wife work there. The store is open from 7:00 a.m. to 11:00 p.m. every day of the year, and at least one of the Kimura parents must be in the shop at all times. Busy hours require the presence of both. After a classroom discussion of the lives they lead, students compose the sentences as homework. Students are happy to imagine activities that do *not* cleave to conventional gender expectations and produce expressions of appreciation for things such as Grandpa cooking dinner, Mrs. Kimura moving heavy boxes, and Mr. Kimura making breakfast for the family. Sharing these sentences in class soon reveals the fact that students gravitate toward descriptions that run against the grain of gender conventions.

As a whole, this unit underscores the points made in the earlier one: whether conscious of it or not, people absorb a set of gendered expectations that they inevitably reference when describing behaviors. This second unit also shares with the first an engagement with evidence that even the rhetorical strength of denunciations of gender expectations rely, in a backhanded sort of way, on the existence and communal knowledge of them. What this unit adds to students' understanding of how language acquisition inscribes gender in its users is an awareness of the degree to which a privileged social class tends to dictate heteronormative gender roles for an entire nation.

Sample Unit 3: Okumura Chiyo's "Slave to Love" ("Koi no dorei," 1969)

My third sample unit is based on a pop song (*kayōkyoku*) by the singer Okumura Chiyo. Debuting in March 1965 at the tender age of eighteen, Okumura catapulted into the national spotlight in 1969 with the release of "Slave to Love" (Koi no dorei). With lyrics penned by Nakanishi Rei and music composed by Suzuki Kunihiko, this single went on to sell over one million copies. The class's engagement with this "text" is less experiential than the previous examples, relying more on a conventional critical analysis. The history of the song and its reception, however, provide a very nice complement to the workings of language in the units introduced above.

Okumura sings "Slave to Love" in a slightly nasal but nevertheless sultry voice, and the sound amplifies the message delivered by the lyrics. The female protagonist confesses to having become a "slave to love" from the very day she met her counterpart, about whom we learn nothing. The impact of the song is rooted in the excessive degree to which the protagonist is willing to subjugate herself to her love. She offers to wrap herself around his knees "like a puppy" and to "follow him like his shadow" though he may pay her no mind. Furthermore, she insists that "if told to turn right, I'll turn right, and be so happy about it." In the most shocking line, she invites him "to hit [her] when she's bad." Each verse ends with the following statement: "I want to become a woman that suits your tastes."

As with all units in the class, time is devoted to studying the vocabulary and grammar appearing in the material. Here the grammar pattern for review is "X *no yō ni* Y," meaning "to do Y in the manner of X." There are two examples: "to wrap myself around your knees like a puppy" (*anata no hiza ni karamitsuku, koinu no yō ni*) and "to follow you around like a shadow" (*kage no yō ni tsuite yuku wa*). The lyrics of this song also lend themselves to the introduction or review of another grammatical point: the inverted sentence, in which the order of grammatically bound phrases is reversed. The line about being puppylike is one example. A second is *anata dake ni iwaretai no, "kawaii yatsu" to* (You are the only one I want to tell me I'm a cutie). Strictly speaking, the Japanese phrases separated by the comma should be in reverse order, but this sort of inversion is a common feature of the spoken language.

Students exhibit two reactions to the lyrics of this song. Some find they cannot but laugh in disbelief as the lyrics strike them as so exaggerated that the song can only be considered a parody. Others are somewhat disturbed by the lyrics. The self-abjection of the protagonist is hard for them to fathom, particularly the request to be struck when "bad." Neither group is inclined to seriously consider the song until it hears about the sales record or discovers that older host family members remember the song and can even reproduce some of the lyrics. This unit becomes increasingly interesting when we examine history of the song's reception. It was so popular in 1969 that the national television station, NHK, felt obligated to invite Okumura to appear on the aforementioned New Year's Eve songfest (*Kōhaku uta gassen*). However, being the nation's flagship television studio, NHK had rather stringent regulations about what might be aired. It found the theme and lyrics of "Slave to Love"offensive and subsequently withdrew the invitation to perform it.[10] Okumura was pressured to sing instead "Love Bandit" (Koi dorobō), a song with far more moderate lyrics.

This incident is explained to the students orally in Japanese, followed by a short essay I composed expressly for this class communicating the same set of facts. The discussion then revolves around whether or not the censorship of a very popular song, albeit with an anachronistic, reactionary message in the lyrics, is in keeping with the broader goals of a democratic society. There is no easy conclusion to be reached here, of course. The song and its reception history, however, provide an important counterpoint to the earlier units in the course. Izumiya's song and the hand towels serve as case studies of how language can be empowering in its capacity for meaningful communication only when it simultaneously coerces its users into accepting *some* dimension of (possibly repressive) discursive conventions. The history of Okumura's song, on the other hand, shows the inverse of this equation: how a reactionary set of statements can set the stage for a battle for a progressive agenda, namely, freedom of speech. In fact the essay describing the NHK suppression of this song is titled "Might Choosing to Be a Slave Be One Sort of Freedom?"

Sample Unit 4: Personal Pronouns and Gendered Subjectivities

Over the course of this ten-week class, students study eight or nine pop songs from postwar Japan. Toward the end of the course there is a sufficient archive of textual evidence for an investigation of the function of personal pronouns in Japanese. Unlike English, where the only first-person pronoun is "I," Japanese provides a range of options: *watashi, atashi, boku,* and *ore,* to name but a few of the more common. The same is true of second-person pronouns. This list might include *anata, omae, temē,* and *kimi.* Students arrive in Japan generally using only the most formal, generic versions of these words: *watashi* and *anata.* Interacting with their Japanese host families and Japanese college students, however, they soon become curious about the various referents for what most English speakers, anyway, have always assumed is a single, coherent, cohesive self. This provides an ideal opportunity to explore again how language inculcates gendered identities.

The first step of this unit builds on the archive of song lyrics and other "texts" that students have worked with in the class. As the song lyrics are already familiar to the students, it is possible to add texture by viewing performances of some of the singers on DVD or YouTube. Adding a visual component to the music provides an opportunity to review vocabulary related to clothing, and as such it contributes to the language acquisition portion of the class. It is also a time to consider the semiotics of fashion/clothing. As Jan Bardsley argues in chapter 5 of this volume, fashion "makes statements about national culture, often in ways that index social position, gender, race, and age."[11] Students quickly and largely intuitively understand the "code" of musician fashion, and they are quick to point out how the positions implied by dress most often amplify the gendered subjectivities linguistically constructed in the lyrics.

The review of our archive of song lyrics at this late point in the course focuses on the relationship between the first- and second-person pronouns used and the nature of the subjectivities and relationships represented. The task is fairly easy. In the folk and new music genres popular among the postwar generation in the radical late 1960s and early 1970s, the preferred pronouns are *boku* (I) and/or *kimi* (you). Representative examples include Izumiya's "I Love Ya" ("Ai shite ru yo"), Izumiya's "Bedroom Serenade" ("Nedoko no serenade," 1972), Yoshida Takurō's "Let's Get Married" ("Kekkon shiyō yo," 1971), and Inoue Yōsui's "Got No Umbrella" ("Kasa ga nai," 1972). In all cases here the lyrics suggest a vision of a "modern" relationship in which the couples represented interact on roughly equal terms and strive, at least, for a mutually fulfilling relationship. Songs featuring either of the other conventional pairings—either the *ore* (I) and *omae* (you) or the *watashi* (I) and *anata* (you)—inevitably lean toward more traditional, and more hierarchical, relationships. Sada Masashi's 1979 hit "Lord of the Manor" (Kanpaku sengen), for example, uses *ore* and *omae* throughout and takes the form of a male protagonist dictating the terms of the marital relationship he is about to enter. Almost all the verbs are in the imperative form as the man commands his betrothed to "cook well" (*meshi wa umaku tsukure*) and "always be beautiful" (*itsumo kirei de iro*). Through an initial review and analysis of the paradigmatic relationships, students are sensitized to the "communal language" that dictates the nuances of these pronouns.

The second step is to interview two or three individuals, preferably varying in age and gender, to ascertain the pronouns they and those around them use, as well as the personality traits associated with the individuals using them. Although the first-person pronouns in everyday use parallel closely those represented in song lyrics, students inevitably discover a disconnect in the interviewees' perceptions of second-person pronoun usage and nuance. Contrary to what the song lyrics would suggest, most members of our admittedly limited and homogeneous circle of program family and friends, as well as students at the host institution, indicate an aversion to almost any use of the second-person pronoun. This is particularly strong in female interviewees, who far prefer the use of personal names in place of pronouns, both for themselves and for those to whom they speak.

In order to explain this discrepancy, I introduce students to Kinsui Satoshi's concept of "character language" (*yakuwarigo*).[12] Kinsui categorizes and analyzes various registers or dialects that appear in popular, as well as highbrow, culture in Japan, arguing that these distinct "languages" are unique and easily identifiable to native speakers in spite of the fact that they exist largely if not entirely in the realm of media and pop culture (hence "virtual *nihongo*"). The simple linguistic anthropological work done by students in our summer program in Japan suggests that this is also true for the various second-person pronouns. While popular song suggests a triad of widely used second-person pronouns (*anata*, *kimi*, *omae*), our ethnographic research indicates that for the most part these words exist largely as "role-playing language."

This prolonged engagement with personal pronouns sensitizes students to them, and often a number of male students will begin to experiment with them in their daily lives. With the range of options for female first-person pronouns rather limited, it is not surprising that the experimentation takes place chiefly among the men. Although the evidence is only anecdotal, my observations of such students suggest that, for a time at least, they are incapable of using *any* first-person pronoun in anything other than a parodic mode. With the knowledge that each pronoun carries with it strong gendered associations, and aware that native speakers will switch codes depending on context, native English speakers will experience disorientation on being thrust into a realm where gendered identity is not treated linguistically as "natural" and stable. An English-language discussion of such issues allows the class to translate experiential learning in the linguistic "performance" of gender into a heightened awareness of how entrance into a communal language shapes subjectivities overall, and particularly in terms of gender.

Conclusion

The above has been a description of a course incorporating foreign-language acquisition with an exploration of the linguistic roots of gendered subjectivities. The intention is, again in Henry A. Giroux's terms, to provide "students with the skills, knowledge, and authority they need to inquire into and act upon what it means to live in a radical multicultural democracy, to recognize anti-democratic forms of power, and to fight deeply rooted injustices in a society and world founded on systemic economic, racial, and gender inequalities."[13] As a part of that quest, the course introduced here is designed and executed with the goal of offering students an opportunity to consciously and critically analyze the processes by which entry into a communal language coercively indoctrinates them into the acceptance of certain linguistic and cultural conventions. The exercises and activities of the course provide an experiential engagement with linguistic and cultural conventions that represents both the limits of what might be thought or said in language and, ironically, the foundation for challenging those limits. The paradox of language acquisition, whether first or foreign, is that it both empowers by offering access to community (*kyōsei gengo toshite no Nihongo* or "Japanese as a communal language") *and* represses by forcing at least nominal acceptance of linguistic and societal conventions in order to communicate at all (*kyōsei gengo toshite no Nihongo* or "Japanese as a coercive language"). The hope is that by experiencing consciously and critically as adults a linguistic indoctrination similar to that undergone as a child in the course of learning a native language students will be more aware, more wary, and more appreciative of the power of language to construct identities in terms of gender, social class, or any of a host of other possibilities.

Perhaps the most succinct expression of the project comes from Friedrich Nietzsche's 522nd aphorism in his *Will to Power*: "We have to cease to think, if we refuse to do it in the prisonhouse of language; for we cannot reach further than the doubt which asks whether the limit we see is really a limit. All rational thought is interpretation in accordance with a scheme that we cannot throw off."[14] And so we reach for the doubt, we seek cognizance of the limit, and we attempt to alter the scheme.

Notes

[1] Henry A. Giroux, "Public Pedagogy and the Politics of Resistance: Notes on a Critical Theory of Educational Struggle," *Educational Philosophy and Theory* 35, no. 1 (2003): 5–16.

[2] See Sally McLaren and Alwyn Spies, "Risk and Potential: Establishing Critical Pedagogy in Japanese Popular Culture Courses," chapter 1 in this volume.

[3] William Spencer Armour, "Learning Japanese by Reading 'Manga': The Rise of 'Soft Power Pedagogy,'" *RELC: A Journal of Language Teaching and Research* 42 (2011): 125–40.

[4] Ibid., 128–29. Armour glosses the phrase as "Japanese as a language for co-living."

[5] Miyo Junpei and Kyung Hee Chung, "'Tadashii Nihongo' o oshieru koto no mondai to 'kyōsei gengo to shite no nihongo' e no tenbō" [The issue of teaching "proper Japanese" and perspectives on "Japanese as a communal language"], *Gengo Bunka Kenkyū* 5, no. 89 (2006): 80–93. All translations from Japanese are mine unless otherwise noted.

[6] Judith Butler, "Performative Acts and Gender Constitution: An Essay in Phenomenology and Feminist Theory," *Theatre Journal* 40, no. 4 (December 1988): 520.

[7] Ferdinand de Saussure, *Course in General Linguistics* (New York: McGraw-Hill, 1959).

[8] Izumiya Shigeru, "Ai shite ru yo," on *Uta no ichi dai isshū*, Bappu ASIN: B000BV7STO, 2005, CD. This is a rerelease of an album originally produced in 1972. The song is available with lyrics offered in both original Japanese and English translation on YouTube, http://www.youtube.com/watch?v=LbFjZtcCOR0.

[9] "Sarariiman senryū: fūfu katei hen" [Salaryman *senryū*: Married couples and homelife edition], Dai-ichi Seimei, http://event.dai-ichi-life.co.jp/company/senryu/theme/home.html.

[10] Ishibashi Harumi, *Fūin kayo daizen* [Complete collection of censored songs] (Tokyo: Sansai Books, 2007).

[11] See Jan Bardsley, "Teaching Fashion as Japanese Popular Culture," chapter 5 in this volume, 101–2.

[12] Kinsui Satoshi, *Baachuaru Nihongo: Yakuwarigo no nazo* [Virtual Japanese: The mysteries of role-playing Japanese] (Tokyo: Iwanami Shoten, 2003).

[13] Giroux, "Public Pedagogy," 11–12.

[14] Friedrich Nietzsche, *The Will to Power*, trans. Walter Kaufmann (New York: Random House, 1967), aphorism 522.

Works Cited

Armour, William Spencer. "Learning Japanese by Reading 'Manga': The Rise of 'Soft Power Pedagogy.'" *RELC: A Journal of Language Teaching and Research* 42 (2011): 125–40.

Butler, Judith. "Performative Acts and Gender Constitution: An Essay in Phenomenology and Feminist Theory." *Theatre Journal* 40, no. 4 (December 1988): 519–31.

Giroux, Henry A. "Public Pedagogy and the Politics of Resistance: Notes on a Critical Theory of Educational Struggle." *Educational Philosophy and Theory* 35, no. 1 (2003): 5–16.

Ishibashi Harumi. *Fūin kayo daizen* [Complete collection of censored songs]. Tokyo: Sansai Books, 2007.

Izumiya Shigeru. "Ai shite ru yo" ("I Love Ya"). On *Uta no ichi dai isshū (Song Market Volume One)*. Bappu ASIN: B000BV7STO, 2005. CD.

Kinsui Satoshi. *Baachuaru Nihongo: Yakuwarigo no nazo* [Virtual Japanese: The mysteries of role-playing Japanese]. Tokyo: Iwanami Shoten, 2003.

Miyo Junpei and Kyung Hee Chung. "'Tadashii Nihongo' o oshieru koto no mondai to 'kyōsei gengo to shite no nihongo' e no tenbō" [The issue of teaching "proper Japanese" and perspectives on "Japanese as a communal language"]. *Gengo Bunka Kenkyū* (Studies in Language and Culture) 5, no. 89 (2006): 80–93.

Nietzsche, Friedrich. *The Will to Power*. Translated by Walter Kaufmann. New York: Random House, 1967.

"Sarariiman senryū: fūfu katei hen" [Salaryman *senryū*: Married couples and homelife edition]. Dai-ichi Seimei. http://event.dai-ichi-life.co.jp/company/senryu/theme/home.html.

Saussure, Ferdinand de. *Course in General Linguistics*. New York: McGraw-Hill, 1959.

10

POP(ULAR) CULTURE IN THE JAPANESE HISTORY CLASSROOM

PHILIP SEATON

Introduction

This chapter begins with a confession. I have never been a particular fan of manga, anime, and J-pop.[1] I am a historian or, more accurately, a researcher of historical memory interested in what the past means to us in our daily lives. My interest in Japanese pop culture developed primarily out of necessity. Understanding how the Japanese perceive and narrate their own history requires examining historical narratives in cinema, manga, and other forms of popular culture. In other words, the power of pop culture to shape historical memory has attracted my attention more than the appeal of Japanese pop culture per se.

Now, as a teacher of Japanese history and/or memory, I consciously include popular culture into my classes. I am conscious of the significant role of Japanese pop culture in driving the interest of students in learning Japanese and about Japan. But my aim is not to meet student expectations, entertain the students, or provide light relief from the serious business of studying history, in other words, the problematic "pop to prop" approach outlined in chapter 1, by Sally McLaren and Alwyn Spies, in this volume. First, I routinely use popular culture as a research resource, so it inevitably works its way into my teaching. Second, I believe the use of popular culture in the classroom hones critical-thinking skills (a theme developed by a number of other contributors to this volume) and the traditional historian's skill of evaluating primary sources, especially when used in tandem with academic or educational texts.

This chapter discusses how pop culture may be used in the Japanese history classroom. It addresses teaching history *using* Japanese pop culture rather than teaching *about* Japanese pop culture. I start by defining and distinguishing popular culture and pop culture. I also use the shorthand "pop(ular) culture" to mean "primarily pop (but also popular) culture."

The second section looks at curriculum guidelines for history education at schools in Japan, England, and the United States and discusses the potential for using popular culture in the classroom under different styles of educational system. It then considers whether there are any characteristics of Japanese history that make the use of popular culture particularly suitable in the Japanese history classroom.

The third section presents four examples of my own use of pop(ular) culture in university classes. I discuss how a computer graphic may be used to introduce a technique for cultural analysis, how fictional cinema can be used when teaching history, how manga may be used to supplement official narratives in Japanese textbooks, and how popular culture informs understandings of Ainu history in Hokkaido. Underpinning all the case studies is the philosophy that popular culture is never used in isolation but in conjunction with academic literature to elucidate key historiographic themes in an accessible way. The conclusions, while derived from the use of Japanese popular culture in a Japanese history classroom, are intended to be more universal in nature and of relevance to teachers focusing on other parts of the world and even teaching subjects other than history, too.

Pop(ular) Culture

First, let us define *popular culture* and *pop culture*. In vernacular usage the terms are often used interchangeably, but in this chapter they are distinct.

Andrew Jones defines *pop culture* as follows when considering the relative merits of "high culture versus pop culture" in the religious education classroom.

> [Pop culture is] culture which is popular, easy to understand and entertaining to the majority of young people. For example, pop music, romantic Hollywood comedies and soap operas. High culture, on the

other hand, may include renaissance art, classical music and opera. The latter is arguably more sophisticated, intellectually challenging and intrinsically rewarding.[2]

This useful working definition suffices when dealing with relatively clear examples of "high" and "pop" culture. However, distinguishing low culture from high culture or art from populist entertainment can descend into subjectivity or elitism in the absence of widely accepted objective criteria for such distinctions. Overall, however, pop culture tends toward being light, popular, entertaining, and accessible.

Popular culture has a broader meaning. Kirwin R. Shaffer, in an essay on a topic similar to mine, defined *popular culture* as "those religious, artistic, athletic, and political expressions arising from different segments of society, and thus reflecting a society's dominant culture as well as its diversity."[3] This broad definition—which is close to the definition of *pop culture* (*poppu karuchā*) used by the Japanese government in relation to its Cool Japan campaign [4]—allows almost any cultural production to be termed "popular culture."When juxtaposed with Jones's definition it highlights how *popular* may mean both "liked by many people" and "of the people." In this chapter, *pop culture* is defined broadly as "entertainment liked by many people," which is a subset of *popular culture*, the collective cultural production "of the people." The term *pop(ular) culture* is also used to mean "primarily pop (but also popular) culture."

These definitions of *popular* and *pop culture* can be developed further using key concepts from historiography.

First, popular culture is unofficial. It excludes anything written, commissioned, funded, or screened by local or national governments. Therefore, official histories, publicly funded museums, state-written or state-screened textbooks, government statements on the past, and documents in government archives are not considered to be popular culture. Sometimes governments utilize genres commonly associated with pop culture to disseminate their message, such as an anime publicity film. These are easily confused with pop(ular) culture, but they are not "of the people" and therefore not popular culture.

Second, distinguishing fiction and nonfiction is vital for historians. Nonfiction—including academic scholarship, trade press publications, news journalism, and documentaries—is categorized as popular culture (and not pop culture) and may be used for teaching historical content, but fiction—as in novels and films—will typically only be useful for indicating images, attitudes, myths, or stereotypes about the past. The primary aims of pop culture are assumed to be self-expression, entertainment, and financial profit. While historical accuracy or "authenticity" might be a sales point for individual works of pop(ular) culture, in general pop(ular) culture is assumed to operate outside professional academic/journalistic codes of historical accuracy.

Third, items of popular culture can be thought of as historical sources. For the historian, contemporary popular culture is a secondary source produced at a distance from the historical period under study. Over time the status of popular culture metamorphoses. As the period in which the popular culture was produced recedes into the past, the popular culture is transformed into a primary source: an "authentic" document from the past that tells historians something about the period in which it was produced, a theme raised by James Dorsey in chapter 9 of this volume, in which the use of popular songs for language learning also affords opportunities for insights into the cultural landscape of postwar Japan.[5] The use of popular culture in the history classroom, therefore, depends on when it was produced. The more contemporary the popular culture, the more insights it provides into *memories* of the past (how the past is viewed in the present); the older the popular culture, the more it becomes part of the very *history* that is being taught.

The Japanese History Classroom

Next I consider the potential for using pop(ular) culture in the Japanese history classroom. First, I consider the *history classroom* through comparison of curriculum guidelines in Japan, England, and the United States. Second, I examine the potential for *Japanese history* (as a distinct area of study within world history) to be taught using pop(ular) culture.

The History Classroom

The Japanese Ministry of Education outlines the purpose of history education in junior high school as follows.

> To raise interest in historical phenomena and to provide understanding of the grand flow of our country's history against the background of world history and the characteristics of each period. Through history education students are made to think from a broad perspective about our country's

traditions and culture, while students' love of our nation's history is also deepened and their consciousness as citizens developed.[6]

The characteristics of Japanese history education, therefore, are studying chronological flow, contextualizing Japanese history within world history, and developing a positive sense of national identity via history. In addition to these broader objectives, the type of exams students take affects the style of history teaching. Students at both the junior- and senior-high-school levels take entrance exams dominated by multiple choice or short-answer questions that test factual recall, particularly of dates, treaties, events, and people.

Consequently, opportunities for using popular culture in the Japanese school history classroom are limited. There is little time for diversions from the task of teaching students the textbook-based factual content needed for exams. Indeed, it is often said that Japanese students do not learn enough about modern history (particularly World War II) because the teacher "runs out of time" to teach that period. Furthermore, given that exams test primarily factual recall, only popular culture that helps students absorb "the facts" or acts as a motivational aid to (re)stimulate interest is beneficial. Using popular culture to stimulate critical thinking is largely superfluous when preparing Japanese students for their entrance exams.

Nevertheless, as I have argued elsewhere, many history teachers in Japan *do* use supplementary materials in class, particularly documentaries and news media.[7] Pop culture elements are also used extensively in the vast educational materials market that exists alongside government-screened textbooks. Educational manga (*gakushū manga*) is widely available. The Shōgakukan publishing company, for example, produces extensive manga series in which the popular characters Doraemon and Detective Conan "teach" everything from Japanese history to science. In Japan, therefore, pop(ular) culture is used primarily in a motivational context for supplementing official textbooks or making unofficial educational materials more engaging.

In the Anglo-American school history classroom there is more potential for using popular culture. The history National Curriculum for England (Key Stage 3, 2007–2013) identifies the following "key concepts" in history education: chronological understanding (the terminology and flow of periods); cultural, ethnic, and religious diversity (how different peoples have shaped and viewed the world); change and continuity (both within and across periods); cause and consequence (analysis of historical change); significance (considering the significance of people and events then and now); and interpretation.

The guidelines regarding interpretation directly relate to the classroom use of popular culture.

> People represent and interpret the past in many different ways, including in pictures, plays, films, reconstructions, museum displays, and fictional and non-fiction accounts. Interpretations reflect the circumstances in which they are made, the available evidence, and the intentions of those who make them (e.g. writers, archaeologists, historians and film-makers).[8]

"Interpretation" is almost the realm of historical memory rather than history per se. Nevertheless, schoolchildren in England have analysis of popular culture written into their national curriculum for history. The format of exams includes both short-answer and essay questions that test analytical skills. As part of exam preparation, teachers must provide various texts—whether popular culture or authentic historical documents—for students to discuss and analyze.

Caroline Hoefferle lists a similar set of skills tested within the American system.[9] Of particular relevance are Standard 3H, "Hold interpretations of history as tentative, subject to changes as new information is uncovered, new voices heard, and new interpretations broached," and Standard 3I, "Evaluate major debates among historians concerning alternative interpretations of the past." Both standards emphasize the contemporary context and the need for analysis of both primary and secondary sources. For Hoefferle teaching historiography is akin to teaching critical thinking, and she proposes a six-stage process for analyzing sources: students identify the author, topic, thesis, evidence, and theory, and then perform critical analysis. This method works for primary and secondary sources, including popular culture texts. How many history teachers actively use popular culture materials in the Anglo-American setting is unclear, but Anglo-American teachers have more curriculum-based justifications for introducing popular culture into the history classroom than their Japanese counterparts at the junior and senior high school levels do.

We should not overstate, however, the dichotomy between a "Japanese model" centered on chronology, factual recall, and national identity creation and an "Anglo-American model" promoting understanding of diversity and critical thinking. The Japanese guidelines cited above were drafted following revisions to the Basic Law on Education in 2006. The prime minister at that time, Abe Shinzō, admired former British prime minister Margaret Thatcher for opposing history teaching that "harmed British pride." In the 1980s Thatcher introduced the National Curriculum, which both forms the basis of English school history education today and inspired Abe's 2006 patriotically minded educational reforms.[10] Furthermore, Hoefferle comments:

> Many of my undergraduate students had never before thought critically about the histories that they read. . . . [M]ost high school and undergraduate courses heavily rely on textbook readings. History textbooks are normally written in a narrative format, which sends the message to students that they are simply presenting "the truth" about the past.[11]

This closely resembles the Japanese situation.

Ultimately, government guidelines and what actually happens in the classroom need clear distinction. Whatever incentives or disincentives exist within a national system according to government guidelines on history education, the decision to use popular culture in the classroom rests with the teacher.

Japanese History

Is there something specific about Japanese history that might encourage the use of popular culture in the classroom? In some ways, yes. A major factor driving student interest in studying the Japanese language and about Japan these days is an interest in Japanese pop(ular) culture. Teachers, therefore, are responding to many students' interests by using pop(ular) culture. Furthermore, historical representations in Japanese television dramas, manga, and computer games are so ubiquitous that there is a wealth of potential material to use.

In other ways, the answer is no. Among historians of Japan, as among historians elsewhere, many remain skeptical about using popular culture. William M. Tsutsui writes, "Popular culture, I've been told, just doesn't seem that important. It's not the stuff for a 'serious' history course."[12] Using pop(ular) culture may also generate a sense of vulnerability among history teachers, either because of a relative lack of knowledge among teachers about pop(ular) culture compared to their students,[13] or because of a fear of being put on the spot by difficult questions such as "what really happened?" if historically inaccurate popular culture has been used in class. Ultimately, historians will take many different approaches. Positivist historians who do mainly archival work are probably less enthusiastic about using popular culture, while social or oral historians whose primary sources are the "voices of the people" are more likely to feel comfortable doing so.

My own research profile is toward the cultural history and memory studies end of the spectrum, which helps explain my enthusiasm for using popular culture in the classroom. I also believe that the history narrated in pop(ular) culture forms is often too powerful even for positivist historians to ignore. In Japan, for example, the annual Taiga Drama on NHK television greatly impacts "serious history."[14] Museums put on special exhibitions, academic historians appear on television, publishers commission books, and tourists flock to historical sites related to the drama.

Popular culture can even trigger serious historical debate on the mysteries of the past. For example, it is not known for sure who assassinated Bakumatsu period (1853–68) visionary Sakamoto Ryōma. However, as Robert A. Rosenstone argues:

> Film offers us history as the story of a closed, completed, and simple past. It provides no alternative possibilities to what we see happening on the screen, admits of no doubts, and promotes each historical assertion with the same degree of confidence.[15]

Unlike academic histories, films and dramas cannot use the passive voice ("Sakamoto was assassinated") or evasive language ("debates continue about exactly who was responsible"). The drama chooses its version of history from one of the hypotheses on offer, and the historians respond to the interest generated by the pop(ular) culture. Just as Oliver Stone's movie *JFK* triggered debate about the Kennedy assassination, every time Sakamoto's assassination is depicted onscreen it reignites a historical debate about who killed him.

In sum, on methodological and pedagogical grounds the arguments and opportunities for using popular culture in the history classroom are basically the same in Japan as elsewhere; on practical grounds Japanese popular culture has a large global fan base, and the ubiquity of representations of history in Japanese popular culture means there are plentiful potential teaching resources from which to choose.

When Tsutsui conducted a small survey of Japanese history courses at universities in the United States and Canada, he found that just over half included popular culture in some way. He comments, "So historians don't seem to have entirely missed the bus on Japanese popular culture, but at present they are sitting in the back of that bus, not driving it, when it comes to teaching and research on Cool Japan."[16] However, given the current global interest in Japanese popular culture, Japanese historians are in a good position to occupy the driver's seat in broader debates about popular culture and pedagogy within the discipline of history.

Japanese Pop(ular) Culture in the Japanese History Classroom

In this third section, I describe popular culture teaching materials and classroom activities that I have used. The classes were taught at one major Japanese university and one medium-sized private university. Classes at both universities were taken by a mixture of Japanese and non-Japanese students (at the undergraduate level mainly exchange students from partner universities and at the postgraduate level mainly Chinese masters students).

The underlying principle in all the activities is that popular culture is never used in isolation but always linked to academic discourse. Furthermore, the activities have one or more of the following educational aims: the introduction of a historiographic or analytical technique, the performance of critical textual analysis, the debate of a particular historical theme, or the teaching of historical knowledge.

Teaching Cultural Analysis Using a "Cute" Image

Popular culture can be used to introduce analytical techniques. Hoefferle's methodology was introduced above: students identify the author, topic, thesis, evidence, and theory and then perform critical analysis. This is useful for analyzing written texts or documents; however, it is less appropriate for analyzing nonacademic or nondocumentary sources. I prefer a cultural studies approach, which can be used for both text and nontext sources. The following exercise was used in an undergraduate course about World War II history and memories.

In *Doing Cultural Studies*, Paul du Gay and his colleagues propose a "circuit of culture" that highlights five key words: *representation, identity, production, consumption*, and *regulation*. In order to analyze any text or artifact culturally, "one should at least explore how it is represented, what social identities are associated with it, how it is produced and consumed, and what mechanisms regulate its distribution and use."[17] Using a methodology from cultural studies in a history and memory class also

Figure 10.1. A royalty-free graphic (*left*) from the collection
"Kawaii katto daizenshū DVD" (*right*).

provides an opportunity to discuss interdisciplinarity: how researchers
working in different disciplines can learn from each other about best
research practice.

The graphic used for analysis (fig. 10.1) is from a collection of over
twelve thousand royalty-free images called "Kawaii katto daizenshū
DVD" (Cute Images Collection DVD) produced by the software company
MPC World.[18] The images, all in a "cute" manga style, can be divided
into various categories: people, seasons, food, and other stock images of
Japan. This image (VD-01-27) is part of a collection of summer event and
anniversary images.

Discussion starts with issues of representation: What does this image
mean? Three main components can be identified: a Japanese flag, an origami
crane, and the numbers 8.15. The flag is not the national Japanese flag (*hi
no maru*) but the rising sun flag (*kyokujitsuki*), Japan's military flag. The
coloring is conspicuous: the sun and rays are black rather than the original
red. This could mean "ignominious" or "death." It is shattered, seemingly
indicating Japan's military downfall. The shattering motif might also be
a reference to *gyokusai*, literally "shattered jewel," the suicide charges
of the Japanese army toward the end of the war. The flag appears to have

been shattered by the tail of the origami crane. The origami crane in the context of World War II is particularly associated with the story of Sadako, a young girl exposed to the A-bomb in Hiroshima who folded chains of a thousand origami cranes in a bid to overcome radiation sickness. So, perhaps it is peace that shatters militarism, or even the A-bomb.

The number at the bottom signifies August 15 to Japanese. However, British people do not use the month-day ordering of dates, so for them it means the time 8:15, which happens to be the time at which the atomic bomb was dropped on Hiroshima. Considering who produced the graphic, 8.15 surely refers to the anniversary of the end of the war, but within cultural studies such distinctions between the intended message of the sender and the actual message received by the consumer are significant.

Ultimately, which interpretation is "correct" is of less importance than the discussion about the semiotics of the graphic and students' diverse interpretations of it. The analysis then proceeds to the other elements of the circuit of culture. The identities associated with the graphic are more likely to be antiwar than prowar. A collection of "cute" images seems incongruous with militarism, and the other war-related graphics featured on the DVD refer to the A-bombs or air raids, namely, civilian victimhood. A pacifist, mildly critical historical consciousness seems most likely, although the semiotics of the graphic are ambiguous enough to permit a more conservative view, too: mourning the demise of the Japanese military.

In terms of production, we know the company that produced the graphic but not the individual artist. It is consumed (purchased) by people presumably with no specific interest in the war: there are fewer than ten war images out of the twelve thousand available. The graphic is consumed (viewed and analyzed) by only a fraction of those who purchased the DVD, but through being used (including in my class) its message has been consumed by some people who did not purchase the DVD. Concerning the regulations surrounding its use, it is a royalty-free image, and as a nonoffensive image it does not generate any censorship issues.

In this way, the image has been used to introduce a method for analyzing an object culturally. The aim is to introduce theory, so the simpler the object being analyzed the better (an archive document or history book could equally be used, but a visual image has the advantage that it can be "read" quickly). Discussion is stimulated via simple questions: what does it mean, where did it come from, and how can it be used? Students experience the essence of a cultural studies approach to textual analysis before the circuit of culture is presented. In this way, an appropriate popular culture text provides a way to introduce serious academic skills.

Using Fictional Cinema in the History Classroom

There are many documentaries or largely accurate historical films that can be used as lecture materials to add variety to a course and/or give students a break from the lecturer's voice. However, the great events of history are popular topics of or backgrounds for cinematic storytelling, too. These (semi)fictional films may be immensely powerful in shaping popular consciousness of history, but they pose considerable problems as classroom materials. History teachers are obliged to teach fact, not fiction, and showing a movie and pointing out factual errors is of limited educational benefit, especially if the film is more memorable than the lecture listing the inaccuracies.

This section considers how fictional or semifictional historical films may be used in the classroom without getting stuck at the level of correcting inaccurate historical representations. I consider two films: *The Last Samurai* and *Grave of the Fireflies*. They were discussed during a course on modern Japanese history for exchange students that met for two consecutive ninety-minute classes once a week. Classes of this length were often grueling for both teacher and students, but they enabled a film to be introduced, watched, and analyzed all in one session.

The Last Samurai was used to introduce Robert Rosenstone's framework for analyzing the "historical practices of mainstream film."[19] First students were introduced to issues such as time compression (events that took much longer in reality are compressed into one scene in a film) and dramatization (events are fabricated or glamorized for the sake of attractive cinema).[20] Then, rather than watching the actual film, a History Channel documentary about the film contained within the DVD bonus materials was used.[21] The documentary introduced the making of the movie, including how the filmmakers strove for historical authenticity in the sets and period costumes. This generates discussion about why filmmakers are often highly concerned with accurately re-creating the "look of the past" even if they are largely unconcerned about accurately re-creating the events of the past.

The Last Samurai is loosely based on the life of Saigō Takamori, a leading figure in the Meiji Restoration of 1868. After watching the documentary, the real history of Saigō is told with reference to academic history, such as Mark Ravina's *The Last Samurai: The Life and Battles of Saigō Takamori.*[22] This includes discussion of where the film is and is not historically accurate. The last charge in the film, for example, takes place on an open battlefield in spring, whereas Saigō's real last stand during the Satsuma Rebellion was in September 1877 on a hillside in Kagoshima. This last scene also provides a chance to discuss how the representation of exactly the same act may change significantly across historical periods. The charge of sword-wielding samurai in *The Last Samurai,* for example, is depicted as a noble act of "death before dishonor" that epitomizes the virtues of the warrior code Bushidō, but similar charges in the television series *The Pacific* are depicted as the acts of a brutal enemy during World War II and the fanaticism instilled in Japanese soldiers by Bushidō (the so-called way of the warrior).[23]

This lesson plan template can be used for any historical period and location. First, introduce an analytical framework (in this case Rosenstone's historical practices of mainstream film); second, view the film or an excerpt; third, compare and contrast the cinematic narrative with the historical record with particular reference to why the filmmakers might have wanted to alter history for dramatic and/or narrative effect; and, finally, discuss issues of representation in the film (along with identity, production, consumption, and regulation to complete the cultural analysis of the film).

The second film is *Grave of the Fireflies* (Hotaru no haka), one of Japan's best-known anime films.[24] Typically, in any class a number of students will have seen it before. *Grave of the Fireflies* tells the story of Seita and his little sister Setsuko, who lose their mother during an air raid on Kobe and have to fend for themselves at the end of World War II. The suffering of innocent children—with the levels of tragedy and pathos ratcheted up to intolerable levels by the "cuteness" of the protagonists, soundtrack, and flashbacks to childish joy—inevitably leaves many students in tears.

At the end of the film, just as students are at the peak of experiencing what Sabine Frühstück terms the "emotionalising power of popular culture,"[25] I ask a question: Did you cry when we discussed the suffering of people in China during atrocities committed by the Japanese army? The tears are quickly replaced with discussion. The emotions are turned down, and the intellect is turned up. "Spoiling the moment" is a visceral lesson in how the form of historical narration affects people's engagement with history. In contrast to the emotional reaction to *Grave of the Fireflies*, when students are in "concentrate seriously in class" mode they can absorb high levels of disturbing information without becoming emotional. Frühstück makes similar observations and found that far fewer students cried during the screening of a documentary film about Korean "comfort women" than did so while watching *Grave of the Fireflies*.

With *Grave of the Fireflies,* there is also an important lesson related to historical accuracy. The original novel is "semiautobiographical." The author, Nosaka Akiyuki, experienced the war as a teenager and saw one of his sisters die in his arms, just as Setsuko dies in the film. However, Nosaka survived, and rather than being the caring Seita figure in *Grave of the Fireflies*, he hit his sixteen month old sister when she cried. "In the end," writes Hiroko Cockerill, "Nosaka condemns himself for having written a complete fabrication in *Hotaru no haka*, in order to justify the actions of the boy who let his sister die of malnutrition."[26]

The revelation that the historical events behind *Grave of the Fireflies* differ significantly from the events depicted in the film sets up a discussion about the key themes in historiographic debates over autobiography and oral history: can testimony be trusted as a historical source, what are the processes for ensuring that testimony is accurate, and why might people intentionally or unintentionally falsify their narratives of the past? In this way, a famous work of popular culture viewed in combination with related academic texts can be used to introduce historiographic and methodological issues related to the use of autobiography and testimony.

Manga as Counternarrative

I teach a graduate school class titled History and Education in which we compare and contrast the content related to World War II in school history textbooks from Japan and abroad. We also consider the type of lessons children receive on educational visits to war and peace museums. A key theme in this course is distinguishing official and unofficial history. In Japan, history textbooks screened by the government count as official history, while educational materials produced without government involvement are considered popular culture. We also examine three museums: Yūshūkan, the Hiroshima Peace Memorial Museum, and Peace Osaka. Yūshūkan is not official because it is the private museum of an

Figure 10.2. Three educational manga focusing on the war years.

autonomous religious organization (the Yasukuni Shrine). The other two museums are funded by local governments.[27]

In this section, I describe how unofficial narratives in manga can be used as a counternarrative to official narratives. The first example uses educational manga (*gakushū manga*) narrating Japanese history that targets the elementary schoolchild market. Such manga is typically consumed (i.e. read) by young children at home or in school libraries, tells history from the standpoint of a young Japanese child, and is not subjected to any government screening or regulations. These manga form an interesting comparison with the official school textbooks used by Japanese children.

First, the manga typically tell a personalized version of history through the eyes of a young central character and his or her family. By contrast, textbooks are impersonal and contain dry prose listing the events and facts that students need to know for their entrance exams.

Second, the manga focus on a few particular episodes of history in some detail rather than presenting a broad overview. This is a characteristic of manga because a number of panels (amounting to a page or more) are required to develop even a short story line. Textbooks, by contrast, can cover the same content in a few lines and can therefore fit more episodes onto one page. In other words, textbooks provide a high density of content in words, while the meanings in manga are conveyed more visually.

Third, both textbooks and educational manga engage in sanitization or emotional distancing. Neither really captures the horrors of the war.

In textbooks the chronological approach to history means the text is a collection of statements each deemed to be "factually correct" by the Ministry of Education. There might be some emotive comments, such as how people suffered, but most value judgments are excised during the screening process. Sanitization in educational manga operates more on a visual level. Seeing people killed in an anime or manga is quite different from seeing people actually being killed in photographs or newsreel footage. On the one hand, this sanitization enables visual depictions of historical violence to be introduced to children from a relatively young age: indeed, educational manga usually depict major atrocities from the war in some visual detail.[28] On the other hand, neither the perpetrators nor the victims of atrocity are main characters with whom the reader is encouraged to identify.

The issue of sanitization relates to a recurrent debate within Japanese history education: what is appropriate to show children (and adults, too) in class. An R-rated film, for example, should not be shown to young children without parental permission. But when does "R-rated material" such as graphic images or testimonies of sexual violence become acceptable in the history classroom? These arguments cover educational activities outside the classroom, too. For example, in *Sensōron* ("On War"), nationalist manga artist Kobayashi Yoshinori is highly critical of school trips to Peace Osaka, a museum run by the Osaka municipal and prefectural governments whose displays used to include graphic photos of Japanese atrocities in Asia.[29] Kobayashi was more concerned with the "masochistic views of history" that he believed were instilled in schoolchildren by such trips, but the issue of whether it is right to expose children to such images in the name of education is important nonetheless.

Notwithstanding Kobayashi's concern with shocking imagery shown to children, his own manga contains a section in which he dismisses various grisly atrocity photographs as fakes. This section is excellent material for a postgraduate class on how and how not to do primary source analysis. Kobayashi argues that the atrocity photographs in some Japanese scholarly books cannot be what the captions say they are. A picture of a Japanese soldier about to decapitate a prisoner (fig. 10.3) could not have been taken during the Nanjing Massacre (December 1937 to February 1938), he argues, because the soldier is only wearing a shirt and Nanjing is freezing in winter.[30] Kobayashi has a point. This picture also appears in a Filipino school textbook we use during the course. In the Filipino book the photo does not have a caption but appears near a section stating, "[The

Figure 10.3. An atrocity picture of disputed origin.

Japanese Military Administration] also issued a proclamation stating that for every Japanese killed, ten Filipino lives would be taken in return."[31]

Exactly when and where the picture was taken remains unclear, but it is an archetypal image of Japanese brutality freely available on the Internet (it comes up in a Google search for "Japanese atrocities"). Kobayashi, therefore, has done half the job of the historian well by skeptically questioning suspect evidence. But as a nationalist who denies or downplays Japanese atrocities, Kobayashi is unconcerned with positively identifying under what circumstances the photo was actually taken. This is where he falls short as a historian, and where the real lesson to students lies: to authenticate primary sources can be difficult; to invalidate them is relatively easy. Even so, Kobayashi has not actually invalidated the photo, only the caption. He has only succeeded in questioning where the decapitation took place. He has not disproved the existence of the killing in the photograph. Nevertheless, Kobayashi has achieved his aim: to instill doubt. With the authenticity of the photo now "disputed," it cannot be allowed in a Japanese textbook, even if it passes the "appropriate for schoolchildren" test. This exemplifies a classic tactic of nationalist historians in Japan: casting doubt on any historical evidence that portrays Japan in a bad light and thereby preventing its inclusion in "factually correct" official narratives such as textbooks.

Visiting Historical (Web)Sites

Finally, I discuss using the Internet in the history classroom to visit historical (web)sites. I teach a course on Hokkaido history that draws heavily on historical narratives at tourist sites, particularly museums, their guidebooks, and their websites. During class we go as virtual tourists to various historical (web)sites and discuss what we find.

First, as we did when using cinematic materials, we start by considering the historical practices of museums. Museums are extremely expensive to establish and run. Typically they rely on taxpayers or benefactors to sustain them. Local governments fund museums as sites of local identity creation and/or for creating a critical mass of local tourist sites that will encourage tourists to visit the locality. Benefactors, meanwhile, have a business interest or political agenda to promote. A company museum is essentially an advertisement for the business. "Following the money" ("production" in the terminology of the circuit of culture), therefore, is a good starting point when culturally analyzing tourist sites because the vested interests behind the museum affect the usefulness of museum materials as teaching resources. In sum, the advantages of using museum materials are that they are self-contained historical narratives from an identifiable perspective and compact because they are designed to be consumed by tourists during a reasonably short visit. The disadvantages are that the historical narrative is inevitably colored by the vested interests behind the museum and particularly marketable narratives may receive more attention at the expense of other, "less profitable" ones.

The local history example I will use here is (web)sites depicting the culture of the indigenous Ainu people in Hokkaido. Hokkaido was annexed and settled by Japanese following the Meiji Restoration of 1868. Culture played a critical role in this history. Ainu were not exterminated, but rather they were dispossessed of their land and stripped of their cultural identity via assimilationist policies. As Michele Mason illustrates, from Meiji period literature through the "conspicuous visual erasure of Hokkaido's Ainu" in the blockbuster film *Year One in the North* (Kita no zero nen), literature, cinema, and other forms of popular culture helped construct a dominant narrative of Hokkaido that excluded the Ainu from the island's history.[32] The Ainu are present, of course, in scholarly histories and museum exhibits (such as the Hokkaido Museum),[33] but for the Ainu to feature too prominently means exposing the fallacy that Hokkaido was "unsettled land" waiting to be colonized by the pioneers, who are the real central characters in Hokkaido's dominant narrative.

However, the policies of assimilation could not extinguish Ainu culture, and eventually the Japanese government did a U-turn. With the 1997 Ainu Culture Promotion and Dissemination of Information Concerning Ainu Traditions Act and the Japanese government's belated attribution of "indigenous people" status in 2008,[34] national policy has switched from cultural assimilation to cultural promotion. In this project the various Ainu museums have a vital role. The most important museums are at Shiraoi (an open air museum), Biratori (a standard museum housing artifacts), and Lake Akan (containing the most important craft market and performance space for Ainu culture).[35] They not only display Ainu culture, making money for the community in the process, but are also sites of cultural preservation. The museum websites are a rich source of visual images and explanations about Ainu history and culture.

However, while traditional Ainu culture can be preserved in such museums, there is a danger that it will become a historical museum piece. The challenge, therefore, is to create new culture, too. One example of new culture is the music of the Ainu Rebels, a band created by young Ainu. The Ainu Rebels only existed from 2006 to 2010, but their legacy and significance will endure much longer. The Ainu Rebels mixed traditional Ainu music with modern music forms, such as hip-hop and rap, and asserted Ainu pride rather than attempting to conceal the musicians' identities.

In class I show a YouTube clip of the Ainu Rebels performing live.[36] Ainu-influenced hip-hop might seem out of place in the history class, but the music is less important than the act of the Ainu Rebels and other bands in producing pop culture.[37] The experience of the Ainu and other minority groups worldwide shows that in the absence of a vibrant popular culture, the cultural heritage of the community becomes fossilized—trapped in history and slipping ever farther away from the present. A vibrant contemporary popular culture gives a community a reservoir of future primary historical sources on which future generations of historians will base their research. Together with the efforts of museums and other actors to preserve traditional Ainu culture, the creation of new culture by the Ainu Rebels and others has given Ainu the opportunity to reclaim their history from the grip of the dominant narrative of Hokkaido. The colonial takeover of Hokkaido was too "successful" (from the colonizer's perspective) for

Ainu to regain meaningful territorial and political sovereignty, but through pop(ular) culture they can maintain an important place for themselves in the cultural history of Japan.

By using popular culture to teach Ainu history, we gain not only insights into Ainu history but also the understanding that to be culturally assimilated ultimately means to be forgotten by history. Having pop(ular) culture means having a history.

Conclusions

Historians, history teachers, and history classes come in many different forms, but unless we have a rigid "this is what happened and why" approach to history, popular culture clearly has much to offer in the history classroom. These days there are no technological excuses for not using popular culture. The onus is on teachers to devise pedagogy and debate best practice. Clearly some historical topics lend themselves to the use of popular culture more than others, and some cultural forms are of more value as teaching resources than others. But, with pedagogical creativity, most popular cultural forms on a historical theme can be of use.

I have proposed some guiding principles for the use of popular culture in the classroom. The materials are never used "for the sake of it" or "for light relief" but always support a set of clear educational aims: the introduction of a historiographic or analytical technique, the performance of critical textual analysis, the debate of a particular historical theme, or the teaching of historical knowledge. Furthermore, popular culture should be situated within academic discourse. Much of the bibliography for this essay is from the reading lists I give my students in class. In this vision, teaching and research go hand in hand. The scholar-educator sometimes engages in research-driven teaching and sometimes in teaching-driven research.

Historians are well qualified to lead discussions on the use of popular culture in teaching. Their training in the use and selection of historical source materials is invaluable in assessing the worth of potential teaching materials. The popular culture around us today is not irrelevant for history. It is not only an invaluable window into what our societies now think about the events of the past, but it is also the source material that subsequent generations of historians will be looking to incorporate into their future scholarship about us and our age.

Notes

[1] See also chapter 6, by Melanie King, in this volume.

[2] Andrew Jones, "High Culture versus Pop Culture: Which Is Best for Engaging Students?," *Guardian,* February 20, 2013.

[3] Kirwin R. Shaffer, "Popular Culture and the Teaching of History: The Modern Caribbean History Course," *History Teacher* 37, no. 3 (2004): 368.

[4] A Japanese Ministry of Foreign Affairs report defines *pop culture* as "culture produced in the everyday lives of ordinary people," which allows forms categorized as "traditional culture" by many, such as ukiyo-e, pottery, and tea ceremony, to be categorized as *poppu karuchā* along with anime and manga. Ministry of Foreign Affairs. "Poppu karuchā no bunka gaikō ni okeru katsuyō ni kansuru hōkoku," http://www.mofa.go.jp/mofaj/annai/shingikai/koryu/h18_sokai/05hokoku.html.

[5] For another fine example of this sort of study, see Jason G. Karlin's monograph about popular culture in the Meiji and Taisho periods, which illuminates how people in Japan at that time viewed their own present and the even more distant past. Jason G. Karlin, *Gender and Nation in Meiji Japan: Modernity, Loss, and the Doing of History* (Honolulu: University of Hawai'i Press, 2014).

[6] Ministry of Education, Culture, Sports, Science, and Technology [Japan], "Chūgakkō gakushū shidō yōryō kaisetsu" (Junior High School Government Curriculum Guidelines), 2006, 79, http://www.mext.go.jp/component/a_menu/education/micro_detail/__icsFiles/afieldfile/2011/01/05/1234912_003.pdf.

[7] Philip A. Seaton, *Japan's Contested War Memories: The "Memory Rifts" in Historical Consciousness of World War II* (London: Routledge, 2007), 148–50.

[8] Department for Education [United Kingdom], "History: Key Concepts," http://www.education.gov.uk/schools/teachingandlearning/curriculum/secondary/b00199545/history/programme/concepts.

[9] Caroline Hoefferle, "Teaching Historiography to High School and Undergraduate Students," *OAH Magazine of History* (Organization of American Historians) 21, no. 2 (2007): 40–44.

[10] Shinzō Abe, *Utsukushii kuni e* (Toward a Beautiful Country). (Tokyo: Bunshun Shinsho, 2006), 203.

[11] Hoefferle, "Teaching Historiography," 40.

[12] William M. Tsutsui, "Teaching History and/of/or Popular Culture," *electronic journal of contemporary japanese studies* 13, no. 2 (2013), http://www.japanesestudies.org.uk/ejcjs/vol13/iss2/tsutsui.html.

[13] Ibid. See also Melanie King's discussion in chapter 6 of this volume.

[14] Taiga Dramas run throughout an entire year and are an epic biopic of a historical figure. Broadcast on Sunday evenings from 20:00 to 20:45 on the national TV network NHK (Nippon Hōsō Kyōkai), and with viewing figures in the 15 to 25 percent range, Taiga Dramas are a truly national media event.

[15] Robert A. Rosenstone, "Oliver Stone as Historian," in *Oliver Stone's USA: Film, History, and Controversy*, ed. Robert Brent Toplin (Lawrence: University Press of Kansas, 2000), 30.

[16] Tsutsui, "Teaching History."

[17] Paul du Gay et al., *Doing Cultural Studies: The Story of the Sony Walkman* (London: Sage, 1997), 3.

[18] This company went bankrupt in 2009.

[19] *The Last Samurai*, dir. Edward Zwick, Warner Bros. Pictures, 2003.

[20] Rosenstone, "Oliver Stone as Historian," 29–31.

[21] *History vs. Hollywood*, dir. Steven Jack, The History Channel, 2003.

[22] Mark Ravina, *The Last Samurai: The Life and Battles of Saigō Takamori* (Hoboken NJ: John Wiley & Sons, 2004).

[23] *The Pacific*, dir. Tim Van Patten et al., Dreamworks Television, 2010.

[24] *Grave of the Fireflies* (Hotaru no haka), dir. Takahata Isao, Studio Ghibli, 1988.

[25] Sabine Frühstück, "The Uses of Popular Culture for Sex and Violence," *electronic journal of contemporary japanese studies* 13, no. 2 (2013), http://www.japanesestudies.org.uk/ejcjs/vol13/iss2/fruhstuck.html.

[26] Hiroko Cockerill, "Laughter and Tears: The Complex Narratives of Shōwa Gesaku Writer Nosaka Akiyuki," *Japanese Studies* 27, no. 3 (2007): 300.

[27] See the Yūshūkan website, http://www.yasukuni.or.jp/english/yushukan/; Hiroshima Peace Memorial Museum website, http://www.pcf.city.hiroshima.jp/top_e.html; Peace Osaka website, http://www.peace-osaka.or.jp.

[28] In one of the most popular series, published by Shōgakukan, there are frames depicting civilians being machine-gunned in Nanjing and Singapore and prisoners of war worked to death on the Burma Railroad. See *Nihon no Rekishi* (*History of Japan*), vol. 20: *Ajia to Taiheiyō no tatakai* (Tokyo: Shōgakukan, 1983), 53, 81, 94.

[29] Kobayashi Yoshinori, *Sensōron* (Tokyo: Gentōsha, 1998), 157. In April 2015 Peace Osaka reopened after major renovations. Peace Osaka bowed to pressure from Osaka Mayor Hashimoto Toru and rightwing campaigners to change the contents of its exhibits. All references to and photographs of Japanese atrocities have been removed.

[30] Ibid., 162.

[31] Reynaldo Oliveros et al., *Philippine History and Government* (Quezon City: Ibon Books, 2007), 189.

[32] Michele M. Mason, *Dominant Narratives of Colonial Hokkaido and Imperial Japan: Envisioning the Periphery and the Modern Nation-State* (New York: Palgrave Macmillan, 2012), 166; Year One in the North (Kita no zero nen), dir. Isao Yukisada, Tōei, 2005.

[33] Hokkaido Museum, http://www.hm.pref.hokkaido.lg.jp (formerly called the Historical Museum of Hokkaido). The museum was renovated and reopened in April 2015. The new exhibits contain expanded displays of Ainu history and culture.

[34] Ministry of Land, Infrastructure, Transport, and Tourism, "Promotion of Ainu Culture," http://www.mlit.go.jp/hkb/ainu_e.html; ann-elise lewallen, "Indigenous at Last! Ainu Grassroots Organizing and the Indigenous People's Summit in Ainu Mosir," Asia-Pacific Journal 48-6-08 (November 2008), http://www.japanfocus.org/-ann_elise-lewallen/2971.

[35] Ainu Museum Poroto Kotan: http://www.ainu-museum.or.jp/en/; Nibutani Ainu Culture Museum: http://www.town.biratori.hokkaido.jp/biratori/nibutani/; Akan Ainu Kotan: http://www.akanainu.jp.

[36] "Ainu's New Identity," TITV Weekly, http://www.youtube.com/watch?v=9dgexEvTEjs.

[37] Examples include the various performers at the Indigenous Music Festival in 2008. See ann-elise lewallen, "Indigenous at Last! Ainu: Grassroots Organizing and the Indigenous People's Summit in Ainu Mosir." *Asia-Pacific Journal* 48-6-08 (2008), http://www.japanfocus.org/-ann_elise-lewallen/2971.

Works Cited

Abe, Shinzō. *Utsukushii kuni e* (*Toward a Beautiful Country*). Tokyo: Bunshun Shinsho, 2006.

Cockerill, Hiroko. "Laughter and Tears: The Complex Narratives of Shōwa Gesaku Writer Nosaka Akiyuki." *Japanese Studies* 27, no. 3 (2007): 295–303.

Department for Education [United Kingdom]. "History: Key Concepts." http://www.education.gov.uk/schools/teachingandlearning/curriculum/secondary/b00199545/history/programme/concepts.

Du Gay, Paul, Stuart Hall, Linda Janes, Hugh Mackay, and Keith Negus. *Doing Cultural Studies: The Story of the Sony Walkman*. London: Sage, 1997.

Frühstück, Sabine. "The Uses of Popular Culture for Sex and Violence." *electronic journal of contemporary japanese studies* 13, no. 2 (2013). http://www.japanesestudies.org.uk/ejcjs/vol13/iss2/fruhstuck.html.

Hoefferle, Caroline. "Teaching Historiography to High School and Undergraduate Students." *OAH Magazine of History* (Organization of American Historians) 21, no. 2 (2007): 40–44.

Jones, Andrew. "High Culture versus Pop Culture: Which Is Best for Engaging Students?" *Guardian*, February 20, 2013.

Karlin, Jason G. *Gender and Nation in Meiji Japan: Modernity, Loss, and the Doing of History*. Honolulu: University of Hawai'i Press, 2014.

Kobayashi Yoshinori. *Sensōron* (On War). Tokyo: Gentōsha, 1998.

Kodama Kōta. *Nihon no Rekishi* (*History of Japan*). Vol. 20: *Ajia to Taiheiyō no tatakai* (Asia and the Pacific War). Tokyo: Shōgakukan, 1983.

lewallen, ann-elise. "Indigenous at Last! Ainu Grassroots Organizing and the Indigenous People's Summit in Ainu Mosir." *Asia-Pacific Journal* 48-6-08 (November 2008), http://www.japanfocus.org/-ann_elise-lewallen/2971.

Mason, Michele M. *Dominant Narratives of Colonial Hokkaido and Imperial Japan: Envisioning the Periphery and the Modern Nation-State*. New York: Palgrave Macmillan, 2012.

Ministry of Education, Culture, Sports, Science, and Technology [Japan]. "Chūgakkō gakushū shidō yōryō kaisetsu" (Junior High School Government Curriculum Guidelines), 2006. http://www.mext.go.jp/component/a_menu/education/micro_detail/__icsFiles/afieldfile/2011/01/05/1234912_003.pdf.

Ministry of Foreign Affairs. "Poppu karuchā no bunka gaikō ni okeru katsuyō ni kansuru hōkoku" (Report on "Applications of Popular Culture Diplomacy"). 2006. http://www.mofa.go.jp/mofaj/annai/shingikai/koryu/h18_sokai/05hokoku.html.

Oliveros, Reynaldo, Ma. Concepcion M. Galvez, Yolanda R. Estrella, and John Paul Andaquig. *Philippine History and Government*. Quezon City: Ibon Books, 2007.

Ravina, Mark. *The Last Samurai: The Life and Battles of Saigō Takamori*. Hoboken NJ: John Wiley & Sons, 2004.

Rosenstone, Robert A. "Oliver Stone as Historian." In *Oliver Stone's USA: Film, History, and Controversy*, edited by Robert Brent Toplin, 26–39. Lawrence: University Press of Kansas, 2000.

Seaton, Philip. A. *Japan's Contested War Memories: The "Memory Rifts" in Historical Consciousness of World War II*. London: Routledge, 2007.

Shaffer, Kirwin R. "Popular Culture and the Teaching of History: The Modern Caribbean History Course." *History Teacher* 37, no. 3 (2004): 365–83.

Tsutsui, William M. "Teaching History and/of/or Popular Culture." *electronic journal of contemporary japanese studies* 13, no. 2 (2013). http://www.japanesestudies.org.uk/ejcjs/vol13/iss2/tsutsui.html.

Movies and Television Programs

"Ainu's New Identity." TITV Weekly. http://www.youtube.com/watch?v=9dgexEvTEjs.

Grave of the Fireflies (Hotaru no haka). Dir. Takahata Isao. Studio Ghibli, 1988.

History vs. Hollywood. Dir. Steven Jack. The History Channel, 2003.

The Last Samurai. Dir. Edward Zwick. Warner Bros. Pictures, 2003.

The Pacific. Dir. Tim Van Patten et al. Dreamworks Television, 2010.

Year One in the North (Kita no zero nen). Dir. Yukisada Isao. Tōei, 2005.

THE ONLINE FUTURE(S) OF TEACHING JAPANESE POPULAR CULTURE

CHRIS McMORRAN

Introduction

One thread winding its way through this volume has been the importance of technology in teaching *about* and *with* Japanese popular culture (JPC). During the past few decades, instructors gradually replaced grainy audiocassettes and VCR tapes with CDs and DVDs, before eventually finding much popular culture on the Internet. This has meant fewer technical problems such as incompatible DVD region codes, and it has meant the availability of seemingly endless content. Contributors to this volume cite the Internet's usefulness for allowing students and instructors to virtually travel or quickly locate media, such as images (both historical and contemporary), music videos, print and television advertisements, or film and television clips, all of which hopefully will do more than just be a hook to attract students. Even content originally intended to be held in one's hand, like manga, may be scanned, uploaded, and translated for global consumption, turning it into digital media. There seems to be a consensus among our contributors that the Internet has vastly enhanced teaching JPC and in fact would be virtually impossible without it.

Additionally, many contributors acknowledge the importance of the Internet and other technologies not only for exposing students to JPC but also for providing them with a way to communicate with like-minded individuals around the world. For students interested in games, cosplay, J-pop, television dramas, and more, the Internet has become an indispensable tool for keeping abreast of the latest trends and participating in geographically dispersed communities. Indeed, it is clear that the Internet and related technologies are a driving force in attracting students to JPC courses.

Clearly, the Internet has become indispensable to teaching JPC. This seems likely to remain the case in the future. However, although those who teach about Japan have long been at the forefront of using popular culture to cross physical and intellectual borders, they have been very slow to actually teach JPC *via* the Internet. In other words, Japanese studies instructors and students have been tapping into online sources to discover content and build communities for years, but they have not actually created or taken courses online. In this chapter, I analyze why this is the case by outlining some of the potential rewards and obstacles associated with Massive Open Online Courses (MOOCs). MOOCs may vastly expand the global population of students learning about Japanese popular culture. However, in order to reach such a goal, those who teach with or about Japanese popular culture must navigate the confusing waters of copyright.

What might the future hold for MOOCs about or incorporating Japanese popular culture? This chapter addresses this question and explains the relevance of the topic for anyone engaged in teaching Japanese popular culture. This includes not only individuals who teach courses in film, media, or cultural studies departments specifically about Japanese film, anime, manga, games, cosplay, literature, music, television dramas, and so on, but also those who use examples from popular culture to teach *about* something else, such as history, sociology, anthropology, geography, politics, international relations, marketing, business, and more. This chapter should help anyone who relies on Japanese popular culture to make a point, provide an example, define a term, or even entertain, to understand how MOOCs might shape what they do and how they do it. It reviews literature about MOOCs in general and incorporates the comments of scholars from around the world who have developed MOOCs rich in popular culture in order to (1) define MOOCs and trace their recent growth, acclaim, and controversy; (2) discuss challenges that must be overcome to take advantage of MOOCs, most notably copyright; and (3) suggest future applications of MOOCs, including in "flipped classrooms."

Defining MOOCs

Since 2012 the growth of MOOCs has stirred excitement and controversy in higher education. Open-access, fully online courses are but the latest advance in a long history of distance learning. However, the recent combination of advanced course-hosting technologies, enthusiasm for MOOCs at institutions like Harvard and Stanford, and vast start-up capital for MOOC providers like Coursera, edX, and Udacity has led to speculation that MOOCs may drastically alter higher education, for better or worse. They have been called "the single most important experiment in higher education."[1] Others see them as a "game changer" that will open higher education to "hundreds of millions of people."[2] And still others consider them a "massive, terrible idea for the future of college."[3] They have stirred almost religious fervor among advocates and doomsday scenarios among opponents. However, for anyone unfamiliar with the term MOOC, some explanation is necessary.

By definition a MOOC can have a *massive* number of learners. For instance, over 160,000 students from over 190 countries signed up for Sebastian Thrun and Peter Norvig's Artificial Intelligence course in 2011, spurring Thrun to give up tenure at Stanford and found the MOOC provider Udacity.[4] Because it is online and can be fully automated, in theory a MOOC can have an unlimited number of participants and be running constantly.

By definition a MOOC should be *open* to learners regardless of institutional affiliation, academic status, age, sex, religion, race, or geographic location. In addition, most MOOCs are still free of charge, allowing anyone access to classes taught by faculty at some of the world's top institutions. In theory anyone with a computer and Internet access can enroll in any MOOC.

By definition a MOOC is *online*. Like radio, television, VHS tapes, cassette tapes, CDs, and DVDs before, the Internet ushered in a new era in distance learning. Advanced course-hosting technologies now allow nearly all materials to be accessible through one online portal, including lectures, discussion forums, and assessments. While some MOOCs show lectures videotaped in front of students, others are specially produced for online learners, with an instructor speaking directly to the camera or over lecture slides, and include homework, discussion forums, and assessments specially designed for an online learning environment.

Finally, a MOOC is a *course*. It is not a single lecture, or even a series of lectures one can view online. Nor is it learning materials or lesson plans found online that can be used to supplement a course. Instead, a MOOC is a self-contained course that follows a syllabus and includes assessment. Unlike most courses, however, successful completion of a MOOC typically does not earn the student credit toward the completion of a degree. In lieu of credit, instructors may offer a certificate of completion.

The term *MOOC* was coined by Dave Cormier in 2008 in reference to the University of Manitoba's Connectivism and Connective Knowledge course.[5] Precursors like Open Educational Resources (OER) have been praised for their potential to assist developing countries by enabling anyone to pursue higher education.[6] However, the MOOC idea did not garner much attention until Stanford's "AI" course in 2011, with its startling enrolment of 160,000.[7] In the intervening years, MOOCs have continued to grow in ways none of their pioneers ever imagined, with established MOOC providers now located around the world, including Australia, Canada, Germany, Great Britain, Spain, and the United States.

Godzilla-Size Growth

The *New York Times* declared 2012 "The Year of the MOOC," stating, "The shimmery hope is that free courses can bring the best education in the world to the most remote corners of the planet, help people in their careers, and expand intellectual and personal networks."[8] Indeed, most MOOC providers portray themselves as democratizing education. For instance, Udacity claims, "Our mission is to bring accessible, affordable, engaging, and highly effective higher education to the world. We believe that higher education is a basic human right, and we seek to empower our students to advance their education and careers."[9] Coursera has similar aims: "We envision a future where everyone has access to a world-class education that has so far been available to a select few. We aim to empower people with education that will improve their lives, the lives of their families, and the communities they live in."[10] Finally, edX also sees itself opening the doors to learning: "We present the best of higher education online, offering opportunity to anyone who wants to achieve, thrive, and grow."[11]

The admirable goal of opening higher education to anyone, coupled with a world of potential learners, has led to immense growth in the number of MOOC platforms, partner universities, course offerings, and enrolled students over the past few years. For instance, Coursera, founded in April

2012, maintains a ticker on its homepage that in mid-2015 boasted more than 11 million students, 900 courses, and 118 partner institutions.[12] Such growth may be unsustainable. Massive open online courses might be a fad.[13] However, the growth has been too sudden and widespread to ignore. With enrollment figures for courses about Japan constantly in flux due to unpredictable economic and cultural factors,[14] faculty members who teach about Japan might see MOOCs as a way to reach more learners, including the possibility of reaching more students in a single MOOC than in a thirty-year career in the classroom.[15] While some may argue that education should be focused more on quality than quantity, dwindling enrollments have justified the closure of many departments over the decades, and there is nothing sacrosanct about Japanese studies or courses on Japan in general. At some point, faculty members may need to decide whether to create, reject, or adopt the MOOC platform.

The stakes for joining (or not) the MOOC revolution are higher for institutions. Given the ever-increasing costs of higher education and growing student debt, MOOCs provide an opportunity for highly selective and/or expensive institutions to be seen as opening their (online) doors to anyone who wants to learn, regardless of their financial circumstances.[16] Moreover, in a globally competitive higher education marketplace, many institutions consider MOOCs a major pedagogical shift that cannot be missed. Early advocacy of MOOCs by top-tier institutions like Stanford and Harvard has left some others scrambling to join existing MOOC platforms, create their own, or even actively reject the model.[17]

Democratizing Education?

Enthusiasm for the potential of MOOCs to democratize education recently has become tempered by serious questions about the centralization of knowledge, academic freedom, and the potential hollowing out of institutions. Some of these concerns were sparked by a MOOC titled Justice, offered by edX and taught by Harvard government professor Michael Sandel. Japan scholars might recall Sandel's recent popularity in Japan, where his public lectures attracted tens of thousands.[18] In early 2013, a dean at San Jose State University suggested that its Philosophy Department assign Sandel's MOOC lectures as homework, which students would watch before class, then discuss with the instructor during class. Some experts consider this "flipped classroom" approach a promising innovation enabled by MOOCs, a point to which I return later. In this case, however, the San Jose State Philosophy Department balked.[19] In an open letter to Sandel published in the *Chronicle of Higher Education*, it implicated him in a process that may one day dismantle departments and narrow the production of knowledge in higher education: "We fear that two classes of universities will be created: one, well-funded colleges and universities in which privileged students get their own real professor; the other, financially stressed private and public universities in which students watch a bunch of videotaped lectures and interact, if indeed any interaction is available on their home campuses, with a professor that this model of education has turned into a glorified teaching assistant."[20]

Indeed, the contention that MOOCs help democratize education may be undermined by the possibility that they could lead to a concentration of knowledge production and dissemination in the hands of a few elite institutions and celebrity academics, as well as less academic freedom for faculty members required to use MOOCs in "flipped" or "blended" environments.[21] As the San Jose State faculty note: "Teaching justice through an educational model that is spearheading the creation of two social classes in academia thus amounts to a cruel joke."[22] Sandel responded to the letter, supporting the department's academic freedom. However, he admitted, "The worry that the widespread use of online courses will damage departments in public universities facing budgetary pressures is a legitimate concern that deserves serious debate, at edX and throughout higher education."[23]

In an era of cost cutting throughout higher education it will be difficult for many institutions to resist the dual allure of (1) reducing labor costs by reducing new hires or hiring qualified scholars as lower-paid "glorified teaching assistants" and (2) offering students at less prestigious institutions credit for MOOCs from global brand-name universities.[24] As the San Jose State Philosophy Department points out, this may lead to "the creation of two social classes in academia,"[25] a division that might be further exacerbated among those who teach about or with Japanese popular culture. The reason is simple: copyright.

Copyright and Fair Use in MOOCs

Continued expansion of course offerings by Coursera, edX, Udacity, and others means students can choose from hundreds of courses in STEM (science, technology, engineering, math) disciplines, the humanities, and the social sciences. However, only a handful of courses focus on popular culture (see table C.1), and only two incorporate any type of Japanese popular culture. One is *Visualizing Japan (1850s–1930s): Westernization, Protest, Modernity* (MITx and HarvardX).[26] The other is *Visualizing Postwar Tokyo* (UTokyoX).[27] Both courses are offered by edX. The former is made by the collaborators at MIT and Harvard behind Visualizing Cultures, a website that contains images, narratives, and lesson plans devoted to image-driven scholarship about East Asian history.[28] To be clear, neither of these would fit most people's definition of a popular culture course, nor do they advertise themselves that way. Both are history courses that rely heavily on the visual historical record: woodblock prints, postcards, magazine advertisements, TV programs, and other media that were the popular culture of their day.[29] For instance, in Visualizing Postwar Tokyo, students "Analyze the history of change and development in postwar Tokyo from different perspectives using archived photographs, films, and TV programs."[30] These courses are an important first step, but no one has yet built a MOOC specifically about Japanese film, anime, manga, games, characters, fashion, literature, music, television, and so on. Whoever does so will face hurdles.

Existing online technologies enable any course to reach millions of learners; however, it is no wonder that the first and most common MOOCs have been in STEM fields. Particularly at the introductory level, such courses do not require major adjustments each year. Students can simply watch a series of video lectures and do online problem sets that scaffold their learning of content and skills. Courses like those mentioned in this volume, on the other hand, involve more interaction between students and faculty. Plus the content constantly shifts to keep up with trends in popular culture and scholarship on it.

This is not the only disadvantage suffered by humanities and social science courses in online education though.[31] Of particular concern is the issue of fair use: the informal doctrine that in the case of the United States allows the "performance or display of a work by instructors or pupils in the course of face-to-face teaching activities of a nonprofit educational institution, in a classroom or similar place devoted to instruction."[32] Fair use allows instructors to show film or television clips, artwork, music, or anything else protected by any country's copyright laws without fear of prosecution by copyright holders.[33] Without such protection, the classroom would be a space absent of all media other than that specifically created by the instructor and students.

Provider (courses related to popular culture / total courses)	Course Title	Instructor and Affiliation
Coursera (14/939)	Marriage and the Movies: A History	Jeanine Basinger, Wesleyan University
	Scandinavian Film and Television	Ib Bondebjerg, University of Copenhagen
	Music's Big Bang: The Genesis of Rock 'n' Roll	David Carlson, University of Florida
	Online Games: Literature, New Media, and Narrative	Jay Clayton, Vanderbilt University
	History of Rock, Pt One History of Rock, Pt Two The Music of the Rolling Stones The Music of the Beatles	John Covach, University of Rochester
	Warhol	Glyn Davis, The University of Edinburgh
	The Language of Hollywood: Storytelling, Sound, and Color	Scott Higgins, Wesleyan University
	Comic Books and Graphic Novels	William Kuskin, University of Colorado, Boulder
	Listening to World Music	Carol Muller, University of Pennsylvania
	Live: A History of Art for Artists, Animators, and Gamers	Jeannene Przyblyski, California Institute of the Arts
	The Camera Never Lies	Emmett Sullivan, Royal Holloway, University of London
edX (4/411)	Visualizing Japan (1850s–1930s): Westernization, Protest, Modernity	John Dower, MIT; Andrew Gordon, Harvard University; Shigeru Miyagawa, MIT; Gennifer Weisenfeld, Duke University
	Music in the 20th Century (in Mandarin)	Bryan Minghui, Peking University
	Visualizing Postwar Tokyo, Part 1 Visualizing Postwar Tokyo, Part 2	Shunya Yoshimi, University of Tokyo
Udacity (0/57)	None	

Table C.1. Courses About, or Widely Incorporating, Popular Culture Offered by Major MOOC Providers (mid-2015)

In general, the fair use doctrine applies to MOOCs. For instance, Coursera, one of the leading providers, states that the fair use doctrine applies when:

> (1) The image shown is being directly criticized. For example, in a photography course, a photo is being shown to illustrate the problems with over-exposing film; (2) The image is being used in a transformative way; that is, the purpose for use in the course is completely different than its original purpose. For example, in a course about web design it is acceptable to show web screen shots to demonstrate good and bad web design techniques.[34]

Criticism and transformation have long been central to the fair use argument for including media in classrooms,[35] and based on its statement, Coursera appears to recognize the importance of fair use. In fact, however, MOOC providers and institutions have been advising instructors designing MOOCs to secure copyright permissions or remove anything protected by copyright.

Caution stems from two points. First, like all digital scholarship and learning platforms (e.g., websites, wikis, blogs, Moodle), MOOCs are not confined to the physical classroom. Therefore, the "face-to-face" requirement mentioned above does not necessarily apply. Also, fair use protection is limited to "nonprofit educational institutions." Since many MOOC providers are actually for-profit corporations that only partner with educational institutions, this protection may not apply. Some MOOC providers charge students for course access (e.g., Udacity's nanodegree programs incur a monthly fee) or completion certificates (e.g., Coursera's verified certificate), while some providers charge institutions to use their MOOCs for credit-earning courses.[36] For these reasons, MOOC providers urge caution when using third-party content, which Coursera defines as "content that is not self-created, such as graphs, charts, artwork, photos, screenshots, clip art, trademarks and videos."[37] The company provides this advice to faculty making MOOCs: "While this is not to rule out fair use as an option, it is to be used with care, and in parallel with consultation with your university's attorneys or legal personel [sic]."[38] In fact it recommends securing permission for all copyright-protected materials "as if you were the author of a textbook, obtaining rights for materials you would like to include in your book."[39] Many instructors will find it unrealistic to consult with university legal personnel about every piece of third-party content to be shown in class, since this is precisely what the fair use doctrine is meant to help them avoid.

Taking this cautious approach to copyright requires altering many teaching practices. For instance, Ib Bondebjerg, whose course Scandinavian Film and Television premiered in 2014 with Coursera, acknowledged, "The question of copyright is indeed much more complicated in a MOOC course like this reaching many thousand students from a wide variety of countries."[40] During the planning stages Bondebjerg met with others who have created MOOCs: "We were advised not to upload or show any clips ourselves. I do this all the time in my normal classes, so this is indeed a restriction. I had hoped to be able to imbed clips in my video presentations, but unless I somehow clear the rights (which I am working on) this cannot be done."[41]

If this cautious approach prevails, I believe the limitations of fair use in MOOCs may create a chasm between institutions with sufficient financial, staffing, and legal support to produce media-rich MOOCs and those without. Developing any MOOC related to Japanese popular culture will require one of three options: (1) stripping the course of all copyright-protected material, (2) testing the limits of fair use protection, or (3) securing copyright permission from all content creators. For the majority of instructors, only the second option is feasible for teaching popular culture. Despite the potential for effective education via the other two options, I argue that testing the limits of fair use protection is necessary for retaining the integrity of the fair use principle in education and maintaining the greatest potential for the democratization of learning via MOOCs.

Playing It Safe: The Content-Free Course

The first option, not including any third-party content protected by copyright, is already the norm for MOOCs in STEM fields. Here courses rely on images (graphs, animations) created by MOOC faculty and their support teams. For courses in the humanities and social sciences that may have included copyright-protected content in the past, it may be easy to remove such material that simply illustrates a concept or phenomenon. For instance, in my Introduction to Japanese Studies course, a residential course for 460 students at the National University of Singapore, when I teach about the recent decline in lifetime employment and the emergence of dispatched workers, I do not need to show a five-minute clip from the 2007 NipponTV drama *Haken no hinkaku* (Dignity of Special Temporary Staff).[42] The clip may grab student attention and help introduce the topic, but it is not essential. If I developed this module into a MOOC, I could drop the television clip without much sacrifice.

However, how could one teach a media studies course without showing at least something protected by copyright? How could one teach a course on manga using only work in the public domain? How could one teach a film studies course? Screenshots are acceptable in MOOCs, but they are insufficient to achieve the kind of close and repetitive viewing necessary when teaching about the *moving* image. While television and film clips are covered by fair use in the classroom due to the tireless efforts of the Society for Cinema and Media Studies and others,[43] in the area of MOOCs, Bondebjerg and others have been encouraged to err on the side of caution, to the point of removing all third-party content from their online courses. If the fair use doctrine fails to transfer to MOOCs and all copyright-protected material is excised from film and media studies classes, many departments and scholars around the world will be unable to fully participate in this new world of online education, hamstrung by the inability to include the very object of criticism and debate in their lectures.

Alternatively, one could remove all copyright-protected material from a MOOC and encourage students to purchase it. This has been the strategy for some popular culture MOOCs. For instance, on the course description page for History of Rock, Part One, John Covach notes, "Unfortunately, the expense of licensing music to support a course like this is prohibitive. Students are therefore asked to seek out the music discussed here (most of which is readily available on the internet). Because artists cannot be paid otherwise, we encourage all students to purchase the music they enjoy when possible."[44] Of course, this assumes that students can purchase content regardless of their location. Similarly, in his film course entitled The Language of Hollywood: Storytelling, Sound, and Color, instructor Scott Higgins points students to potential outlets for the required films: "They are readily available on DVD and available for RENTAL via NETFLIX or a similar service. Some of them are available streaming on the internet. All are available for purchase from AMAZON or another vendor."[45] Of course, the requirement that students view films outside class in this MOOC means Higgins's film choices are restricted to what is available for rental or purchase, possibly limiting what he can teach about filmmaking in the early twentieth century. More disconcertingly, prohibitive shipping costs, incompatible DVD region codes, and inaccessible online versions will make the films unobtainable for many potential learners outside the United States and may prevent students from registering for or completing the course.

After removing all copyright-protected content, one can also point students to it elsewhere on the Internet. However, linking to external sites is only feasible if one is certain a link will remain active and if the content is legally accessible to students around the world.[46] Of course, when creating a MOOC, one should not link students to pirated content; however, can one mention that such websites exist, letting students find them on their own? How should one react if students use discussion forums to provide other students with links to sites that violate copyright? In his film studies class, Higgins soon discovered that students turned to alternative methods for the sake of learning. He writes, "As soon as the course launched some students set up a Facebook page for it where they listed torrents for most of the movies. I monitored the Coursera discussion board and removed any reference to this, and any attempt to provide links to the films directly."[47]

Those who teach about or with Japanese popular culture understand well the barriers to learning erected by prohibitive shipping costs, incompatible DVD region codes, and online inaccessibility. Like Higgins's students, many instructors engage in legally questionable tactics in order to stay on top of popular culture trends in Japan and curate pedagogically appropriate materials for the classroom. After decades of sharing these works with students under the protection of fair use, instructors will be unable to incorporate them into a MOOC without bending the rules or insisting on fair use protection through transformative use of the original.

Pushing the Limits of Fair Use Online

For those who cannot conceive of a course on Japanese popular culture without any third-party content directly in the course, one can push the limits of fair use in the MOOC era. To do so, instructors must insist on including popular culture content in their courses and constantly stand by the "transformative" principle in the fair use doctrine. One example of this in practice is Scott Higgins and his MOOC. When creating his MOOC, Higgins took the issue of copyright very seriously, as did the legal and administrative teams at his institution and Coursera. Still, he proceeded with using third-party content. He explains, "I did use quite a few clips in my lectures, but always with running commentary and/or interrupted. Also I used Screenflow to produce the lectures, so the film clip is always embedded, never full frame."[48] In this way, he contends he is criticizing and transforming the original. In preparation for potential copyright issues, Higgins composed a letter to his provost justifying his incorporation of stills and clips into lectures. His rule of thumb is useful for anyone considering a MOOC on popular culture: "My personal litmus test for this practice is to ask, 'Am I ruining the sequence in some way?' In other words, if I am destroying the entertainment value of the sequence through a critical intervention, then I am probably safe."[49]

Higgins is not the only MOOC instructor incorporating film clips. In a piece in the *New Yorker*, Nathan Heller introduced The Ancient Greek Hero, a MOOC from edX led by Gregory Nagy. Heller describes a lecture relevant to the discussion of fair use.

> The segment started with a head shot of Nagy talking about the 1982 movie *Blade Runner*. His lecture was intercut with a muted clip showing the rain-drenched death soliloquy of Roy Batty, the movie's replicant antagonist. "I've seen things you people wouldn't believe. ... All those moments will be lost in time, like tears in rain. *Time to die*." Nagy spoke the crucial words and started teasing them apart.[50]

Nagy pushes the boundaries of fair use by showing the clip in its entirety, but he voices the character's last words himself.

William Kuskin has taken a less cautious approach with his course Comic Books and Graphic Novels. The course, on Coursera, is entirely image driven. Therefore, while planning it he explained, "I will definitely show images, by hook, by crook, by copyright, or by fair use. I can't teach the class otherwise".[51] Two years, two iterations, and seventy thousand students later, Kuskin admits, "[I] freely incorporated as much material as I wanted, both visual and textual, from a variety of sources."[52] In fact, he says, "We never asked for copyright, and none was given, but I cited everything as carefully as if I were writing a textbook."[53] In his videos, Kuskin fits the "transformative" model of fair use by thumbing through comic books, directing students' attention to key aspects of the design, ink, and more. In other words, while the course may increase the entertainment value of comic books and graphic novels in general for students, they could not watch his videos in lieu of purchasing this third-party content. For this reason, he is testing the limits of Coursera's advice and counting on the transferability of the fair use doctrine from the classroom to the MOOC.

Playing It Safe: Negotiating Permissions

For those who wish to remain as cautious as possible in the MOOC era while still retaining the vibrancy of a course that teaches *about* or *with* popular culture, one can contact the necessary publishers, production companies, website administrators, and advertising agencies for permission to use each image, film and television clip, advertisement, or song used in class. Some copyright holders may be generous with their assets and willing to cooperate. A prime example is the cosmetics company Shiseido, which allowed the edX course Visualizing Japan (1850s–1930s): Westernization, Protest, Modernity to use its advertisements from the 1920s and 30s.[54] Thanks to Shiseido's generosity, the course could use these vivid images to make points about gender, consumption, and modernity of the era. In fact, MIT negotiated a creative commons copyright license with Shiseido years before the MOOC was proposed, when the images and associated essays and lesson plans were posted on the Visualizing Cultures website mentioned earlier. As Shigeru Miyagawa, one of the MOOC's producers, explains, "For copyright, we were in the unusual situation of basing our virtually entire work on *Visualizing Cultures*, a 10-year project in which we cleared the copyright to the images. ... We have Creative Commons agreement with over 200 museums and other collections."[55] Similarly, in creating the course Visualizing Postwar Tokyo, instructors at the University of Tokyo needed to negotiate (and sometimes purchase) rights to show archived photographs, films, and TV programs, specifically footage from the national broadcast network NHK. It is unclear how much impact the institutions (MIT and Harvard in the former case, in the former case, the University of Tokyo in the latter) had in convincing the copyright holders to cooperate. However, it is clear that similarly content-rich MOOCs will require vast institutional support (staff, legal assistance, course release for instructors, and financial support for the purchase of usage rights when needed) to negotiate the inclusion of third-party content.

Given these demands, even the most enthusiastic faculty member and institution may conclude that developing a Japanese popular-culture-focused MOOC is not worth the effort. The thought of liaising with university lawyers (assuming one's institution has full-time lawyers with time to devote to copyright issues) and chasing down the copyright holders for bottled green tea commercials or out-of-print manga may sound unreasonable to many.[56] And even if copyright is secured for enough material to create a course, instructors may have to settle on a second- or third-best example. More seriously, securing permissions may require an investment of time and money beyond the reach of most scholars and institutions. Much as McLaren and Spies emphasize the importance of understanding who is producing popular culture and under what conditions,[57] the emergence of MOOCs highlights the need to make clear who is producing academic knowledge about Japan and Japanese popular culture. Specifically, if one takes the cautious approach to including third-party content encouraged by Coursera, it is likely that only institutions with deep pockets, large legal teams, and savvy tech support will be able to produce MOOCs of the highest scholarly caliber. Echoing the concerns of the San Jose State Philosophy Department, such practices threaten to widen the gap between higher education institutions by ensuring that top-tier schools strengthen their hold on the production of knowledge about Japan and Japanese popular culture.

MOOCs as Teaching Tools

Despite the challenges related to developing MOOCs outlined above, I believe they will soon prove instrumental in teaching Japanese popular culture. One promising avenue relates to the controversy involving Michael Sandel. In that case the Harvard professor's video lectures were to be viewed by San Jose State philosophy students as homework, then discussed in class. While the San Jose State faculty protested, due in part to its lack of input in the decision, I argue that such a "flipped classroom" approach may one day offer a potential future for the teaching of Japanese popular culture online. Two MOOCs related to Japanese popular culture already exist, and it seems inevitable that other scholars will eventually assemble the creative energies, financial resources, time, and technological know-how to create more. Depending on who builds these MOOCs, concerns may linger about the concentration of the construction and dissemination of knowledge in a handful of top-tier institutions. However, hopefully there will eventually be a range of content-rich MOOCs that bring the study of Japanese popular culture to a wide global audience, and that through the flipped classroom approach even instructors without the resources to develop their own MOOC can take advantage of the work of others. In this final section I introduce the idea of the flipped classroom and some ways in which one might take advantage of MOOCs.

The flipped classroom is defined by the displacement of the traditional lecture to a time and space outside regular class time, thereby freeing class time for discussion, problem solving, group work, peer instruction, and so on.[58] The idea of using class time for something other than lectures is not new. In some courses in the humanities and arts the bulk of class time has always been devoted to the discussion of novels, films, artwork, and other works that were read or viewed beforehand. However, for disciplines that rely heavily on the lecture, and particularly those whose classes have been scaled up over the years to fill larger lecture theaters, the idea of students gathering in a lecture theater to do something *besides* listen to a lecture remains relatively new. Professor Shigeru Miyagawa of MIT used the online lectures from his course Visualizing Japan (1850s–1930s): Westernization, Protest, Modernity to flip his classroom, using class time to ask questions of the students and reinforce what they had learned beforehand. The experience was summarized this way.

> In the classroom, the MOOC material became a new form of textbook. The students found the video lectures easy to follow. They could watch each bite-sized two- to seven-minute video in its entirety and retain the information. The finger exercises following the video further reinforced their learning. Instead of teaching the information covered in the assignment, Miyagawa was able to delve deeper into the subject matter.[59]

Miyagawa believes that the real promise of MOOCs is in this flipped classroom format, causing him to declare, "I don't think I can ever go back to a pure lecture-style teaching."[60]

Once a library of MOOCs related to Japanese popular culture is available online, students around the world will be able to learn about their passions from a scholarly perspective, whether they be anime, film, manga, fashion, drama, or J-pop. Moreover, instructors based anywhere will be able to curate and select high-quality, engaging lectures on popular culture topics from around the world. The use of these lectures before class could replace time typically spent in content delivery, such as historicizing a particular television drama, with more time for classroom discussion or other learning activities. Students could be assigned lectures from a series of experts, or they could be charged with finding and reviewing lectures on topics of their choice from within the available MOOCs. Instead of just using the Internet to follow their interests and build fan communities, they could participate in learning communities. Moreover, instructors would have the intellectual freedom to challenge the lectures they assign as required viewing. The MOOC lecture videos could be treated not as the authoritative voice on a particular aspect of Japanese popular culture but as just another perspective to be analyzed critically.

Of course, this future will require some significant changes. First, more instructors will have to take the plunge and develop MOOCs taught *about* or *with* Japanese popular culture. These individuals will need strong support networks in their institutions and MOOC providers willing to support their content-heavy endeavors. Second, more MOOCs will need to remain permanently accessible. Currently, most MOOCs run for six to ten weeks, with a definite start and stop date. This is deemed necessary to maintain the flow of a course, as well as to facilitate the assessments that require deadlines, participation in online forums, and more. However, for instructors to take full advantage of the flipped classroom potential of MOOCs, they will need access to the lecture videos year-round. At present, few MOOCs provide this option, including the two Visualizing Japan courses at edX mentioned here. Although instructors and students cannot take advantage of any of the interactive learning tools associated with the full course, they can freely view all the videos. It is hoped that more MOOCs will follow this pattern in the future, enabling others to utilize these tools and further broadening the audience for learning about Japanese popular culture.

Conclusion

It is both exhilarating and daunting to think about how MOOCs may affect the future of Japanese studies and higher education as a whole. Because of their relative newness, it may be years before we understand either the full repercussions of creating MOOCs or their effectiveness in learning and instruction. There are still many issues that need to be resolved about MOOCs. For instance, how will they affect graduate-training, hiring, salary, and promotion decisions? Might MOOCs raise the bar on teaching in higher education, not only by encouraging more carefully planned courses and sound pedagogical choices by MOOC instructors but also by providing faculty members around the world an opportunity to keep abreast of pedagogical innovations and cutting-edge content delivered by peers at other institutions? Might scholarly journals that already feature book reviews add MOOC reviews? Although speculative, these are all questions that the emergence of MOOCs suggest.

The open and online nature of MOOCs and the extremely cautious application of fair use by institutions and providers threaten to limit the global, democratizing impact envisioned by MOOC advocates and create two classes of institutions. If we fail to properly address fair use and copyright in MOOCs, those who teach about or with Japanese popular culture may find themselves on either side of a chasm. On one side will be those with the institutional support to develop media-rich courses that offer the greatest level of academic freedom and attract the largest number of students. On the other side will be those marginalized by MOOCs, unable to contribute to student learning with the same resources and on the same scale.

The flipped classroom provides one potential bridge across this gulf, enabling instructors anywhere not only to take advantage of the hard work of others but also to build widespread learning communities that could reduce the alienation often associated with teaching Japanese popular culture. Moreover, as was stated in the introduction, many new faculty members feel an acute lack of pedagogical training when they create new courses and lectures on popular culture. With a library of excellent MOOCs available in the future, maybe future instructors will no longer feel such anxiety and tap into the hard work of others. The future of teaching Japanese popular culture may depend on it.

Notes

I would like to thank all the faculty members quoted in this chapter for their willingness to share their experiences. I also thank Deborah Shamoon for her feedback at several critical stages of the work's development. Portions of this chapter previously appeared as a journal article, "Teaching Japanese Popular Culture in the MOOC World," *electronic journal of contemporary japanese studies* 13 no. 2 (2013). I thank the editor for permission to reproduce those sections here.

[1] Jordan Weissmann, "The Single Most Important Experiment in Higher Education," *Atlantic*, July 18, 2012, http://www.theatlantic.com/business/archive/2012/07/the-single-most-important-experiment-in-higher-education/259953/.

[2] Tamar Lewin, "Universities Reshaping Education on the Web," *New York Times,* July 17, 2012, http://www.nytimes.com/2012/07/17/education/consortium-of-colleges-takes-online-education-to-new-level.html?smid=pl-share.

[3] Maria Bustillos, "Venture Capital's Massive, Terrible Idea for the Future of College," *The Awl*, January 31, 2013, http://www.theawl.com/2013/01/venture-capitals-massive-terrible-idea-for-the-future-of-college.

[4] Laura Pappano, "The Year of the MOOC," *New York Times*, November 2, 2012, http://www.nytimes.com/2012/11/04/education/edlife/massive-open-online-courses-are-multiplying-at-a-rapid-pace.html?smid=pl-share.

[5] David T. Boven, "The Next Game Changer: The Historical Antecedents of the MOOC Movement in Education," *eLearning Papers* 33 (2013), http://www.openeducationeuropa.eu/en/article/The-Next-Game-Changer%3A-The-Historical-Antecedents-of-the-MOOC-Movement-in-Education. See also Alexander McAuley et al., "The MOOC Model for Digital Practice," 2010, http://www.elearnspace.org/Articles/MOOC_Final.pdf.

[6] Organization for Economic Co-operation and Development [Paris, OECD Publications], *Giving Knowledge for Free: The Emergence of Open Educational Resources,* 2007, http://www.oecd.org/edu/ceri/ngknowledgeforfreetheemergenceofopeneducationalresources.htm.

[7] Fred G. Martin, "Will Massive Open Online Courses Change How We Teach?," *Communications of the ACM* 55, no. 8 (2012): 26–28, http://cacm.acm.org/magazines/2012/8/153817-will-massive-open-online-courses-change-how-we-teach/fulltext.

[8] Pappano, "Year of the MOOC." See also Clay Shirky, "Napster, Udacity, and the Academy," November 12, 2012, http://www.shirky.com/weblog/2012/11/napster-udacity-and-the-academy/.

⁹ Udacity, "About Us," https://www.udacity.com/us.

¹⁰ Coursera, "About Coursera," https://www.coursera.org/about.

¹¹ edX, "About Us," https://www.edx.org/about-us.

¹² Coursera, "Homepage," https://www.coursera.org/. This represents significant growth since June 10, 2013, when Coursera had more than 3.7 million students, 384 courses, and 81 partner institutions.

¹³ See, for instance, Robert Zemsky, "With a MOOC MOOC Here and a MOOC MOOC There, Here a MOOC, There a MOOC, Everywhere a MOOC MOOC," *Journal of General Education: A Curricular Commons of the Humanities and Sciences,* 63, no. 4 (2014): 237–43. Zemsky calls 2012 the high-water mark for MOOCs and cites a number of negative appraisals since, particularly due to incredibly low completion rates of courses.

¹⁴ See Mark McLelland, "Ethical and Legal Issues in Teaching about Japanese Popular Culture to Undergraduate Students in Australia," *electronic journal of contemporary japanese studies* 13, no. 2 (2013), http://www.japanesestudies. org.uk/ejcjs/vol13/iss2/mclelland.html; and William M. Tsutsui, "Teaching History and/of/or Japanese Popular Culture," *electronic journal of contemporary japanese studies*, 13, no. 2 (2013), http://www.japanesestudies.org.uk/ejcjs/ vol13/iss2/tsutsui.html.

¹⁵ A colleague at the National University of Singapore's Department of Philosophy recently put it this way. His MOOC, titled Reason and Persuasion: Thinking through Three Dialogues by Plato, enrolled more students in its first iteration (ten thousand plus) than he could reach in three decades of typical classes. See the Coursera website, https://www.coursera.org/course/ reasonandpersuasion.

¹⁶ Michael Ritter, "Tomorrow's College Will Be Free: Massive Open Online Courses," *Digital Professor*, October 26, 2012, http://thedigitalprofessor. wordpress.com/2012/10/26/tomorrows-college-will-be-free-massive-open- online-courses/.

¹⁷ The best-known example is Amherst College. See Steve Kolowich, "Why Some Colleges Are Saying No to MOOC Deals, at Least for Now," *Chronicle of Higher Education*, April 29, 2013, http://chronicle.com/article/Why-Some- Colleges-Are-Saying/138863/.

¹⁸ Tomoko Otake, "Thinking Aloud," *Japan Times*, September 19, 2010, http://www.japantimes.co.jp/life/2010/09/19/to-be-sorted/thinking-aloud/#. UbWXj-C9f3G; Tōhoku University, *Maikeru Sanderu no hakunetsu kyōshitsu @ Tōhoku Daigaku* [Justice with Michael Sandel at Tōhoku University], video, March 25, 2013, http://www.youtube.com/watch?v=-npwdBWgP9A.

[19] Steve Kolowich, "Why Professors at San Jose State Won't Use a Harvard Professor's MOOC," *Chronicle of Higher Education*, May 2, 2013, http://chronicle.com/article/Professors-at-San-Jose-State/138941/.

[20] Philosophy Department, San Jose University, "An Open Letter to Professor Michael Sandel from the Philosophy Department at San Jose State University," *Chronicle of Higher Education*, May 2, 2013, http://chronicle.com/article/The-Document-an-Open-Letter/138937/.

[21] Tamar Lewin, "Colleges Adapt Online Courses to Ease Burden," *New York Times*, April 29, 2013, http://www.nytimes.com/2013/04/30/education/colleges-adapt-online-courses-to-ease-burden.html?smid=pl-share.

[22] Philosophy Department, San Jose University, "Open Letter."

[23] Michael Sandel, "Michael Sandel Responds," *Chronicle of Higher Education*, May 2, 2013, http://chronicle.com/article/Michael-Sandel-Responds/139021/.

[24] Tamar Lewin, "Adapting to Blended Courses and Finding Early Benefits," *New York Times*, April 29, 2013, http://www.nytimes.com/2013/04/30/education/adapting-to-blended-courses-and-finding-early-benefits.html?smid=pl-share.

[25] Philosophy Department, San Jose State University, "Open Letter."

[26] edX, Visualizing Japan, https://www.edx.org/course/visualizing-japan-1850s-1930s-harvardx-mitx-vjx#.VL3AaC7sSqP.

[27] edX, Visualizing Postwar Tokyo, https://www.edx.org/course/visualizing-postwar-tokyo-part-1-utokyox-utokyo001x#.VL3AUy7sSqM.

[28] M.I.T., Visualizing Cultures. http://ocw.mit.edu/ans7870/21f/21f.027/home/index.html.

[29] See chapter 10, by Philip Seaton, in this volume.

[30] edX, Visualizing Postwar Tokyo.

[31] Digital Media Project, "The Digital Learning Challenge: Obstacles to Educational Uses of Copyrighted Material in the Digital Age," http://cyber.law.harvard.edu/media/files/copyrightandeducation.html.

[32] US Code, Title 17, Chapter 1, §110, 2013, "Limitations on Exclusive Rights: Exemption of Certain Performances and Displays," Legal Information Institute, Cornell University, http://www.law.cornell.edu/uscode/text/17/110.

[33] Susan M. Bielstein, *Permissions, a Survival Guide: Blunt Talk about Art as Intellectual Property* (Chicago: University of Chicago Press, 2006).

[34] Coursera, personal communication, May 9, 2013.

[35] Society for Cinema and Media Studies, "The Society for Cinema and Media Studies' Statement of Best Practices for Fair Use in Teaching for Film and Media Educators," *Cinema Journal* 47, no. 2 (2008): 155–64.

[36] Melissa Korn, "Coursera Makes a Case for MOOCs," *Wall Street Journal*, May 14, 2013, http://online.wsj.com/article/SB1000142412788732471570457848 3570761525766.html.

[37] Coursera, personal communication, May 9, 2013.

[38] Ibid.

[39] Ibid.

[40] Ib Bondebjerg, personal communication, June 11, 2013.

[41] Ibid.

[42] See NipponTV, http://www.ntv.co.jp/haken/.

[43] Society for Cinema and Media Studies, "Society for Cinema and Media Studies' Statement of Best Practices."

[44] John Covach, History of Rock, Part One, Coursera, https://www.coursera.org/course/historyofrock1.

[45] Scott Higgins, The Language of Hollywood: Storytelling, Sound, and Color, Coursera, https://www.coursera.org/course/hollywood.

[46] See McLelland, "Ethical and Legal Issues."

[47] S. Higgins, personal communication, June 11, 2013.

[48] Ibid.

[49] Ibid.

[50] Nathan Heller, "Laptop U: Has the Future of College Moved Online?" *New Yorker*, May 20, 2013, http://www.newyorker.com/reporting/2013/05/20/130520fa_fact_heller.

[51] William Kuskin, personal communication, June 18, 2013.

[52] William Kuskin, personal communication, January 22, 2015.

[53] Ibid.

[54] Gennifer Weisenfeld, personal communication, January 21, 2015.

[55] Shigeru Miyagawa, personal communication, January 21, 2015.

[56] A colleague at the National University of Singapore who teaches Japanese language told me of her efforts to secure permission to use a bottled green tea advertisement in an academic conference paper. She contacted the company and waited months before finally receiving permission. In the meantime, the conference was already over, and she had not used the clip.

[57] See chapter 1, by Sally McLaren and Alwyn Spies, in this volume.

[58] Jonathan Bergmann and Aaron Sams, *Flip Your Classroom: Reach Every Student in Every Class Every Day* (Washington, DC: International Society for

Technology in Education, 2012); Dan Berrett, "How Flipping the Classroom Can Improve the Traditional Lecture," *Chronicle of Higher Education*, February 19, 2012, http://chronicle.com/article/How-Flipping-the-Classroom/130857/.

[59] Office of Digital Learning, MIT, "A MOOC Sees Its Greatest Impact in the Classroom at MIT," http://newsoffice.mit.edu/2014/mooc-sees-its-greatest-impact-classroom-mit-1114.

[60] Ibid.

Works Cited

Bergmann, Jonathan and Aaron Sams. *Flip Your Classroom: Reach Every Student in Every Class Every Day.* Washington, DC: International Society for Technology in Education, 2012.

Berrett, Dan. "How Flipping the Classroom Can Improve the Traditional Lecture." *Chronicle of Higher Education*, February 19, 2012. http://chronicle.com/article/How-Flipping-the-Classroom/130857/.

Bielstein, Susan M. *Permissions, a Survival Guide: Blunt Talk about Art as Intellectual Property.* Chicago: University of Chicago Press, 2006.

Bondebjerg, Ib. Scandinavian Film and Television. Coursera. https://www.coursera.org/course/scanfilmtv.

Boven, David T. "The Next Game Changer: The Historical Antecedents of the MOOC Movement in Education." *eLearning Papers* 33 (May 2013). http://www.openeducationeuropa.eu/en/article/The-Next-Game-Changer%3A-The-Historical-Antecedents-of-the-MOOC-Movement-in-Education.

Bustillos, Maria. "Venture Capital's Massive, Terrible Idea for the Future of College." *The Awl*, January 31, 2013. http://www.theawl.com/2013/01/venture-capitals-massive-terrible-idea-for-the-future-of-college.

Coursera. "About Coursera." https://www.coursera.org/about.

———. "Homepage." https://www.coursera.org/.

Covach, John. 2013. History of Rock, Part One. Coursera. https://www.coursera.org/course/historyofrock1.

Digital Media Project. "The Digital Learning Challenge: Obstacles to Educational Uses of Copyrighted Material in the Digital Age." http://cyber.law.harvard.edu/media/files/copyrightandeducation.html.

edX. "About Us." https://www.edx.org/about-us.

———. Visualizing Japan. https://www.edx.org/course/visualizing-japan-1850s-1930s-harvardx-mitx-vjx#.VL3AaC7sSqP.

———. Visualizing Postwar Tokyo. https://www.edx.org/course/visualizing-postwar-tokyo-part-1-utokyox-utokyo001x#.VL3AUy7sSqM.

Heller, Nathan. "Laptop U: Has the Future of College Moved Online?" *New Yorker*, May 20, 2013. http://www.newyorker.com/reporting/2013/05/20/130520fa_fact_heller.

Higgins, Scott. The Language of Hollywood: Storytelling, Sound, and Color. Coursera. https://www.coursera.org/course/hollywood.

Kolowich, Steve. "Why Professors at San Jose State Won't Use a Harvard Professor's MOOC." *Chronicle of Higher Education*, May 2, 2013. http://chronicle.com/article/Professors-at-San-Jose-State/138941/.

——. "Why Some Colleges Are Saying No to MOOC Deals, at Least for Now." *Chronicle of Higher Education*, April 29, 2013. http://chronicle.com/article/Why-Some-Colleges-Are-Saying/138863/.

Korn, Melissa. "Coursera Makes a Case for MOOCs." *Wall Street Journal*, May 14, 2013. http://online.wsj.com/article/SB1000142412788732471570457848 3570761525766.html.

Lewin, Tamar. "Adapting to Blended Courses and Finding Early Benefits." *New York Times*, April 29, 2013. http://www.nytimes.com/2013/04/30/education/adapting-to-blended-courses-and-finding-early-benefits.html?smid=pl-share.

——. "Colleges Adapt Online Courses to Ease Burden." *New York Times*, April 29, 2013. http://www.nytimes.com/2013/04/30/education/colleges-adapt-online-courses-to-ease-burden.html?smid=pl-share.

——. "Universities Reshaping Education on the Web." *New York Times*, July 17, 2012. http://www.nytimes.com/2012/07/17/education/consortium-of-colleges-takes-online-education-to-new-level.html?smid=pl-share.

Martin, Fred G. "Will Massive Open Online Courses Change How We Teach?" *Communications of the ACM* 55, no. 8 (2012): 26–28. http://cacm.acm.org/magazines/2012/8/153817-will-massive-open-online-courses-change-how-we-teach/fulltext.

McAuley, Alexander, Bonnie Stewart, George Siemens and Dave Cormier. "The MOOC Model for Digital Practice," 2010. http://www.elearnspace.org/Articles/MOOC_Final.pdf.

McLelland, Mark. "Ethical and Legal Issues in Teaching about Japanese Popular Culture to Undergraduate Students in Australia." *electronic journal of contemporary japanese studies* 13, no. 2 (2013). http://www.japanesestudies.org.uk/ejcjs/vol13/iss2/mclelland.html.

MIT. Visualizing Cultures. http://ocw.mit.edu/ans7870/21f/21f.027/home/index.html.

Office of Digital Learning, MIT. "A MOOC Sees Its Greatest Impact in the Classroom at MIT." http://newsoffice.mit.edu/2014/mooc-sees-its-greatest-impact-classroom-mit-1114.

Organization for Economic Co-operation and Development [Paris. OECD Publications]. *Giving Knowledge for Free: The Emergence of Open Educational Resources.* 2007. http://www.oecd.org/edu/ceri/ledgeforfreetheemergenceofopeneducationalresources.htm.

Otake, Tomoko. "Thinking Aloud." *Japan Times*, September 19, 2010. http://www.japantimes.co.jp/life/2010/09/19/to-be-sorted/thinking-aloud/#. UbWXj-C9f3G.

Pappano, Laura. "The Year of the MOOC." *New York Times*, November 2, 2012. http://www.nytimes.com/2012/11/04/education/edlife/massive-open-online-courses-are-multiplying-at-a-rapid-pace.html?smid=pl-share.

Philosophy Department, San Jose University. "An Open Letter to Professor Michael Sandel from the Philosophy Department at San Jose State University." *Chronicle of Higher Education*, May 2, 2013. http://chronicle.com/article/The-Document-an-Open-Letter/138937/.

Ritter, Michael. "Tomorrow's College Will Be Free: Massive Open Online Courses." *Digital Professor*, October 26, 2012. http://thedigitalprofessor.wordpress.com/2012/10/26/tomorrows-college-will-be-free-massive-open-online-courses/.

Sandel, Michael. "Michael Sandel Responds." *Chronicle of Higher Education*, May 2, 2013. http://chronicle.com/article/Michael-Sandel-Responds/139021/.

Shirky, Clay. "Napster, Udacity, and the Academy," November 12, 2012. http://www.shirky.com/weblog/2012/11/napster-udacity-and-the-academy/.

Society for Cinema and Media Studies. "The Society for Cinema and Media Studies' Statement of Best Practices for Fair Use in Teaching for Film and Media Educators." *Cinema Journal* 47, no. 2 (2008): 155–64.

Tōhoku University. *Maikeru Sanderu no Hakunetsu Kyōshitsu @ Tōhoku Daigaku* [Justice with Michael Sandel at Tōhoku University]. Video, March 25, 2013. http://www.youtube.com/watch?v=-npwdBWgP9A.

Tsutsui, William M. "Teaching History and/of/or Japanese Popular Culture." *electronic journal of contemporary japanese studies* 13, no. 2 (2013). http://www.japanesestudies.org.uk/ejcjs/vol13/iss2/tsutsui.html.

Udacity. "About us." https://www.udacity.com/us.

US Code, Title 17, Chapter 1, §110, 2013. "Limitations on Exclusive Rights: Exemption of Certain Performances and Displays." Legal Information Institute, Cornell University. http://www.law.cornell.edu/uscode/text/17/110.

Weissmann, Jordan. "The Single Most Important Experiment in Higher Education." *Atlantic*, July 18, 2012. http://www.theatlantic.com/business/archive/2012/07/the-single-most-important-experiment-in-higher-education/259953/.

Zemsky, Robert. "With a MOOC MOOC Here and a MOOC MOOC There, Here a MOOC, There a MOOC, Everywhere a MOOC MOOC." *Journal of General Education: A Curricular Commons of the Humanities and Sciences* 63, no. 4 (2014): 237–43.

Contributors

WILLIAM S. ARMOUR is Honorary Senior Lecturer at the University of New South Wales, Australia. He has taught several courses on Japanese popular culture spanning more than a decade. In 2012 he received the Vice-Chancellor's Award for Teaching Excellence and an Australian Award for University Teaching (Citation for Outstanding Contributions to Student Learning) together with his former Japanese studies colleagues. His recent publications include "Learning Japanese by Reading 'Manga': The Rise of 'Soft Power' Pedagogy," (*RELC Journal, 2011*) and "Are Australian Fans of Anime and Manga Motivated to Learn Japanese Language?" (*Asia Pacific Journal of Education* 2014), with coauthor Sumiko Iida.

JAN BARDSLEY is Professor of Asian Studies at the University of North Carolina at Chapel Hill. She is the author of *Women and Democracy in Cold War Japan* (Bloomsbury, 2014) and *The Bluestockings of Japan: New Women Fiction and Essays from Seitō, 1911–1916* (Center for Japanese Studies, University of Michigan, 2007) and coeditor with Laura Miller of *Manners and Mischief: Gender, Power, and Etiquette in Japan* (University of California Press, 2011) and *Bad Girls of Japan* (Palgrave, 2005). She is the recipient of several campus teaching awards.

JAMES DORSEY is Associate Professor of Japanese and a department chair at Dartmouth College. His chapter in this volume emerged out of a class he teaches regularly in Dartmouth College's summer program at Kanda Gaigo Daigaku in Chiba, Japan. He is the author of *Critical Aesthetics: Kobayashi Hideo, Modernity, and Wartime Japan* (Harvard University Asia Center, 2009) and coeditor of *Literary Mischief: Sakaguchi Ango, Culture, and the War* (Lexington Books, 2010). A piece of his next book has been published as "Breaking Records: Media, Censorship, and the Folk Song Movement of Japan's 1960s" and is included in *Asian Popular Culture: New, Hybrid, and Alternate Media* (ed. Lent and Fitzsimmons, Lexington Books, 2014).

SUMIKO IIDA is Lecturer of Japanese Studies at the University of New South Wales, Australia. Apart from Japanese language courses, she has taught and researched Japanese popular culture courses with William Armour since 2002. Her current popular culture courses include Japan in Popular Culture and Learning Japanese by Manga and Anime. Her latest publication in this field is "Are Australian Fans of Anime and Manga Motivated to Learn Japanese Language?" (*Asia Pacific Journal of Education* 2014), with coauthor William S. Armour. She has received awards for teaching excellence, including the Australian Award for University Teaching with New South Wales Japanese studies colleagues.

MELANIE KING is a member of the Art History faculty at Seattle Central College in Seattle, Washington. In addition to teaching art history full time to a diverse, dynamic student body, she instructs K–12 teachers about East Asia from a humanities-based perspective, originally through the University of Colorado at Boulder and currently at the University of Washington's East Asia Resource Center. She has experience working as a curator of Japanese and Korean art at the Seattle Art Museum. She is the author of "What Should Be Displayed? Native Arts in Museums and on the Runways" (Evergreen State College, 2014) and a 2014 League for Innovation recipient of the John and Suanne Roueche Excellence Award.

SALLY MCLAREN has a PhD from Ritsumeikan University (Kyoto) and is currently Assistant Professor in the School of International Studies at Kwansei Gakuin University (Nishinomiya), where she teaches Japanese popular culture and media studies courses. Her research focuses on gender, media, and politics in the Asia-Pacific region. As a journalist, she has been writing about Japan for domestic and international media since 1997, as well as guest-editing *Kyoto Journal* (no. 64, "Unbound: Gender in Asia," 2006) and contributing to *The Rough Guide to Japan* (Pearson, 2014).

CHRIS MCMORRAN is Senior Lecturer in the Department of Japanese Studies at the National University of Singapore. A cultural geographer by training, he teaches courses related to Japan's environment-society relations and political economy, as well as an annual field studies course in Kyūshū. He has won multiple teaching awards and published research articles on heritage tourism, labor mobility, Japanese feminism, and field-based learning. He is currently writing a book based on a year of fieldwork conducted in a traditional Japanese inn, *Last Resort: Labor, Tourism, and Identity in Japan.*

PHILIP SEATON is Professor in the International Student Center, Hokkaido University, where he is convener of the Modern Japanese Studies Program. He is the author of *Japan's Contested War Memories* (Routledge, 2007), *Voices from the Shifting Russo-Japanese Border: Karafuto/Sakhalin* (Routledge, 2015, coedited with Svetlana Paichadze), and *Local History and War Memories in Hokkaido* (Routledge, 2015). He also researches tourism at heritage sites induced by historical dramas and recently coedited a special edition of *Japan Forum* with Takayoshi Yamamura, "Japanese Popular Culture and Contents Tourism."

DEBORAH SHAMOON is Associate Professor of Japanese Studies at the National University of Singapore, where she teaches courses in modern Japanese literature and popular culture. She is the author of *Passionate Friendship: The Aesthetics of Girls' Culture in Japan* (University of Hawai'i Press, 2012), as well as several articles on manga, anime, and film. From 2006 to 2011 she was Assistant Professor at the University of Notre Dame in the Department of East Asian Languages and Cultures.

ALWYN SPIES is a Senior Instructor in Critical Studies at the University of British Columbia Okanagan Campus. She teaches Japanese language courses, as well as Japanese modern literature and pop culture in translation.

AKIKO SUGAWA-SHIMADA is Associate Professor at Yokohama National University. She is the author of a number of books and articles on anime, manga, and cultural studies, including *Girls and Magic: How Have Girl Heroes Been Accepted?* (in Japanese, NTT Shuppan, 2013), which received the Japanese Society of Animation Studies Award in 2014); "Grotesque Cuteness of Shōjo: Representations of Goth-Loli in Japanese Contemporary TV Anime" (in *Japanese Animation: East Asian Perspectives*, University of Mississippi Press, 2013); "*Rekijo*, Pilgrimage, and 'Pop-Spiritualism': Pop-Culture-Induced Heritage Tourism of/for Young Women" (*Japan Forum*, 2015); and "Japanese Superhero Teams at Home and Abroad: Super-*Sentai* in Japan and Their Adaptation in South Korean Cinema" (*Journal of Japanese and Korean Cinema*, 2014).

COSIMA WAGNER is Scientific Coordinator of the Cluster East Asia at the Campus Library and Research Fellow at the Japanese Studies Institute of Freie Universität Berlin. From 2003 to 2013, she was Lecturer and Research Fellow in the Japanese Studies Department of Goethe-University in Frankfurt, where she initiated the Cool Japan Working

Group as an extracurricular research-oriented learning project on Japanese popular culture. She is the author of *Robotopia Nipponica: Research on the Acceptance of Robots in Japan* (in German, Tectum, 2013), where she explored interfaces between (popular) culture and robot technology development in Japan.

MARC YAMADA is Assistant Professor of Interdisciplinary Humanities at Brigham Young University. He received his PhD in Japanese literature and culture from the University of California, Berkeley. He has published articles on modern Japanese literature, film, and manga and is currently working on a project on the cultural reactions to Japan's "lost decade" of the 1990s and 2000s. He has taught classes in Japanese language and culture at the University of California, Berkeley; University of Iowa; and Wake Forest University and is currently teaching classes on Japanese film and popular culture at Brigham Young.

INDEX

3.11 disasters (March 2011 disasters), 62, 64, 71, 147–8

Abe Shinzō, 237
Adichie, Chimamanda Ngozi, 153
Ainu, 232, 248–250, 253n33
Ainu Rebels, 249
Alda, Frances, 111, 112, 114
All She Was Worth (*Kasha;* Miyabe Miyuki), 171
Ambassadors of Cute (*Kawaii Taishi*), 27
anime: fans of, 4–6, 26, 28, 34, 50, 61, 80; legal issues, 25, 204; studies, 82; in teaching analytical skills, 170–173; in teaching culture, 4–6, 8, 9, 47, 65, 69, 71; 79–95, 137, 139, 140, 146–147, 153; in teaching history, 11, 246; in teaching language, 6, 10, 45, 51–57, 170; in translation, 1, 2, 26
Anime Festival Asia (Singapore), 1
Allison, Anne, 28–29
Althusser, Louis, 190
Anpō (US-Japan Joint Security Treaty), 216
anthropology, 3, 4, 258
anti-area studies, 29–30
area studies, 3, 6, 29–30
art history, 137, 138, 144
Asia-Pacific, 22, 32
Asian studies, 20, 83

assessment: creation of, 12, 35, 53–54, 56; curriculum design and, 20, 46–47, 167; exam, 122–123; online teaching and, 259–260, 273; oral exam, 123. *See also* outcomes
Association for Social Science Research on Japan (VSJF), 65–66
Auburn University, 168
Australia, 1, 3, 9, 21, 32–33, 54, 84, 166, 260
authentic materials, 6–8, 10, 161, 165, 166, 175
Azuma Hiroki, 2, 71

Berg Fashion Library, 103, 105, 125n3
Blade Runner (Ridley Scott), 269
Blow, Charles M., 145
Bologna Process, 61–62
Bondebjerg, Ib, 264, 266, 267
Buck, Elizabeth B., 190
Burdick, Jake, 6
Butler, Judith, 214

Cammarata, Laurent, 165–166
Canada, 3, 25, 32–33, 238, 260
Canagarajah, A. Suresh, 174
capitalism, 22, 26
Center for the Study of Languages and Cultures (CSLC), 168
Chandler-Olcott, Kelly, 6
Chijin no ai (Naomi, Tanizaki Jun'ichirō), 118, 119